America Today

CURRENT PROBLEMS AND THEIR ORIGINS

SECOND EDITION

Henry Brun
Principal (Ret.), John Jay High School
New York City

AMSCO

AMSCO SCHOOL PUBLICATIONS, INC.
315 Hudson Street / New York, N.Y. 10013

When ordering this book, please specify either **R 643 P** or AMERICA TODAY

ISBN 1-56765-601-3
New York City Item 56765-601-2

Printed in the United States of America

1 2 3 4 5 6 7 8 9 10 00 99 98 97

Preface

America Today: Current Problems and Their Origins provides a panoramic view of the United States in the 1990's. It affords students and teachers opportunities to move beyond standard textbooks in their exploration of contemporary issues and events. The information found in this book will enable students and teachers to focus on a variety of key topics that illuminate the changing American scene.

Dynamic changes in American life and in the role played by the United States in the world at large are the book's central theme. The causes and immediate effects of the most current of these changes are set in their historical contexts. This perspective helps the reader to see the connection between past and present.

America Today: Current Problems and Their Origins is an instructional tool. To help the teacher develop students' knowledge of current American affairs, the readable text is supplemented by maps, illustrations, and a variety of content and skill-assessment exercises.

The following features are included:

Comprehensive Coverage. Recent developments in the U.S. government, economy, society, and technology are examined, as are foreign relations with Europe, Asia, the Middle East, Africa, and Latin America. Analysis of America's role in these critical regions is followed by a look at the participation of the United States in the building of international security and a new global economic order. Significant attention is given to peacemaking efforts in Somalia, Bosnia, and Haiti. The American position on crises such as Northern Ireland and involvement in the activities of the United Nations, NATO, and other regional security organizations is outlined. The American contribution to the development of GATT and the World Trade Organization is discussed, as are our current relations with old and new trading partners.

These issues are followed by the examination of battles being fought to save the environment and the efforts to protect Americans from the growing threat of terrorism. Finally, the text examines the innovations and trends that are carrying the United States and the world toward the 21st century.

Unit and Chapter Overviews. Each unit and chapter begins with a brief overview that identifies the major developments to be treated.

Maps, Graphs, Charts, and Cartoons. Many maps appear in the text. They provide geographical references. Map exercises reinforce skills development, as do the graph and chart exercises. Students are given the opportunity to analyze and interpret data. Cartoons emphasize and illustrate people and events.

Exercises and Reviews. To enhance the usability of the book as an instructional tool, the text is supplemented by frequent, strategically placed questions and exercises. Additional reviews appear at the conclusion of each section, chapter, and unit. These are designed to require a variety of response efforts—content and data search, reading for factual detail, and the skills of inference, critical thinking, and expository writing.

Reference Section. The back of the text contains the Index. Topics of current importance are identified and listed for quick and easy location.

Henry Brun

Contents

UNIT III / AMERICA'S ROLE IN BUILDING GLOBAL SECURITY AND PROSPERITY *207*

UNIT IV / THE AMERICAN AGENDA FOR THE 1990's: ISSUES AND PROBLEMS *245*

America Today

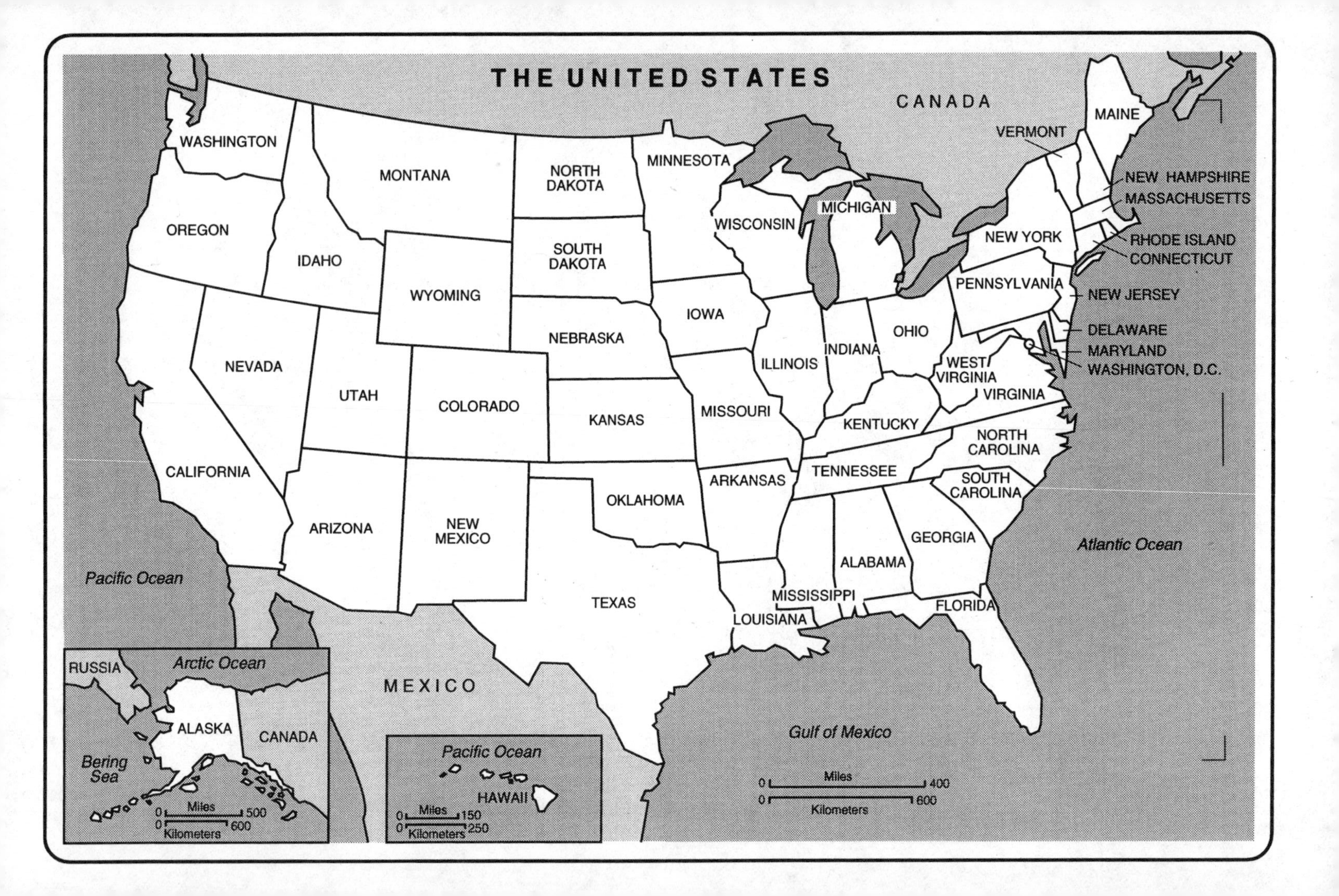
THE UNITED STATES
CANADA
WASHINGTON
MONTANA
NORTH DAKOTA
MINNESOTA
MAINE
VERMONT
NEW HAMPSHIRE
MASSACHUSETTS
OREGON
IDAHO
SOUTH DAKOTA
WISCONSIN
MICHIGAN
NEW YORK
RHODE ISLAND
CONNECTICUT
WYOMING
IOWA
PENNSYLVANIA
NEW JERSEY
NEVADA
NEBRASKA
ILLINOIS
INDIANA
OHIO
DELAWARE
MARYLAND
WASHINGTON, D.C.
UTAH
COLORADO
KANSAS
MISSOURI
WEST VIRGINIA
VIRGINIA
KENTUCKY
NORTH CAROLINA
CALIFORNIA
TENNESSEE
ARKANSAS
SOUTH CAROLINA
OKLAHOMA
ARIZONA
NEW MEXICO
GEORGIA
Atlantic Ocean
ALABAMA
Pacific Ocean
MISSISSIPPI
TEXAS
FLORIDA
LOUISIANA
MEXICO
Gulf of Mexico
RUSSIA
Arctic Ocean
ALASKA
CANADA
Bering Sea
Miles 0 500
Kilometers 0 600
Pacific Ocean
HAWAII
Miles 0 150
Kilometers 0 250
Miles 0 400
Kilometers 0 600

UNIT I

THE UNITED STATES IN THE 1990'S

By the last decade of the 20th century, the United States of America had become a nation at risk. During the cold war, American leaders had been concerned with winning the global struggle against Communism. To win the cold war, American Presidents allocated enormous funds, resources, and energy toward foreign affairs to the neglect of domestic demands. As the cold war subsided, in 1991, America turned its attention to homelessness, unemployment, and inflation. Also troubling to Americans were the social problems of rising crime and violence, health care and welfare reform, failing schools, and ethnic divisiveness.

While Americans sought solutions to these and other problems, advances in science and technology brought the country closer to a new era in space exploration, telecommunications, computerization, and transportation. At the same time, the collapse of the Soviet Union led to political and economic changes in Europe and elsewhere. The emergence of a new world order required the formation of a new American foreign policy, as the United States approached the 21st century. America's continuation as a superpower depends on its willingness and ability to adapt to changing times.

♦ *List some of the major problems facing Americans in the late 20th century.*

Chapter 1

Government and Politics

By the early 1990's, many Americans had lost faith in their government. Although the Republican Administration of George Bush (1989–1993) had achieved a brilliant military victory in the Persian Gulf War, the U.S. economy was weaker than it had been since World War II. The national debt became larger than ever before. In the field of international trade, more markets were lost to Japanese corporations. In 1991, the number of Americans living in poverty rose by 2.1 million to a total of 35.7 million. Many considered President Bush insensitive to the suffering that the poor economy was causing many Americans.

The Presidential Election of 1992

When Governor Bill Clinton of Arkansas, a Democrat, became the 42nd U.S. President in 1992, 12 years of Republican leadership ended. Clinton defeated President Bush and an independent candidate, H. Ross Perot.

During his campaign, Clinton attacked the "trickle-down" economic policies of the Republican Administrations of Ronald Reagan (1981–1989) and George Bush. He argued that wealthy Americans should bear a greater proportion of the tax burden. He also spoke out against the traditional "tax-and-spend" policies of the Democrats. More importantly, Clinton announced that his Administration's main focus would be to solve domestic problems, such as the economy, health care, and education. As the United States struggled through an economic recession and a slow recovery in 1992, more Americans became receptive to Clinton's ideas. Among those who supported him and his Vice-Presidential running mate, Albert Gore, Jr., were blacks, blue-collar workers, and women.

The abortion issue also helped the Democrats. Bush opposed abortion in most cases, while Clinton was pro-choice. Then, too, the promise by Clinton and Gore to "reinvent government" appealed to American youth.

Bush enjoyed great popularity because of the Allied victory over Iraq in the Persian Gulf War of 1991. He had also benefited from the collapse of Communism in the Soviet Union and Eastern Europe during his presidency.

However, his support for a tax increase in 1990, which violated his 1988 pledge of "no new taxes," angered his supporters. Many felt his domestic policies were weak.

Texas billionaire H. Ross Perot entered the race, dropped out, and reentered a month before the election. He spent $60 million broadcasting warnings of an economic crisis resulting from huge federal budget deficits. (These were caused by the federal government's long-standing practice of spending more money than it received in taxes and other revenue.) He offered a plan to reduce the deficit by large cuts in military spending and an increase in the gasoline tax. Although Perot won no electoral votes, he received 19 percent of the popular vote, more than any independent candidate since 1912.

Clinton was victorious, obtaining 370 electoral votes, compared to Bush's 168. However, he won only 43 percent of the popular vote, thus becoming the first President since 1968 to be elected without a majority of the popular vote.

◆ *Explain how the presidential election of 1992 was affected by economic problems.*

Section Review

1. *Complete the table:*

ELECTION OF 1992

Candidates	*Political Parties*	*Ideas or Policies*

2. *List the groups of voters who supported Bill Clinton, and explain why each preferred him to the other candidates.*

The Clinton Presidency

Upon accepting the nomination in 1992, Clinton had said that he would revive the U.S. economy and promised a "New Covenant" that would offer a new approach to government.

In early 1993, with the Democratic Party controlling both the White House and Congress, President Clinton tried to persuade lawmakers to act on his programs. To revive the economy and reduce the deficit, he proposed $246 billion in new taxes, expenditures of another $169 billion to stimulate the economy, and a general spending cut of $247 billion, including substantial cuts in defense spending.

The President's budget plan depended on tax increases to achieve 57 percent of the desired savings needed to reduce the federal deficit. This caused many in Congress to reject it. A compromise plan was designed to slow growth of the federal debt by nearly $500 billion over five years. It raised taxes on people with larger incomes and reduced taxes for the working poor. But it did not succeed in balancing the budget.

Moreover, the budget provided only half the money that Clinton had wanted for programs for the poor. Medicare payments were also far less than those he had proposed.

A poll conducted by *Newsweek* magazine in August, 1993, showed that only 34 percent of the American public approved of Clinton's handling of the budget.

♦ *Explain why many Americans were dissatisfied with Clinton's handling of the budget.*

Clinton vs. the Military

The President challenged the military's refusal to admit homosexuals to the armed forces, a policy approved by General Colin Powell, Chairman of the Joint Chiefs of Staff. After meeting much resistance, Clinton negotiated a compromise. Military recruiters were ordered not to ask enlistees about their sexual orientation. However, enlistees who declared their homosexuality were not admitted and those already enlisted who did so were removed from active duty. Powell also opposed Clinton's desire to use air strikes in Bosnia.

General Powell's retirement allowed Clinton to strengthen his position as commander-in-chief by appointing his own "top soldier," General John Shalikashvili, who did not share Powell's reluctance to use military force.

President Clinton's disagreements with the military did not improve his popularity. Neither did his selection of candidates for high-level positions in the Justice Department. Clinton's first choice for Attorney General, Zoe Baird, had to withdraw when it was disclosed that she had employed illegal aliens. Many were outraged when Clinton withdrew his nomination of Lani Guinier, a civil rights activist, for the post of chief civil rights enforcer for the Justice Department. She had been criticized for her opinions on electoral reform.

Such early setbacks made some people regard the President as amateurish. However, the appointments of Judge Ruth Bader Ginsburg to the Supreme Court and Janet Reno to the post of Attorney General were well received.

◆ *Briefly describe President Clinton's problems relating to the military and the Justice Department in 1993.*

Pursuit of the Presidential Vision

Clinton had several proposals to improve American life. He planned to check rising health care costs, fight crime with more police officers on the streets, and create thousands of new jobs by dropping trade barriers with Mexico and Canada. He also promised to create a National Service Corps as a means for college students to repay tuition loans. He developed a new industrial policy to encourage U.S. automakers to "redefine the world car of the next century."

The Family and Medical Leave Act was the first major legislation passed by Congress at Clinton's request. It permits some workers to take up to 12 weeks of unpaid leave for the birth or adoption of a child, to care for a sick relative, or to deal with their own serious illnesses. Businesses with fewer than 50 employees are exempted.

Developing a plan to provide health care to all Americans

was a key item on the agenda. In January, 1993, he asked his wife, Hillary Rodham Clinton, to head a task force on national health reform (see pages 58–61).

Mrs. Clinton, a successful lawyer and social activist, rapidly established herself as one of the most politically active First Ladies in history. Following her appointment, she dealt skillfully with Congressional committees, medical professionals, and insurance organizations.

In October, 1993, despite several foreign-policy problems, 49 percent of Americans expressed approval of the President's actions. Although low, this rating represented a 10-point improvement since the summer of 1993.

1. *List the programs offered by President Clinton to restore security to American life.*
2. *Identify each of the following:*
   a. *Colin Powell*
   b. *John Shalikashvili*
   c. *Ruth Bader Ginsburg*
   d. *Janet Reno*

Congress and the Democrats

As a result of the 1992 national elections, the Democrats continued to control both houses of Congress. In the Senate, Democrats gained one seat, giving them a 58-to-42 majority over Republicans. In the House of Representatives, the Democratic majority shrank from 260 to 174.

Several circumstances caused turmoil in the election. Because of major population changes, *reapportionment* (changes in the number of Representatives from each state) added many House seats from the South and West, while reducing those from the Midwest and Northeast. Congress angered many voters by voting itself a pay raise. And it was revealed that many House members had written overdrafts on their accounts in the House bank.

Nineteen incumbents (lawmakers elected in a previous election) were rejected in 1992 primaries. Others lost in the November elections. Record numbers of women, blacks, and Hispanic Americans were elected to the House.

In elections for the Senate, women scored a major breakthrough. Eleven won major-party nominations. Five of these, all

Democrats, were elected. Carol Moseley-Braun of Illinois became the first black woman Senator. California's Senate seats went to women: former San Francisco Mayor Dianne Feinstein and Representative Barbara Boxer. Patty Murray was elected Senator from Washington, and Barbara Mikulski was reelected Senator from Maryland.

Representative Ben Nighthorse Campbell (Democrat from Colorado) became the second Native American to win a seat in the Senate. He later switched to the Republican Party.

◆ *State two important ways in which the membership of the U.S. Congress was changed by the election of 1992.*

Problems With Congress

By the end of 1993, many in Congress opposed Clinton's policies. Senate Minority Leader Robert Dole led a fight against the President's budget proposal. That contest ended in compromise, but Congress rejected many of Clinton's plans to stimulate the economy.

In October, 1993, Dole proposed to limit the President's military power to restore Haitian President Jean-Bertrand Aristide to office. The resolution would have required Congress's authorization before Clinton could send troops.

Dole's foreign-policy challenge was not supported by senior Republicans in Congress, who for 12 years had prevented Democrats from limiting the powers of Presidents Reagan and Bush. Dole had to compromise with Clinton, who agreed to ask Congress for authorization before sending troops to Haiti or Bosnia but was not required to do so.

Although Democrats called Dole "Senator Gridlock," he offered, in 1993, to cooperate with the White House on health care reform. He also went along with the Administration's withdrawal of U.S. peacekeeping forces from Somalia.

The former Chairman of the Armed Services Committee, Sam Nunn, also urged Clinton to confer with Congress on domestic and foreign-policy issues. He opposed Clinton in two of the hottest legislative fights of 1993: the President's deficit reduction plan and his proposal to lift the military's ban on homosexuals. By late 1993, however, Nunn had voted in support of Presidential bills 72 percent of the time.

♦ *Identify each of the following:*

a. Ben Nighthorse Campbell *b. Robert Dole* *c. Sam Nunn*

The Republican Victory of 1994

In the 1994 national election, a Republican landslide swept aside Democratic majorities in the Senate and the House. At the state level, Republicans gained control of 18 state legislatures and a majority of governorships.

After the election, Republicans chose Representative Newt Gingrich of Georgia as Speaker of the House. He promised a "Contract With America," a program to reduce government spending and the size of the federal government. Robert Dole became Senate Majority Leader. Together, he and Gingrich were able to influence both appointments to government jobs and the spending of the Clinton Administration.

The extraordinary Republican victory was caused by voter dissatisfaction with elected officials and with Clinton's "big government" policies. This was clear from the fact that no Republican incumbent was defeated. Only Democrats lost.

The Democratic downfall of 1994 appeared to many as a rejection of Clinton's agenda, in spite of the creation of 5 million new jobs, movement toward cutting the deficit, and a foreign-policy success in Haiti (see pages 191–193).

1. *Why was the 1994 election a blow to Clinton's Administration?*
2. *Read the statement below and answer the questions that follow:*

> There are those who would keep us slipping back into the darkness of division, into the snake pit of racial hatred, of racial antagonism and of support for symbols of the struggle to keep African-Americans in bondage.
>
> *—Illinois Senator Carol Moseley-Braun, in a speech to reverse the Senate's vote to extend the patent on a society insignia showing a Confederate flag*

   a. *Explain why Senator Carol Moseley-Braun is an important part of the struggle for racial equality.*
   b. *Indicate why you AGREE or DISAGREE with her statement.*

3. *What did a conservative Republican senator mean by saying that Bill Clinton won the 1994 elections for the Republicans?*

The Federal Courts

Until July, 1993, the Supreme Court had made no sweeping changes in constitutional areas. In its final two weeks, however, the Court demonstrated how conservative it had become. In response to a racial *gerrymandering* case brought in North Carolina, the Justices ruled that carving out legislative districts solely to elect more blacks might violate the constitutional rights of white voters.

Explaining the 5–4 decision, Justice Sandra Day O'Connor wrote that linking people who "may have little in common with one another but the color of their skin bears an uncomfortable resemblance to political apartheid."

In another decision, the Supreme Court made it harder for workers charging discrimination to win their lawsuits. Until this decision, employers could be held liable if they lied about why they had fired someone. The Court ruling requires a worker to prove that the reason for the firing is bias.

In both cases, the five-Justice majority included Sandra Day O'Connor, Antonin Scalia, Anthony Kennedy, Clarence Thomas, and Chief Justice William Rehnquist. They became known as the "Reliable Right." Absent from this group were Justices David Souter, John Paul Stevens, Harry Blackmun, and Byron White. Souter has supported women, minorities, prisoners, and the mentally retarded and worked to maintain separation of church and state. Stevens, Blackmun, and White also aligned themselves with the liberal minority.

The conservative domination of the Court began to change in 1993, when Clinton appointed Ruth Bader Ginsburg, a champion of women's rights. Justice Ginsburg replaced Byron White, who retired in July, 1993. When Justice Blackmun retired in 1994, Clinton appointed Stephen Breyer to the Court. A moderate, Breyer has supported affirmative action programs and separation of church and state. But he has also expressed a willingness to uphold capital punishment and tough sentences for some criminals. These appointments were expected to result in more balanced decisions by the Supreme Court.

1. *Define the term* Reliable Right.
2. *Explain why the Supreme Court decisions during 1992–1993 were considered victories for conservatism.*

The Clinton Legal Team

During the Administrations of Reagan and Bush, conservatives used legal arguments and judicial appointments to promote social goals. These included restriction of abortions, curbing racial preferences in hiring, limiting long-running legal appeals from convicts on death row, and bringing religion into the schools.

In mid-1993, Clinton appeared to lack a consistent social-legal agenda by acting as a liberal on some issues and a conservative on others. At times, however, he firmly opposed Republican views. For example, in July, 1993, Clinton's Justice Department asked the Supreme Court to bar lawyers from rejecting women as jurors because of their gender.

President Clinton began to fill the Administration's top legal jobs in March, 1993, with the appointment of Janet Reno as Attorney General. Drew Days, a Yale law professor, became Solicitor General, the Administration's advocate in the Supreme Court. These appointees became the President's legal team, responsible for moving the following issues through the courts:

- **Abortion.** During the 1993–1994 term, the Supreme Court reviewed a federal law banning the blocking of entrances and violent acts at abortion clinics. (See pages 66–67 for a more detailed discussion of this issue).

- **Privacy.** Solicitor General Days defended Clinton's policy on gays in the military against challenges that it denies full rights to homosexuals.

- **Voting Rights.** Clinton's lawyers supported minority efforts to reverse the Supreme Court's ruling that allowed white voters to contest oddly-shaped districts drawn to ensure election of black representatives.

- **Regulation.** The Clinton team supported a ruling that ordered the National Science Foundation to abide by U.S. environmental laws when conducting research in Antarctica. However, the White House opposed groups that challenged the North American Free Trade Agreement (NAFTA) on environmental grounds.

- **Federal Programs.** Clinton's lawyers have maintained that alcohol and drug abusers denied Social Security benefits may not file a class action suit against the government.

The Clinton legal team found it difficult to pursue their agenda. The Alliance for Justice, a coalition of legal activists, stated in 1994 that conservatives occupied a majority of seats on the Supreme Court and two-thirds of all federal judgeships. As a result, they saw the courts as unsympathetic to extending rights in social and environmental cases.

The White House Counsel is another important attorney on the President's legal team. In 1994, a special federal court appointed an "independent counsel" to continue investigating the 1980's finances of then Governor Clinton and his wife. The main question was whether an Arkansas bank that failed in 1989 had improperly given money to Clinton's campaign for governor in 1984 or to the Whitewater Development Company. This was a real-estate venture co-owned by the Clintons and the failed bank's owner.

1. *Indicate whether the following statements are* true *or* false:
   a. *In 1994, the Supreme Court and the federal courts were dominated by liberal judges.*
   b. *The Clinton Administration supports the realignment of voting districts to favor minorities.*
   c. *Free access to abortion clinics was not part of Clinton's legal agenda.*
   d. *The Solicitor General is the President's advocate in the Supreme Court.*
   e. *Justice Byron White retired from the Supreme Court in 1993.*
2. *List two members of Clinton's legal team. State each one's job.*
3. *List the legal issues pursued by the Clinton Administration.*
4. *How have liberal-conservative divisions in the federal courts affected the Clinton Administration's ability to carry out policy?*

The Federal Bureaucracy

In July, 1993, Clinton became the first President to fire a Director of the Federal Bureau of Investigation (FBI). William Sessions had been appointed by Ronald Reagan to the post of

FBI Director in 1987 for a ten-year term. However, a report issued by the Justice Department in January, 1993, accused Sessions of a range of ethical violations, including a misuse of FBI planes and limousines.

To head the FBI, Clinton appointed Judge Louis Freeh, a former FBI agent and federal prosecutor. Judge Freeh came to the position with considerable experience and an excellent reputation in the law enforcement community.

The FBI has been involved in a reevaluation of both its mission and its structure. Since the end of the cold war, the counterintelligence specialists of the FBI have been focusing on problems such as the international arms trade, industrial espionage, and terrorism. Before statistics showed a decrease in street crime, the FBI was pressured to use its agents to support local police.

As FBI Director, Louis Freeh is subordinate to the Justice Department led by Attorney General Janet Reno. The Attorney General is a member of the President's Cabinet and reports directly to him.

Despite recent efforts to change recruitment policies so that minorities and women can become a significant part of the organization, the FBI is dominated by white males.

Recently, the FBI was sharply criticized for its treatment of Randy Weaver, a white separatist who lived in the remote Ruby Ridge area of Idaho. FBI agents claimed that Weaver had tried to sell two illegal shotguns to a Bureau of Alcohol, Tobacco and Firearms informer. When Weaver resisted arrest, FBI agents surrounded his cabin. During the siege, one of the agents and Weaver's son and wife were shot dead. In 1995, Freeh fired FBI agent Larry Potts, whose orders had been interpreted as authorizing the shootings. Attorney General Reno revised the rules for use of deadly force by the FBI.

In 1996, another incident aroused public disapproval of the

FBI. Agents released information to the press about Richard Jewell, a security guard suspected of planting a bomb in Centennial Olympic Park during the Olympic games in Atlanta, Georgia. As a result, Jewell was widely viewed as guilty before there was sufficient evidence to formally charge him. He was later cleared of the crime.

The federal bureaucracy spans three branches of government—legislative, executive, and judicial. Each includes several bureaus, offices, and other organizations. In the Legislative Branch, for example, the General Accounting Office and the Congressional Budget Office help Congress make laws affecting fiscal matters. In the Judicial Branch, the Supreme Court is supported by Courts of Appeals, District Courts, Claims Courts, and other subordinate courts.

The President presides over the Executive Branch. He is assisted by the Cabinet departments: State, Justice, Treasury, Defense, Interior, Agriculture, Commerce, Labor, Health and Human Services, Housing and Urban Development, Transportation, Energy, Education, and Veterans Affairs. With the exception of Justice, led by the Attorney General, each department is headed by a Secretary appointed by the President with the advice and consent of the Senate. These departments conduct the business of the federal government.

1. *Explain how Clinton provided leadership to the FBI in 1993.*
2. *List the departments that are part of the President's Cabinet.*

The Making of Foreign Policy

The foreign policy of the United States is made by the President in consultation with the Secretary of State. The Clinton Administration received mixed reviews for its initial foreign-policy performance.

- In Somalia, U.S. soldiers were killed on a U.N. peacekeeping mission in April, 1994. The Administration was criticized for changing the U.S. mission from peacekeeping to peacemaking (see page 170).
- Attempts by the United States to return President Aristide of Haiti to power ended in success (see pages 192–193).

- The Administration's support of the North American Free Trade Agreement (NAFTA) was attacked by those who feared the loss of American jobs to lower-paid Mexican labor. Supporters, such as large U.S. corporations, believed that lowered trade barriers would increase U.S. exports and jobs (see pages 183–185).

- The NATO allies rejected Clinton's efforts to halt the war in Bosnia. Clinton's demands had included lifting the embargo on the supply of weapons to the Bosnian government and imposing NATO air strikes against Serb aggressors. (For later developments, see pages 111–113.)

- The Administration had a partial success in persuading North Korea to abandon its nuclear weapons program (see pages 134–136).

Clinton implemented other foreign-policy actions. Chief among them was the September, 1993, peace accord between Israel and the Palestine Liberation Organization. This agreement was a direct result of the Administration's efforts. It was followed by a 1994 settlement between Israel and Jordan, also arranged by the United States. Unfortunately, the talks were halted in 1996. (For the events that led up to this halt, see pages 151–153.)

Clinton sent troops to stop Iraq's aggressive movement toward Kuwait in October, 1996. (For a discussion of Clinton's problems with Iraq, see pages 147–150.)

In December, 1994, Congress approved the General Agreement on Tariffs and Trade (GATT). Negotiated by the Clinton Administration, the 124-nation pact is the most ambitious global trade agreement in four decades.

In pursuit of his policy of reducing the number of nuclear weapons throughout the world, Clinton negotiated with Ukraine's President Leonid Kuchma, who signed the Nuclear Nonproliferation Treaty on December 5, 1994.

President Clinton's political opponents criticized him as lacking skill and determination in foreign affairs. Nevertheless, by 1996, many Americans began to recognize his achievements both at home and abroad.

◆ *Describe Clinton's foreign-policy problems.*

Section Review

1. *Define the term "federal bureaucracy."*
2. *Explain how the Clinton Administration made changes in the federal bureaucracy in order to respond to particular problems.*
3. *Identify the organizations that deal with law enforcement and foreign policy.*
4. *Was Clinton's first term successful or unsuccessful? State reasons for your opinion.*

The Presidential Election of 1996

When the 1996 presidential election campaign began, Americans felt more optimistic about the state of the union; the economy had strengthened, and the crime rate was down. They wanted a President who would foster these improvements while dealing carefully and gradually with other problems. Early in their campaigns, both major parties recognized the nation's desire for a middle-of-the-road approach to government. During his first four years, President Clinton had already adjusted to this attitude by changing how he handled such projects as health care reform.

Republicans responded to the national mood by choosing Senator Robert Dole of Kansas as their candidate, rejecting some of his outspoken rivals. Lamar Alexander, for example, wanted to transfer much of the federal government's power to the states. Patrick Buchanan spoke of outlawing abortion and ending legal immigration for at least five years. Publishing magnate Steve Forbes advocated a flat tax of 17 percent on all taxpayers. Dole's position, while tolerant of such opinions, was less drastic. He proposed a gradual reduction in the size of government, tax cuts for people with low incomes, and the end to federal funding for abortions.

Dole's first choice for Vice President was Colin Powell, who refused the offer, saying he was not a politician. In August, 1996, Dole selected Jack F. Kemp as his running mate. Kemp, a former member of Congress and a former Secretary of Housing and Urban Development, was in favor of tax cuts. He also had a relatively strong standing with black and Hispanic voters.

The Two Campaigns

Clinton identified and responded to the will of the voters more successfully than the Republicans did. He used rival proposals by making similar, more moderate ones. For example, although Clinton and Dole differed on individual income tax rates—Clinton said he would not reduce them, while Dole wanted a 15 percent decrease—their tax ideas had much in common. Dole's proposed 14 percent reduction in capital gains taxes was modified by Clinton to a reduced capital gains tax on the sales of homes. Dole offered families a tax credit for each child under 18; Clinton recommended a tax credit for each child under 13. Although Clinton's suggestions were more modest than Dole's, he succeeded in showing that Democrats as well as Republicans were in favor of "family values." Clinton took the lead in voter polls as early as October, 1995, and never lost it.

Clinton's steady lead was also a response to his claim that the economy had improved during his Administration. Although experts felt that it would have done so no matter who was President, many Americans associated the recent recession with Reagan and Bush economic policies and were reluctant to give a Republican President another chance.

A general sense that the Republican Party favored rich corporations over the "little guy" also helped Clinton. Might not Dole's tax cuts and balanced budget amendment hurt the poor—especially elderly dependents on Social Security and Medicare? Democrats played on this fear by linking Dole with Speaker of the House Newt Gingrich. Gingrich's Contract With America had been aimed at reducing many popular entitlement programs—such as health care and education for immigrants. He was also a major player in the government shut-down during the 1995 budget stalemate. Dole tried to distance himself from Gingrich. He resigned from the Senate to devote more time to his campaign and to weaken his association with the Speaker.

Dole was also hurt by his inability to explain how he would both balance the budget and cut taxes without also deeply cutting Social Security and Medicare. Moreover, he wavered between moderate and more extreme positions. His campaign platform called for a Constitutional amendment to outlaw abortion but, at the same time, recommended tolerance of those with pro-choice views.

When H. Ross Perot entered the race as an independent candidate, Dole feared he would attract a large proportion of Republican votes. Dole, therefore, joined others in barring Perot from the Presidential debates. To general amazement, Dole then asked Perot to drop out of the race and encourage his followers to vote Republican. Perot refused sharply.

Dole's late-campaign attacks on Clinton's integrity were also ineffective. References to Clinton's possible involvement in the Whitewater affair and to several political scandals occurring during his first term failed to sway voters. When Republicans charged Democrats with accepting huge campaign funding from foreign interests and U.S. labor unions, Democrats pointed out that Republicans had benefited from the financial support of big business.

Nothing seemed to damage Clinton's lead. Even when he outraged fellow Democrats by signing a bill to drastically reduce certain welfare benefits, his rating remained high. On November 5, 1996, he was reelected.

- *List the reasons why President Clinton took and kept the lead in the 1996 Presidential race.*

The Outlook for President Clinton's Second Term

The voters did not give President Clinton a mandate to return to former, more liberal positions. The Republicans remained strong in both the House and the Senate. They held a slightly diminished majority in the House, with 227 of the total 435 seats. In the Senate, they gained two seats, for a total of 55 of the 100. Americans had chosen leaders who could prevent anyone from straying either too far left or right.

Clinton's victory showed that the nation generally approved of such policies as encouraging Israeli-PLO peace talks and intervening in Haiti, Bosnia, and the Persian Gulf. There was also strong support for important Democratic positions: maintaining a sound economy by a balanced budget rather than by tax cuts, lowering the deficit, keeping interest rates low, creating more jobs, and assuring the fiscal soundness of Social

Security and Medicare. Those who favored such initiatives were mainly women, minorities, and older people.

Only 49 percent of eligible voters voted. Clinton got 49 percent of this popular vote, Dole, 41 percent, and Perot, 8 percent. Of electoral votes, Clinton got 379, and Dole, 159.

The issue of Clinton's character may indeed have contributed to the small turnout. His supporters hoped that during his second term, he would be able to resolve doubts about Whitewater, the White House travel office firings, the mishandling of FBI files, and campaign fund raising in 1996. Concerning this last matter, many waited to see if the President would fulfill his promise to enact laws against questionable foreign campaign donations.

It was expected that Clinton would profit from first-term experiences and face problem solving in a step-by-step rather than a wholesale manner. Many in both parties hoped that the Republicans would view election results as a rejection of their first-term efforts to cut entitlements and social welfare without first preserving safety nets to protect the needy.

Among Clinton's Cabinet appointments were U.S. Ambassador to the U.N. Madeleine Albright as the first woman Secretary of State and Republican Senator William Cohen as Secretary of Defense. Clinton also hoped to form bipartisan committees to work on future funding for Medicare and Social Security. Other domestic concerns included easing the harsh 1996 Welfare Act, reducing poverty, and reforming education and health care. One foreign-policy priority would be to expand international peacemaking initiatives.

Clinton will be a lame-duck President (one serving a final term in office). Therefore, expectations were high that Democratic leaders would spend the next four years promoting and grooming Vice President Gore as their Presidential candidate in 2000.

♦ *Describe some of the concerns that President Clinton planned to address during his second term.*

Section Review

1. *Explain the effect that the policies supported by Newt Gingrich had on Robert Dole's Presidential campaign.*

2. *Explain why you AGREE or DISAGREE with the following statement: The 1996 election suggests that most Americans have become politically conservative.*

Chapter 1 Review

A. *Write the letter of the correct response.*

1. *In the election of 1992, President George Bush was opposed by (a) Bill Clinton, Democrat; and Ross Perot, Independent (b) Bill Clinton, Republican; and Ross Perot, Democrat (c) Bill Clinton, Independent; and Ross Perot, Republican.*
2. *The issue that proved to be most critical during the election of 1992 was (a) foreign policy (b) the economy (c) technology.*
3. *Among the policies of the Clinton Administration in 1993 were (a) health care reform (b) expansion of the armed forces (c) independence for Puerto Rico.*
4. *During his 1992 struggle with Congress over the budget, Clinton had to compromise on (a) the size of the federal bureaucracy (b) educational funding (c) the energy tax.*
5. *One group elected to the House of Representatives in record-breaking numbers in 1992 comprised (a) African Americans (b) Native Americans (c) Asian Americans.*
6. *A problem faced by Clinton in the area of foreign policy was the attempt by Senator Robert Dole to (a) force the President to support all U.N. peacekeeping efforts (b) prevent the President from deploying troops abroad without the approval of Congress (c) persuade the President to support the admission of Russia to NATO.*
7. *The "Reliable Right" refers to (a) a group of conservative Supreme Court Justices (b) a group of liberal federal court judges (c) the Attorney General and the Solicitor General.*

8. *The federal official who must act as the President's advocate on the Supreme Court is the (a) Attorney General (b) White House Counsel (c) Solicitor General.*

9. *Included in the federal bureaucracy are (a) agencies, bureaus, and offices administered by the Executive Branch of the federal government (b) the General Accounting Office of the Congress (c) a and b.*

10. *Clinton's 1996 campaign was helped by (a) the state of the economy (b) the collapse of Communism (c) his reform of welfare.*

B. *Write the name of the person described.*

1. *A high-ranking military officer, he opposed Clinton's attempt to lift the ban on homosexuals in the armed forces.*

2. *In 1992, he became the second Native American to be elected to the Senate.*

3. *As Senate Minority Leader in 1993, he offered to work with the Clinton Administration on reform of the health care system, but opposed the President in the area of foreign policy.*

4. *She became the first member of Clinton's legal team to be appointed.*

5. *A champion of women's rights, she was appointed to the Supreme Court in 1993.*

6. *A successful lawyer and social activist, she led the health care reform effort.*

7. *In 1993, he became Chairman of the Joint Chiefs of Staff of the Armed Forces.*

8. *His actions as Speaker of the House after the 1994 elections did not help Robert Dole as the Republican Presidential candidate in 1996.*

9. *One of the more extreme persons to campaign in the 1996 Presidential campaign, he advocated outlawing abortion and stopping legal immigration for at least five years.*

10. *He was an independent candidate for President in both the 1992 and 1996 national elections.*

C. *Write a brief essay on ONE of the following themes:*

The victory of Bill Clinton in the election of 1992.

The President and the Congress in the 1990's.

The President and the courts in the 1990's.

The election of 1994.

The election of 1996.

D. *Respond to each of the following statements by writing one or two paragraphs.*

1. *Identify the federal officials connected with the development of foreign policy.*
2. *List three countries that have been foreign-policy problems for the Clinton Administration. Why have they been problems?*
3. *Explain why President Clinton felt that Americans expected him to show a bipartisan spirit after his reelection to the Presidency in 1996.*
4. *Evaluate the Clinton Administration. What have been its successes and failures? How effective do you think President Clinton has been as a leader?*

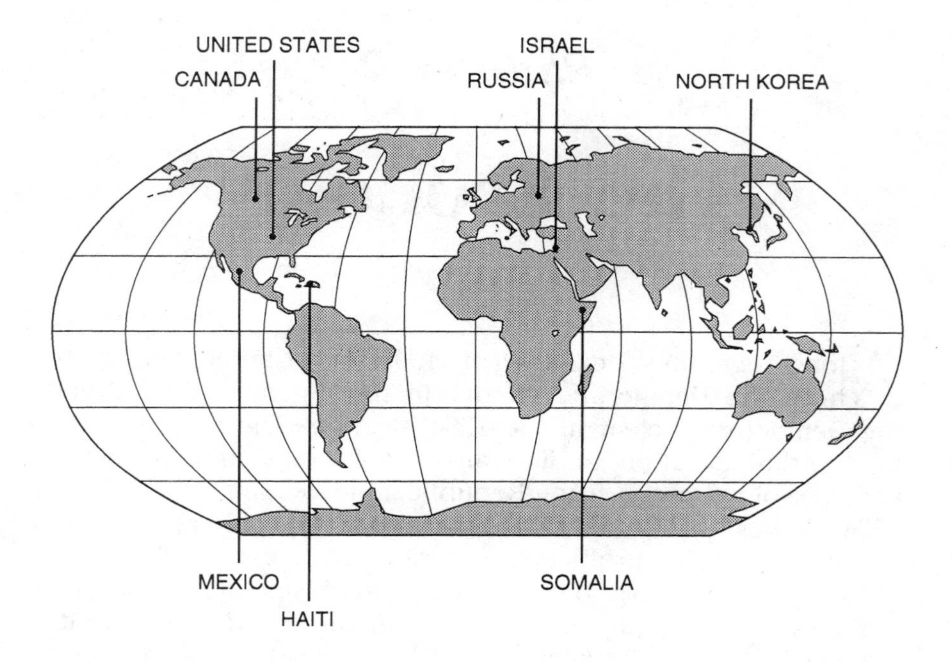
UNITED STATES
CANADA
ISRAEL
RUSSIA
NORTH KOREA
MEXICO
HAITI
SOMALIA

Chapter 2

The Economy

A long recession, beginning in 1990, contributed heavily to both the Democratic victory in the election of 1992 and the Democratic defeat in the 1994 election. The failure of the Bush Administration to find answers to economic problems turned voters away from Republican leadership in 1992. In 1994, it was the Democrats' turn to take the blame for continuing economic problems. American voters turned against elected officeholders because they were unable to provide answers to the problems of unemployment, inflation, corporate downsizing, trade imbalances, and the federal deficit. Some began to fear that despite its military power, the United States might lose economic leadership to other nations. In the spring of 1991, however, economists announced the start of a recovery that was to continue during the decade.

The Slow Recovery

At first recovery was slow, but in the last quarter of 1992, there were positive signs that the recession was ending. The nation's *gross domestic product* (sum total of all goods and services produced) expanded at a rate of 4.7 percent, the highest quarterly growth rate in five years. Productivity increased 2.8 percent, the best showing since 1972. Long-term interest rates declined. Hopes of economic recovery continued into 1993, as auto and housing sales increased and 60 percent of major U.S. companies posted earnings as good as or better than expected. In 1996, not only did the GDP continue to grow steadily, but inflation and, consequently, long-term interest rates remained moderate.

In October, 1993, German Chancellor Helmut Kohl startled

economists and businesspeople by admitting that Germany lagged behind the United States and Japan in adjusting to the economic challenges of the 1990's. Among the reasons for Chancellor Kohl's praise of American efforts to increase performance and competitiveness were the following:

- By 1993, U.S. companies had taken the lead in communications technology. Preparations were begun to design, build, and program the communications systems of the future. These efforts placed the United States in the forefront of one of the world's most important growth industries.

- German carmakers BMW and Mercedes-Benz decided to open plants in the Southeastern United States. Audi has also been considering a U.S. factory. All three have been attracted by the productivity of U.S. workers and by labor costs well below those in Germany. Investors were beginning to notice the competitive turnaround of the American economy.

- Layoffs of middle managers and thousands of other workers at U.S. corporations continued. For those laid off, the job cuts have been painful and depressing. But most economists say that these savings should make American businesses even more competitive in coming years. In short, American firms are developing smaller but more efficient workforces.

The dramatic rise in American competitiveness is expected to bring great benefits to the U.S. economy in the 1990's. The drop in the value of the dollar since 1985, moderation of wage increases, and faster productivity growth have combined to make American labor costs lower than those of other major industrial nations. By 1993, many foreign companies felt that

they had to shift some of their production to the United States to assure continued access to North American markets. Partly as a result of this, the growth rate rose to over 4 percent in the second quarter of 1996, compared to approximately 3 percent in 1993.

The continued recovery of the American economy is linked to the recovery of other nations. In April, 1993, Secretary of the Treasury Lloyd Bentsen expressed concern over a falloff in U.S. exports to Europe and Japan. Weakened foreign demand for U.S. goods can slow American business expansion and employment. However, as the global economy improved in 1994, American manufacturing continued to grow. By the end of 1994, exports had increased to 10.2 percent of America's gross domestic product (GDP). In early 1995, Japan, Mexico, and Canada were the largest markets for U.S. exports. The Japan market was somewhat weakened in 1996 by a trade deficit of 34 percent.

1. *List three developments which showed that the United States was recovering from the global recession by the end of 1992.*
2. *Explain the following headline:*

   U.S. LABOR COSTS BEAT THE COMPETITION

Section Review

1. *Which of the following statements are* true *and which are* false*?*
   a. *American economic expansion will be unaffected by gradual economic recovery in Europe and Asia.*
   b. *The U.S. economic growth rate rose to 4 percent in 1996.*
   c. *A slowdown in the global economy will affect the gross domestic product of the United States.*
   d. *By 1993 the productivity rate increase was 2.8 percent.*

2. *Complete the following sentence:*

   One major problem for the U.S. economy which would result from a slowdown of economic growth abroad is ______.

Employment Trends: The Changing Job Market

Despite the beginning of economic recovery in 1992, anxiety about jobs continued. Experts predicted a long wait before the employment picture significantly improved. Production growth did lead to some reduction in unemployment, the jobless rate declining from 7.8 percent in June, 1992, to 5.4 percent in December, 1994. Such data, however, do not adequately measure hardship. The unemployment rate measures the number of people who are unemployed but actively looking for work. It does not include those who have quit looking. Unemployment increased in 1995 to approximately 5.8 percent, but by July, 1996, it had settled back to 5.4 percent.

The employment picture has also been shaped by the trend toward corporate downsizing. Industrial giants like Kodak, McDonnell Douglas, IBM, and General Motors have eliminated jobs in order to cut costs and increase productivity. The jobs wiped out had been far better paying than those available at companies that were still hiring new employees.

Wal-Mart, for example, the discount store chain, created more jobs in the 1990's than did any other American company. However, these jobs generally paid only five to nine dollars an hour. PepsiCo, still expanding in 1994, offered employment opportunities at the company's Pizza Hut, Taco Bell, and KFC fast-food restaurants. As a result, many people who experienced layoffs and found new employment suffered a large reduction in income. For example, 72 percent of the 2,000 workers let go by RJR Nabisco took other jobs, but at wages that averaged only 47 percent of their previous pay.

◆ *PROVE or DISPROVE: The 1990's economic recovery improved living conditions for the average American.*

Jobless in America

The gap between employment supply and demand created an "industrial reserve army" in the United States in the 1990's.

In October, 1993, for example, the Detroit Post Office announced that it had openings for a few hundred clerks, sorters, and letter carriers and that some of these positions would not be filled for three to five years. The number of applicants reached 20,000. This trend is expected to worsen as the nation's corporations continue to downsize. A recent survey by the American Management Association of 8,000 of its member companies showed that 47 percent reduced their staffs during the 12 months ending June, 1993. Among these firms, an average 10.4 percent of staff was let go, as compared to 9.3 percent in the previous 12 months.

Ever since 1992, new college graduates have had a more difficult time finding a good job than at any other time in the past 20 years. According to a 1992 Labor Department study, 30 percent of each new collegiate graduating class between 1992 and 2005 will join the ranks of the jobless or the underemployed. That would represent a considerable increase in unemployed or underemployed graduates over the 1984–90 period, when an average of 20 percent of each graduating class became "underutilized." In addition, college graduates entering the labor force in the 1990's will earn less than their counterparts did a generation ago.

◆ *Explain the following statement:*

> Why is it that everywhere I go in a hotel, I've got a college graduate coming up to the room bringing food, carrying bags and so on and so forth, waiting until they get their job?
>
> —*Ross Perot, in a November, 1993, debate with Vice President Al Gore*

Hopes and Prospects

Fortunately, the employment situation has not been entirely bleak for job hunters, as some types of jobs are still expanding. However, experts have been able to identify only general trends. Biotechnology, for example, is regarded as an industry that is bound to grow. Health care is also viewed as a high-tech field that will generate more and better-paying jobs.

Temporary help has been one of the fastest-growing employment sectors. Restaurants and social services accounted for significant growth in payroll jobs in the mid-1990's.

Employment experts have offered the following forecast to the job hunters of the 1990's:

- More opportunities will be found with foreign companies, especially those investing in U.S. manufacturing. Although U.S.-owned automakers have been downsizing, Toyota, Honda, and Nissan have been hiring workers for their American plants. Mercedes-Benz and BMW plan to build factories in Alabama and South Carolina.

- The number of women bosses will increase. Women in the 1990's have been starting companies at 1.5 times the rate of men.

- The employment future will belong to the educated "knowledge worker." Specialists in personal computers, fiber optics, E-mail, etc. will be most in demand. This will require continuing education and upgrading of skills. High-tech workers will have to go back to school about every five years.

- Employees will work in small groups or individually, even on assembly lines. The trend toward work teams will be especially strong among knowledge workers. Some of these may not work regularly for a single company, but will contract with different corporations to do specific, limited jobs.

The Clinton Administration has regarded training as the key to putting the unemployed back to work. The President's 1994 plans included a $3 billion proposal. The plan is to merge all current federal job programs and to adopt a unified approach to retrain the more than two million workers who lose jobs each year. In response to the President's call for a national "re-employment" system that would address widespread anxiety over job security, Secretary of Labor Robert Reich developed a plan to improve the nation's unemployment insurance system.

Reich criticized the existing unemployment insurance program, claiming that it prolongs joblessness by paying laid-off workers for remaining unemployed. Reich prefers to encourage states to use benefit checks in more creative ways—as cash rewards for workers who find jobs quickly, as stipends to start small businesses, and as training subsidies for those who wish to improve their skills. The Secretary of Labor has also called for a streamlining of the nation's network of 1,700 unemployment insurance offices. He proposed reorganizing these offices into "one-stop career centers" that would distribute unemployment checks, match job seekers with job openings, and identify workers whose skills are obsolete. In 1993, key elements of Reich's plan were successfully field tested in local pilot projects across the United States.

◆ *Examine the graphs and complete the sentences which follow.*

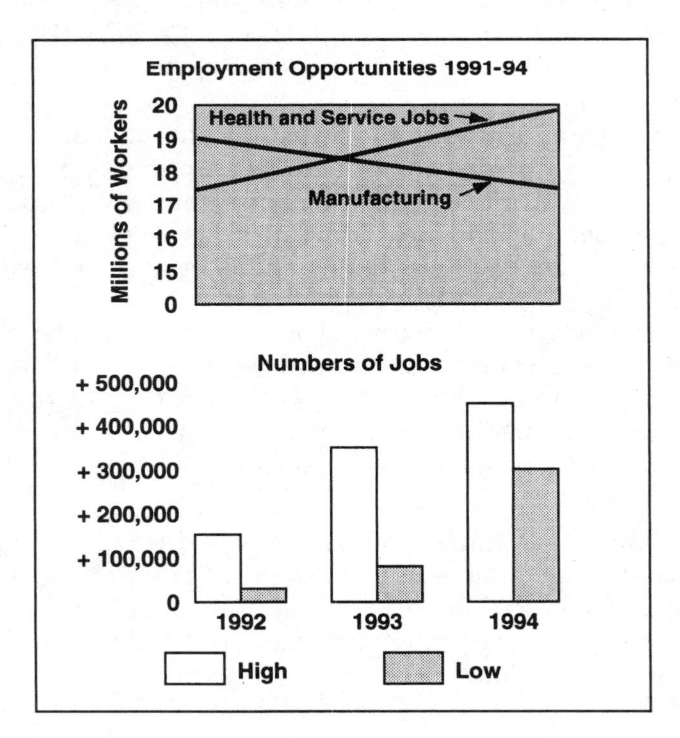

a. *Two areas in which employment opportunities were available in 1993 were ______ and ______.*
b. *Employment opportunities in ______ dropped between 1991 and 1993.*
c. *In 1993, experts predicted that U.S. corporations would ______.*
d. *As compared to manufacturing, wage growth in private sector services ______ between 1990 and 1993.*

Section Review

1. *Explain two employment trends predicted by experts for the 1990's. How might these trends affect your plans for the future?*
2. *State the response of the Clinton Administration to the employment problem. What measures for putting people back to work would you recommend?*

Deficit Reduction: The Long and Complex Struggle

The federal deficit is the amount of money that the federal government spends each year beyond what it collects in taxes. The deficit is paid for by borrowing. This practice has created a large national debt; money owed by the government to the holders of the bonds and notes issued by the U.S. Treasury when it borrows. As the debt grows, the economic growth of the United States is threatened. When President Ronald Reagan took office in 1981, the national debt was $994 billion. Reagan promised a balanced budget in which government spending would equal taxes received. However, during his presidency, the size of the federal deficit increased greatly, and the national debt more than doubled.

Reduction of the federal deficit was the greatest economic challenge facing Reagan's successor, George Bush. The ending of the cold war enabled him to cut military spending, and he approved a tax increase on the very wealthy. Despite these measures, the federal deficit continued to grow. When President Clinton took office in 1993, the national debt stood at $4.4 trillion.

The deficit reduction plan that Clinton pushed through the Congress by a margin of one Senate vote, in August, 1993, provided for spending cuts of nearly $500 billion over a period of five years. The President promised further cuts in the future. Members of Congress and public-interest groups have also developed proposals for the reduction of government spending.

♦ *Define* federal deficit *and* national debt.

Deficit Reduction Strategies

Proponents of deficit reduction believe that the deficit is a serious drag on the economy. Some wish to attack the deficit by radical cutbacks on payments called "entitlements," which embrace Social Security, Medicare, farm-support payments, etc. Such entitlements make up more than half of all federal spending. This path to deficit reduction would require sacrifices by millions of Americans.

Critics of Clinton's deficit reduction plan have claimed that it is inadequate because its main element is a tax increase on a small number of American households—the 1.2 percent earning about $180,000 per year or more. Clinton's opponents would aim for a much broader target. To achieve a balanced budget by the year 2000, they would impose strict standards for the granting of benefits. Households would lose about 10 percent of whatever federal benefits they receive for every $10,000 of income above $40,000. Those earning $120,000 per year or more might lose as much as 85 percent of their benefits. The 58 percent of Americans whose incomes, including entitlements, are $40,000 per year or less would lose nothing.

This particular deficit reduction plan was formulated by the Concord Coalition, a group led by an ex-Secretary of Commerce and two former Senators. They claim to have 100,000 followers in 50 states, and they seek to educate voters as to why sacrifices must be made. To increase federal revenues, the Concord plan also calls for a 50¢ per gallon gas tax and a

$12,000 cap on tax deductions for mortgage interest, a measure that would affect just 5 percent of homeowners.

Economists who disapprove of the Concord plan argue that proposed cuts for retirees violate the trust of people who paid into Social Security and Medicare for years. Most economists agree, however, that the federal deficit must be reduced before the national debt becomes so large that it would be impossible to repay. Those members of Congress who voted against Clinton's deficit reduction package have pledged to introduce a balanced-budget amendment to the Constitution mandating the federal government to maintain a balanced budget.

At a January, 1995, meeting with Republican Speaker of the House Newt Gingrich, President Clinton agreed not to lobby against a balanced-budget amendment. This was a major change in position for the President, who had previously opposed a balanced-budget amendment. It was one of several Republican ideas that Clinton accepted after the 1994 Democratic defeat. In March, 1995, however, a balanced-budget amendment was defeated in the Senate. Its Democratic opponents raised doubts about the future of Social Security funds if the measure became a law. At the end of 1996, the amendment had again been passed by the House of Representatives but not by the Senate.

Meanwhile, by September, 1996, the deficit had dropped to $107 billion, a reduction of 63 percent.

1. *Explain how each of the following has approached the task of deficit reduction:*

   President Clinton
   The Concord Coalition
   Some members of Congress

2. *Examine the graph on page 34 and indicate which statements are* true *and which are* false.

   a. *The federal deficit was higher in 1980 than it was in 1990.*
   b. *The projected federal deficit for the year 2000 will be approximately 5 percent of the gross domestic product.*
   c. *The federal deficit increased greatly in 1990.*
   d. *There is no relationship between the federal deficit and the gross domestic product of the United States.*
   e. *A rising federal deficit is damaging to the national economy.*

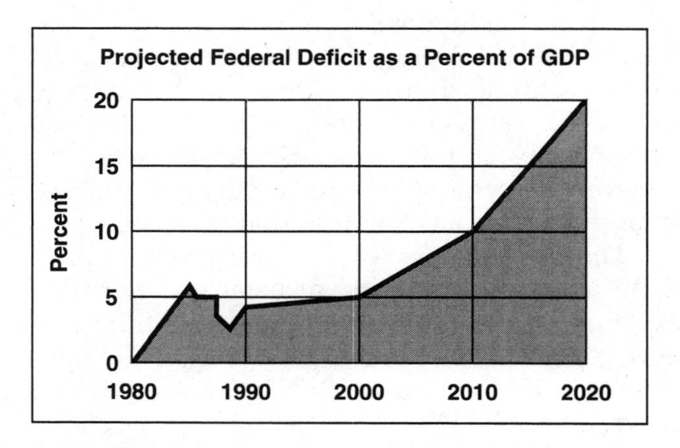

3. *PROVE or DISPROVE: The federal deficit is a problem for economists and political leaders, not the ordinary citizen.*

Taxation and Taxophobia

Increased taxes are essential to the deficit-reduction effort. Reductions in government spending must be matched by increases in government revenues if the budget gap and the national debt are to be decreased. The reluctance of politicians to risk their popularity by raising taxes has been a longstanding obstacle to deficit reduction.

In city and state elections in 1993, Republican candidates were able to benefit from *taxophobia:* the voters' resentment of tax increases. The Republicans won the mayoral race in New York City and the governorships of New Jersey and Virginia. Although these elections were dominated by local issues, such as New York's problems with crime and violence, economic matters also played a role. Each of these areas had experienced a sharp economic downturn, and their growth rates in 1993 were among the lowest in the nation. In New Jersey, the unemployment rate jumped from 7.1 to 7.7 percent in the month before the election.

The defeat of the Democratic candidates was a setback for President Clinton. He had campaigned repeatedly to reelect Mayor David Dinkins in New York and Governor Jim Florio in New Jersey. The latter race, in particular, was viewed by the White House as having national significance. Unable to win approval of his "activist government" and massive tax increases, Florio lost to Republican Christine Todd Whitman.

Four years earlier, Governor Florio had campaigned on the promise of no new taxes. In his first year, however, he pushed through a $2.8 billion tax increase. Part of it was used to finance a fair but unpopular redistribution of resources for the education budget. Money was taken from the wealthier districts to subsidize schools located in poor districts. Florio rode out the voters' anger and attempted to persuade them to accept a government which gave them better services in return for higher taxes. The majority turned to Whitman, who campaigned on a pledge to cut taxes and to slash state spending by $1 billion.

The results of the New Jersey election nullified White House efforts to persuade worried Democratic Congresspeople that voters would not punish supporters of higher taxes and an activist government. During the election year of 1996, Clinton began to look for ways to cut government spending in order to avoid raising taxes.

The new Republican Governor of Virginia, George Allen, celebrated an overwhelming election victory with a promise not to raise any sales or income taxes.

Rudolph Giuliani, the Republican winner of the mayoral race in New York City, inherited a nearly bankrupt city, with a $3 billion deficit in a $31 billion budget. Giuliani campaigned on promises to improve public safety by putting more police on the streets and to keep business and jobs in the city. He may find it difficult to do so without raising taxes.

Voter taxophobia facilitated the Republican attack on "tax-and-spend" Democrats in 1994. Clinton was hard-pressed to defend policies that use tax dollars to improve the quality of American life. Taxophobia contributed to the Republican victory in the 1994 national elections. Health care and other expensive Clinton programs had alarmed many. At the opening of the 104th Congress, in January, 1995, the Republicans promised to cut welfare, taxes, and domestic programs, freeze defense spending, and limit Medicare and Medicaid. By late 1996, the Republican Congress had forced President Clinton to endorse the plan for a balanced federal budget in seven years. Large cuts in Medicare and Medicaid, however, lost the Republicans much public support, which prevented them from passing many of their proposed changes.

1. *Define* taxophobia *and* activist government.
2. *Identify:*
   a. *David Dinkins and Rudolph Giuliani*
   b. *Jim Florio and Christine Todd Whitman*

Section Review

1. *Explain why the Clinton Administration regarded the 1993 election for governor of New Jersey as a race of national significance. How did the race turn out? Do you agree with the voters' decision? Why or why not?*
2. *Discuss the connection between deficit reduction and taxophobia. How have both affected politics in the 1990's?*

The Business Scene

Productivity, or output per hour worked, is an economic yardstick commonly used to measure the ability of a nation to compete. It determines a nation's standard of living and its status among nations. In the 1990's, the United States has remained the world's productivity leader in manufacturing.

A detailed study of American productivity, completed in 1993, compared U.S. manufacturing to that of Germany and Japan, focusing upon individual industries. It revealed that the United States does not lead in all industries and concluded that where it has fallen behind, the reasons have more to do with how goods are produced than with the skills of workers or the quality of technology.

The comparisons of individual industries showed that Japanese output per hour is 15 percent to almost 50 percent higher in cars, car parts, machine tools, consumer electronics, and steel. Germany's productivity is half to three-fourths that of the United States in several industries, including cars and beer. In steel and machine tools, German and American output is equal.

In certain industries, the average German or Japanese factory worker is far less productive than the average American worker. The study suggests that a lack of advanced technology is not that important. The training, organizing, and motivating of workers, for example, have been key factors in the success of Toyota and other Japanese auto manufacturers.

◆ *Study the graph and answer the questions below.*

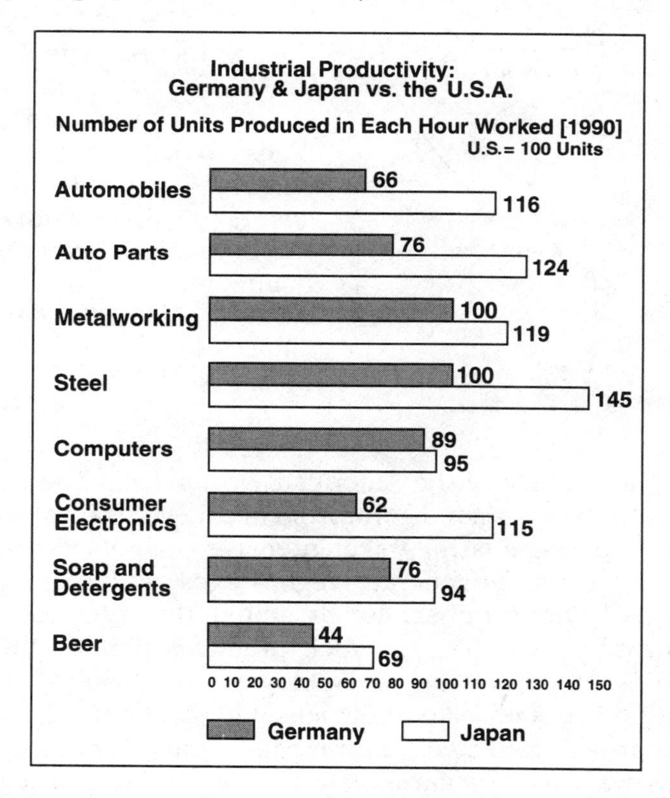

1. *List the industries in which Japanese productivity is greater than that of the United States.*
2. *List the industries in which American productivity is greater than that of Germany and Japan.*
3. *Explain why American productivity is measured against that of Germany and Japan.*

Clinton and the Business Community

Clintonomics, the economic policy of the Clinton Administration, has been described as "business friendly." The President's Council of Economic Advisers has indicated its desire to be a helper and a partner to business. The Administration has developed plans to promote exports and has promised to streamline the bureaucracy.

On the other hand, some businesspeople expressed concern about some of Clinton's bills. Many were angry about the tax increases included in the 1993 budget plan. They were also worried about plans to raise the minimum wage and give health coverage to part-time workers at the employer's expense. The minimum wage was raised to $5.15 in 1997; it seemed to have little impact on small businesses.

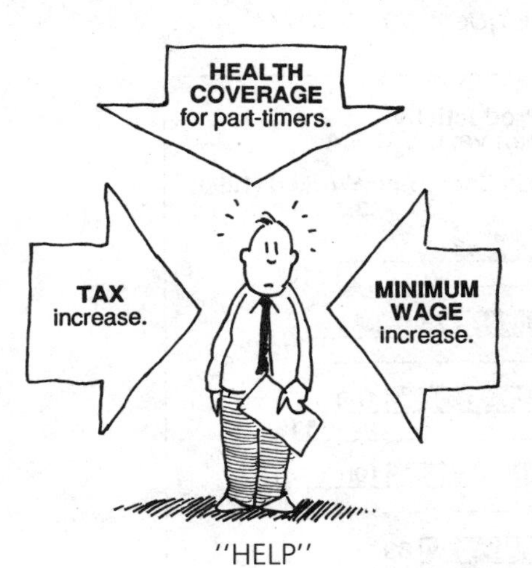

"HELP"

In August, 1993, Clinton hosted a conference in Chicago on the "Future of the American Workplace." The limelight was on employers, such as Motorola and Levi Strauss, who use teamwork, profit sharing, skill-intensive manufacturing, and other techniques to generate high wages and good profits. Secretary of Labor Robert Reich stated the intention of the Administration to encourage such practices across the American economy. Clinton urged employers to prosper and grow by treating workers like indispensable partners. The President's approach reflected a serious imbalance in the economy. U.S. 1993 wages and salaries failed to keep pace with the 3.8 percent inflation rate. This imbalance eased in 1994, when consumer prices rose only 2.7 percent. This was due partly to Clintonomics and partly to steps taken by businesses to increase productivity. Investments in computers and telecommunications enabled companies to improve efficiency and hold down costs.

1. *Define* Clintonomics.
2. *Describe the approach of the Clinton Administration to both business and labor.*

Section Review

1. *Explain why you AGREE or DISAGREE with the claim that American workers are less productive than those of Europe or Asia.*
2. *How "business friendly" do you think the Clinton Administration has been? Explain your answer.*

The Changing Workplace

Most Americans will never work for a blue-chip employer such as Levi Strauss or Motorola. Manufacturing, with its high wages and full-time jobs, employed just 16 percent of American workers in 1993. In contrast, retail and service companies employed 45 percent, but in these industries part-time employment is a common practice.

Part-time jobs accounted for 30 percent of all new jobs created by the economy in the 12 months ending August, 1993. But these part-timers received neither health insurance nor pension benefits. On average, fewer than a third of part-time workers receive health insurance and fewer than one-half are covered by a retirement plan.

A handful of employers in the 1990's began to demonstrate that part-time work need not mean poverty, and that a service job need not mean a dead-end career. Starbucks Coffee Company, a Seattle-based chain of espresso bars, employs 2,800 people. Although more than half of them work part-time, they have been offered health and dental insurance, stock options, and a retirement plan.

Texas-based Whole Foods Market, Inc., is the nation's largest chain of natural foods supermarkets. It defines "full-time employee" as anyone working more than 24 hours a week. Nearly 90 percent of the chain's 3,062 employees were in this category in 1994. They were eligible for health and dental insurance and a retirement plan.

Target Stores, a Minneapolis-based discount chain with 100,000 employees in 32 states, has offered life insurance and a retirement plan to those who work as little as 23 hours a week.

Such generous practices have proven profitable for the employers. By paying 40 percent above minimum wage and funding 75 percent of employees' health and dental insurance,

Starbucks has been able to recruit highly motivated workers who stay with the company three times longer than is standard in the food industry. As a result, sales increased by 68 percent in the second quarter of 1993, and the annual profit far exceeded the $93 million earned in 1992.

Like the Starbucks' example above, more businesses in the 1990's have begun to recognize the link between employee morale, customer satisfaction, and profitability.

1. *Study the graph and answer the questions that follow.*

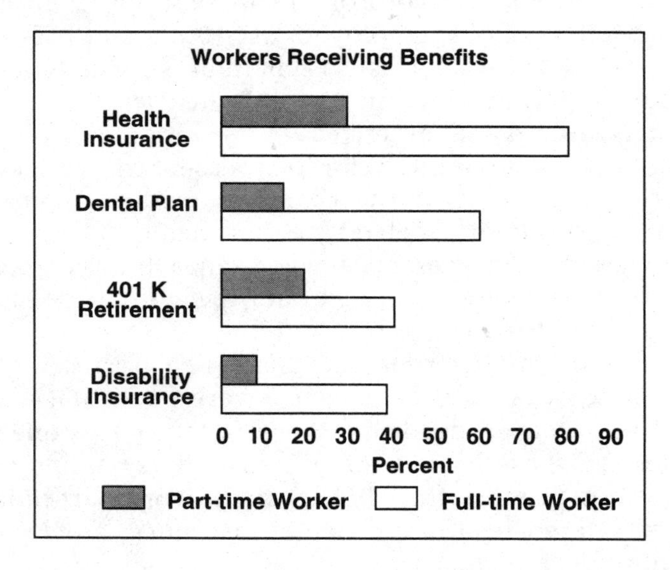

   a. *How have full-time workers received "beneficial treatment?"*
   b. *How have some businesses improved the morale of part-time employees?*

2. *Describe some of the changes taking place in the workplace in the 1990's. Do these changes benefit workers in your age group? Why or why not?*

Labor Unions

Since 1955, when 33.2 percent of the nation's non-agricultural workers were union members, both membership and power have declined. Only 15.8 percent of non-agricultural workers were dues-paying members of traditional trade unions in 1993. A variety of market changes has been responsible for this decline. Most notably, the number of workers in non-union jobs, such as banking and computer technology, has increased. Also, more Americans work in non-unionized part-time jobs, or are self-employed.

Despite their shrinking power base, unions still exercise influence in the economy. This was dramatically demonstrated by the November, 1993, strike of American Airlines' flight attendants. Demanding higher wages, nearly 90 percent of these workers walked off the job when this demand was refused. The union strategy was highly effective. The attendants planned to strike for 11 days, including the peak Thanksgiving holiday travel time, but return to work before the company could train replacements.

The strike ended after five days, when President Clinton intervened with a call for binding arbitration. This was regarded as a victory for the union, which had called for a third-party judge. The President, who had battled the unions over his free-trade policies, welcomed the opportunity to improve relations with organized labor.

The cost of the strike to American Airlines, estimated to be in the tens of millions of dollars, was seen as a victory for women in organized labor. Women comprise about 85 percent of all flight attendants, but their rate of pay is the lowest in an industry dominated by well-paid men.

Labor relations experts predict more frequent use of binding arbitration with a Democrat in the White House. Managements generally oppose the use of this method of settling disputes. Arbitrators usually attempt to find a middle ground between the competing demands of the two sides, thus depriving industry leaders of a way to win a total victory.

Between 1990 and 1993, the nation's airlines lost $10 billion. In response, their managements have been trying to reduce operating costs. However, if the strike by American Airlines' flight attendants reflects a broad resolve among other unions in the industry to fight for improved wages and benefits, future labor disputes are likely.

A 1994 labor dispute led to a Major League baseball strike. To the dismay of millions of fans, the World Series was canceled. The strike was ended in 1995. A new contract was signed in late 1996.

A 1996 agreement between Ford Motor Company and the United Automobile Workers (UAW) improved on the 1993 contract, which had increased wages and pensions, preserved health and other benefits, and let Ford pay lower wages to workers replacing retirees. The new contract guaranteed job security for 95 percent of Ford's workers, while allowing the company to pay workers hired for new plants less than assembly-line workers. Thus, the union sought to end "outsourcing"—the use of nonunion labor. New union contracts with Chrysler and General Motors reflected the Ford agreement.

1. *Explain why labor unions lost some of their power and influence by the 1990's.*
2. *State two important results of the dispute between American Airlines and its flight attendants in 1993.*
3. *List the advantages to both labor and management of the 1996 Ford-UAW agreement.*

Section Review

1. *Research the development of labor unions in the United States. How important have they been to the economic development of the United States and the well-being of American workers?*
2. *Consider what you would regard as an ideal workplace. What working conditions and benefits would be available to you? In which industries or occupations might you find these conditions in the 1990's?*

Investments at Home and Abroad

Mutual funds are pools of stocks, bonds, or other securities that are managed by a professional investment company. Such funds are very popular among American investors. In the 1990's, one in four households has invested in mutual funds. Nearly half of all fund owners earn less than $50,000 a year.

Many American investors have been attracted by the rapid economic growth of the economies of Latin America and Asia.

Discouraged by low-yielding investments at home, they have become increasingly bold about investing abroad, especially in countries once called "underdeveloped," but more recently referred to as "emerging markets." While this has been helpful to the foreign economies and to the bank balances of American investors, the growing trend has reduced the amount of money available for investment in the United States.

By August, 1993, Americans had invested $5.4 billion in foreign-oriented mutual funds. That represented nearly half of all American mutual fund investments.

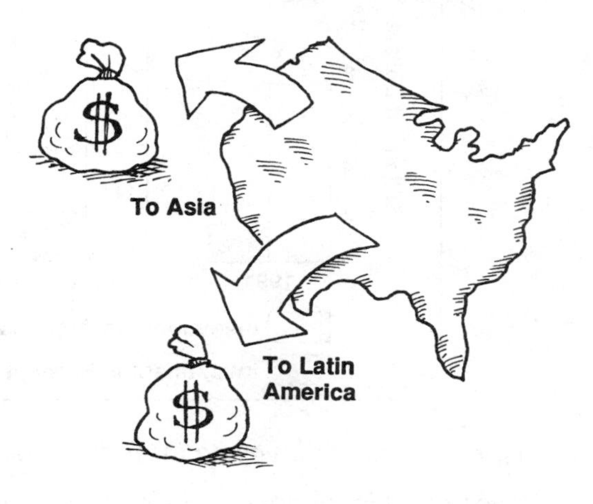

Foreign investments often yield greater profits than do domestic, but they are riskier. In some countries abroad, there is always a potential for political instability and a shortage of regulations to protect investors. Among the factors that make foreign investments attractive to U.S. industrialists have been low labor costs, industrial policies designed to foster growth, and strong work ethics.

Despite the trend toward investment in foreign industries, the U.S. stock markets have outperformed most foreign markets for the past several years. However, the increasing flow of American savings into foreign securities has reduced investment in the American economy.

Americans have also invested heavily in bonds in the 1990's. From mid-1992 to mid-1993, corporate and municipal bonds rose in value by 18 percent. And a recent surge in gold prices has made some market analysts regard it as the great investment of the 1990's.

◆ *Explain this newspaper headline:*

AMERICANS RUSH TO FUNDS THAT INVEST ABROAD

Section Review

Study the graph and indicate whether each of the statements which follow is true *or* false.

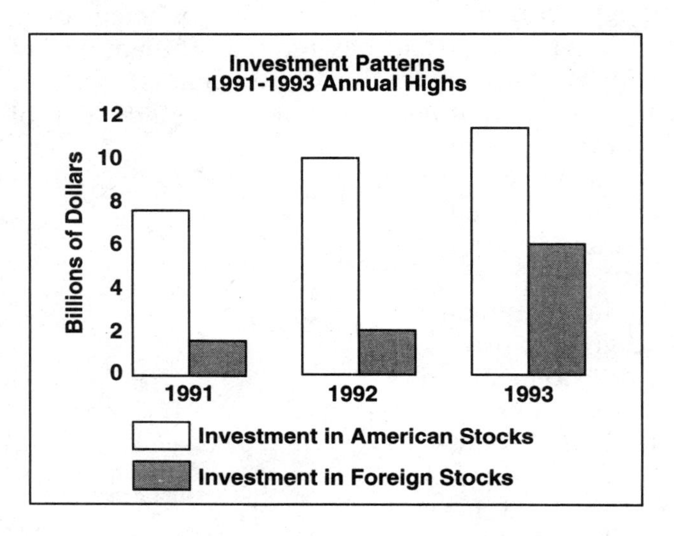

1. *More Americans invested in stock funds in 1991 than in 1993.*
2. *Investment in foreign stocks was higher in 1993 than in any previous year indicated.*
3. *Investment in foreign stocks was at its lowest in 1992.*
4. *In 1993, American domestic investment exceeded $10 billion.*
5. *In 1991, domestic investment far surpassed investment abroad.*

Dynamic Developments in Corporate America

For American corporations, the prospects for growth and profits were excellent in the latter part of 1993. Interest rates were at their lowest in thirty years. This made it easier for companies to pay off the debts they had incurred during the 1980's.

In the 1980's, American companies had borrowed excessively. This changed after 1991, when corporate America earned large amounts of surplus cash. Some companies, such as General Dynamics, a defense contractor, returned cash to shareholders. Others spent their money on acquisitions: the purchasing of other corporations. But much of the cash has been spent for new equipment. Business investment has been crucial to the U.S. recovery from the 1990–1991 recession.

In 1993, corporate America began to benefit from increased consumer spending. Retail sales in September were 6.1 percent higher than they were a year earlier. This mini-boom decreased inventories, and necessitated immediate replacement. Fortunately, the expanding consumer demand came at a time when American companies were downsizing and performing other forms of restructuring to increase productivity. Labor costs fell in 1992 and 1993, enabling corporate profits to grow by 15 percent. The prospect of inflation, however, remained a concern. To prevent it, the Federal Reserve Board raised interest rates in 1994. In 1996, the low inflation rate made it unnecessary for the Board to raise interest rates.

◆ *Explain why American corporations did well after 1991.*

Mergers and Acquisitions

Corporate America made media headlines in the mid-1990's with some large-scale mergers or acquisitions. The Lockheed Corporation and Martin Marietta Corporation agreed to a merger that would create the largest defense contractor in the United States. The annual sales of the two companies were nearly $23 billion. Early in 1997, the two remaining U.S. commercial aircraft manufacturers, Boeing and McDonnell Douglas, also announced their merger.

Two firms, Viacom and QVC, a cable-TV home shopping network, fought a long battle for control of Paramount Communications, a major motion picture producer. Viacom was victorious. The result was the first true multimedia conglomerate, a production and distribution company for publishing, sports, films, television, and telephone service. Other important mergers and acquisitions of the mid-1990's were the merger of NYNEX with Bell Atlantic and Disney's takeover of Capital Cities/ABC—the second largest since Kohlberg Kravis Roberts & Co.'s 1988 purchase of RJR Nabisco, Inc.

A giant of corporate America is Motorola, a firm that has earned large profits from the production of cellular telephones—portable, transportable, and mobile. They have sold in the United States and abroad. In the 1990's, Motorola has held a worldwide lead in this fast-growing market. Motorola is pursuing projects that merge electronics and telecommunications. It envisions a world in which wireless voice and data communications are as common as today's telephone call.

With 107,000 employees and a management training program attended by hundreds of top executives of American, European, and Asian firms, Motorola is regarded as one of the most successful representatives of corporate America.

◆ *Why do you think corporate giants such as Lockheed Martin, Viacom, and Motorola are so important to the U.S. economy?*

Section Review

1. *Study the cartoon below and then answer the questions about it that follow.*

a. *How does the cartoonist indicate that the cellular telephone market is becoming a big business in the United States?*
b. *Compared with stationary public phone installations, cellular*

telephones are (i) safer to use (ii) harder to vandalize (iii) of no use to pedestrians.

2. *Explain why you AGREE or DISAGREE: Corporate America must prosper for the United States to remain a superpower.*

3. *Cite one argument against increasing productivity by means of corporate downsizing.*

Chapter 2 Review

A. *Write the letter of the correct response.*

1. *During the long recession that began in 1990, Americans were hurt by (a) unemployment and inflation (b) expanding foreign trade (c) larger defense contracts.*

2. *The subsequent economic recovery was characterized by (a) an increase in high-wage jobs (b) increased productivity (c) an end to corporate downsizing.*

3. *An employment trend of the 1990's has been (a) a decrease in the number of women executives and managers (b) expanding corporate positions (c) an increase in the number of jobs with smaller and moderately sized business firms.*

4. *Reduced labor costs for American manufacturers have been the result of their efforts to (a) make smaller staffs work more efficiently (b) reduce wages for factory workers (c) reject the demands of labor unions for better benefits.*

5. *Critics of President Clinton's 1993 deficit reduction plan argued that (a) federal spending was not sufficiently reduced, and revenues were not sufficiently raised by new taxes (b) it did not include a balanced-budget amendment (c) both of these.*

6. *Among the new investment opportunities sought by Americans in the 1990's have been (a) defense industries (b) foreign-oriented mutual funds (c) educational institutions.*

7. *A characteristic of the American workplace in the 1990's has been the following: (a) Employers have reduced benefit packages to cut costs. (b) Smaller firms have greatly increased the number of managers they employ. (c) The number of part-time and temporary workers has greatly decreased.*

8. *Two 1993 achievements of labor unions involved (a) contracts for airline and automobile workers (b) a reduction of corporate downsizing in the defense and computer industries (c) increased Social Security benefits for retirees and the disabled.*
9. *Surplus cash generated by corporations in the 1990's was invested in (a) expansion through the purchase of new equipment (b) expansion through the acquisition of other corporations (c) both of these.*
10. *Certain corporations, such as Motorola, can look forward to continued growth because they (a) receive subsidies and tax benefits from the federal government (b) develop new products that reflect technological advances (c) both of the above.*

B. *Use information found in Chapter 2 to write a brief essay on ONE of the following themes:*

Controversy Over the Federal Deficit

The Changing Employment Scene

Corporate America in the 1990's

C. *Pretend that you are an economic adviser to the President of the United States. Help the President by doing the following:*

1. *Prepare a list of the nation's most difficult economic problems.*
2. *Explain why these problems must be solved.*
3. *Develop strategies for solving any two of these problems.*

Chapter 3

The Society

America has traditionally been viewed as a "melting pot" in which people of many ethnicities and cultures would blend and become "Americanized."

In the early 1990's, however, economic problems arising from the recession inflamed anti-immigrant feelings. Radicals and extremists made efforts to turn America away from diversity and multiculturalism.

Other stresses appeared in American society. Crime and violence, often related to the drug trade, moved out from the inner cities to the suburbs and the rural areas. Dissatisfaction with public education increased as schools became places where disruption and failure often took priority over achievement. Rising health costs placed adequate health care beyond the reach of a greater number of Americans. And those who worked to advance the cause of human rights struggled against the growing conservatism of their fellow citizens.

◆ *Explain: American society experienced several changes in the 1990's.*

The Multicultural Society

Across the United States, the teaching of multiculturalism became an educational priority in the 1990's. Schools were encouraged to teach appreciation for the diversity of American society and to foster respect for the beliefs and practices of all cultures. Students were taught to understand and respect both the similarities and differences among the ethnicities, cultures, and religions in their communities. Instruction in multiculturalism included the study of immigration as a building block of American society. The diversity arising from the growth of America as a "nation of immigrants" has been presented as one of the strengths of American society.

However, in a mid-1993 poll conducted by *Newsweek* magazine, 60 percent of those interviewed stated their belief that "immigration was bad for the country." They feared that the nation was losing control of its borders, and they were worried about the long-term prospects for the economy. They were uncomfortable with the fact that so many of the "New Immigrants" have come from Latin America, the Caribbean, and Asia. Some 59 percent stated that immigration had been good for the country in the past. But 66 percent indicated that they did not believe the United States was still a melting pot because newer immigrants maintained their national identities more strongly.

These attitudes have influenced political actions. In August, 1993, Clinton announced his determination to crack down on illegal immigration. The President introduced to Congress a $172.5 million proposal to strengthen the U.S. Border Patrol and reduce visa fraud and false asylum claims.

In 1986, Congress attempted to stop illegal immigration with the Immigration Reform and Control Act (IRCA). The IRCA offered amnesty and eventual citizenship to an estimated 3.7 million illegal aliens. It also aimed to shut down the U.S. job market for these people by making it illegal for employers to hire aliens who lacked immigration documents. The IRCA failed. Despite the amnesty, the estimated number of illegal aliens rose to between 2 to 4 million by 1993.

1. *Define each of the following:*
   a. *multiculturalism*
   b. *the New Immigrants*
   c. *IRCA*
2. *Explain the conflict between the teaching of multiculturalism and the attitudes revealed by the 1993* Newsweek *poll.*

Legal and Illegal Immigrants

Between 1971 and 1990, 10.5 million legal immigrants were admitted to the United States. Ninety percent were from Latin America, the Caribbean, and Asia. Many of the new immigrants came as refugees. In addition, an estimated 500,000 illegal aliens entered each year.

Since 1970, the United States has accepted 1.5 million Vietnamese, Laotians, Cambodians, Cubans, Russians, and other oppressed nationalities. Most immigrants, however, migrated to the United States seeking greater economic opportunity and a better life. Many Chinese, for example, came from those sections of China where capitalism has begun to develop. Having acquired some business experience, they wished to improve their opportunities by settling in the United States. For similar reasons, immigrants have come from Bangladesh, the Dominican Republic, Mexico, the Philippines, and elsewhere. Rising birth rates and exposure to American TV telecasts have also stimulated immigration. Although many Americans have regarded the new immigrants as poor, uneducated, and unskilled, the majority have proven to be enterprising. Many have begun family businesses. Others have taken jobs that few Americans want.

Some economists have claimed that more immigration will lead to more economic growth and more wealth—and progress for all Americans. However, immigration has led to increased social friction. In some cities, such as Los Angeles, immigrants have flooded the labor market and set off bitter competition for jobs with American citizens.

Rising population levels have also been a major concern. In the early 1990's, immigration produced one-third of U.S. population growth. Projections for the future range from a population of about 383 million in 2050 to 436 million in the year 2090. Some environmentalists have urged an immediate halt to immigration to preserve the ecosystem and the quality of life.

Despite the problems caused by immigration, America will continue to be "a nation of immigrants." As a result, our society will become more multicultural as we approach the 21st century. For some Americans, this will result in increased social stress and economic competition. For others, it will be a continuing source of progress and cultural enrichment.

◆ *State three issues or concerns related to immigration.*

Section Review

1. *Describe the flow of immigrants into the United States from 1970 to the present. For what reasons have these people come? What factors have stimulated immigration? How has your school or community experienced immigration in the 1990's?*
2. *Evaluate the American multicultural society of the 1990's. Why is it regarded as a source of both strength and conflict? What responses can you give to critics of immigration?*

Education: Successes and Failures

In early 1994, Walter H. Annenberg, the publisher of *TV Guide* and other enterprises, donated $500 million to public education. Thirty percent of this sum was allocated to the nation's nine largest school systems: New York City, Los Angeles, Chicago, Dade County (Florida), Houston, Philadelphia, Broward County (Florida), Detroit, and Dallas. The five-year grant will be directed at duplicating in failing schools the approaches taken in successful ones.

Annenberg's reason for donating the largest sum ever given to education was his concern about the violence in grade schools and high schools across the United States. The 85-year-old philanthropist stated his belief that continuation of this violence would erode the educational system and destroy the American way of life. He challenged other wealthy Americans and companies to join him in giving financial support to education. President Clinton praised the gift by expressing his hope that instead of hundreds of schools that were working, there would soon be thousands.

By the 1990's, American schools were characterized as the least successful in the industrialized world. In 1990, the American Council on Education determined that only 30 percent of adult Americans possessed a high school diploma, and only 13.1 percent were graduates of a four-year college.

"Adult Literacy in America," a 1993 survey conducted by the Educational Testing Service, reported that roughly 90 million Americans over age 16, or nearly 50 percent of the people in that age group, were unfit for employment. They lacked such skills as the ability to write a letter, calculate the difference between regular and sale prices in a supermarket, or paraphrase the contents of a newspaper story. If the ETS survey is accurate, the United States is populated by a large number of people unprepared for current and advancing technologies.

◆ *Cite evidence that American education, by the 1990's, was less successful than it should have been.*

Strategies for Improvement

Recent educational history provides examples of schools and school systems which have struggled against major difficulties. When New Jersey State officials took control of the failing Jersey City school district in 1989, they declared the city "educationally bankrupt" and began to rebuild its school system. In 1987, only 25.9 percent of Jersey City's ninth graders passed the math, reading, and writing components of the state-required High School Proficiency Test. Only 27,727 of the estimated 52,000 school-age children attended public school.

Under state control, new programs were developed. These included innovative preschool classes, career-oriented educational linkages between schools and local businesses, workshops to enhance parental involvement, home visits by social workers, and adult education classes. Independent auditors gave high ratings to the new programs. By mid-1993, enrollment in Jersey City schools had risen to 30,266. The school system was described as a "model of hope." Encouraged by the success of the Jersey City takeover, the state then moved to take control of Newark's troubled 50,000-student school system.

In California's San Fernando Valley, broad public support has developed for dismantling the giant Los Angeles Unified School District. Some 640,000 children attend the district's 540 schools. Spending for them equals the national average. However, California students have performed below average on standard aptitude and mathematics tests.

By contrast, students in Iowa, the Dakotas, Nebraska, and Utah cost far less to keep in school and achieve far better test results. This success is attributed to having smaller, more responsive school boards. In 1993, a plan was developed to split the Los Angeles school district into seven smaller units with increased decision-making powers given to the schools. Widespread support for the plan appears to assure its adoption in the future.

Other reform efforts under way in California include legislation to give public schools the right to become "charter schools." Charter status enables schools to be largely independent of state or district authority for a period of five years. By early 1994, there were 100 charter schools in California.

◆ *Explain how educational reformers responded to crises in the schools of New Jersey and California.*

Chicago's public schools have been in chaos for years. Teachers' strikes have been frequent, and violence in the schools has been routine. In 1987, an ambitious reform program was undertaken. Each of the city's schools was placed under the authority of a nine-member council of parents, teachers, principals, and community people. In September, 1993, the Consortium of Chicago School Research, a group established to monitor the reform effort, reported that about 60 percent of the teachers thought that things were improving. However, scores in reading and math had dropped since the reform began. Also, the high school graduation rate, which had been over 50 percent for each of the three years before reform, decreased to 45.7 percent in 1994. In response, Chicago's mayor, Richard Daley, began discussion of school vouchers.

Tax-exempt vouchers may be used to pay tuition at private or parochial schools. Parental demand for the use of public funds to defray the cost of sending their children to private schools has risen as dissatisfaction with public education has increased across the United States. This has been especially true in California. A 1993 poll in that state found that 87 percent of people questioned were dissatisfied with the public schools. Of this group, 63 percent favored the use of vouchers. Nevertheless, Californians rejected a voucher plan in the elections of November, 1993. Voters feared that the loss of $1 billion in revenue for the public schools would worsen their condition and performance. In Puerto Rico, however, a voucher plan to cover public and private school tuition up to $1,500 for each child went into effect in the fall of 1993.

Educational reform efforts in Michigan have included a plan to abandon the property tax as the basis of school funding. This was intended to reduce some of the inequities between poor and wealthy school districts. In addition, schools will be required to add an extra hour of teaching each day by the year 2000. And public schools and colleges will be allowed to set up charter schools—specialized institutions funded by the state—to compete with existing schools. The first charter school, which opened in Detroit in September, 1993, received 5,000 applications for 300 places.

The city of Minneapolis, Minnesota, took a rather different approach to school reform. In November, 1993, it voted to negotiate a contract with a private business firm to manage all

98 of its schools. Public Strategies Group, Inc., was paid to administer the city's 6,800 school employees and 44,000 students—the largest school system to be run by a private company. By 1996, the experiment seemed to be working. In August, students in at least 95 percent of Minneapolis's elementary schools earned their highest scores in five years on the reading and math portions of the California Achievement Test. Similar programs in Baltimore, Maryland, and Hartford, Connecticut, however, were discontinued. Nevertheless, Baltimore's experiment with this method of school management suggests that it can be effective.

- *Describe the use of vouchers, charter schools, and privatization to improve education.*

Dangerous Schools

Violence in the nation's schools increased in the 1990's. A 1993 Harris poll of 2,508 schoolchildren suggested that guns are common in American schools. Almost a tenth of those interviewed admitted that they had shot at someone at some time in their lives, and 11 percent said that they had been shot at in the past year. Nearly 40 percent said that they knew someone who had been killed or injured by a gun, and 15 percent said that they had carried a gun within the past thirty days.

Juvenile weapons possession is not limited to inner-city schools. In Fairfax, Virginia, one of the wealthiest suburbs in the country, the authorities recommended, in mid-1993, that 88 students be expelled from school, 42 for possessing guns. In Iowa, 23 percent of the students carried a weapon to school in the 1992–93 school year.

The use of weapons by students has also become more frequent. So have fights between individuals and groups and assaults on teachers and other school employees. Much of this violence is the result of gang wars, spreading in the 1990's from the cities to the suburbs. Some of it is random and impulsive.

As a result, educational authorities have invested heavily in school security. Twenty-five percent of all large urban school systems used hand-held or walk-through metal detectors in 1993 and 1994. New York City's Division of School Safety employs 2,600 uniformed security staff, many with authority to make arrests. Magnetic door locks and photo identification systems also became common features in many large schools. In New York and other cities, police and transit police officers have been assigned patrol and outreach duties in and around schools. In Rochester, New York, teachers have been offered discounts on the purchase of desk alarms.

Many solutions have been offered for the problems of school violence, poor attendance, and substandard academic performance. Among them have been strengthened expulsion authority for administrators, increased community involvement and parental participation, and smaller schools. For many involved in public education, the concept of smallness has become attractive. The giant high schools of the post-1945 era were built on the assumption that size could reduce overhead and increase choice. By the 1990's, such schools had proven to be breeding grounds of violence and academic failure. For that reason, the New York City Board of Education established in 1994 a number of experimental high schools with populations of 150–300 students.

◆ *Describe the extent to which school violence had become a problem by the 1990's.*

Section Review

1. *State an educational program or development in each of the following states:*

   a. New Jersey
   b. New York
   c. California
   d. Michigan
   e. Minnesota

2. *Write a letter to the educational leaders of your community. Give them your suggestions for dealing with violence and failure in schools.*

Health and Medicine: Strategies for Reform

In 1993, President Clinton attempted to back up his campaign promise to assure every American "health care that can never be taken away." While introducing the plan to Congress and a national television audience, Clinton paid tribute to his wife, Hillary Rodham Clinton, the leader of the health reform effort.

The idea of health care reform had gained force during the previous five years. It had been a key element in the 1992 Presidential campaign. By the end of 1993, the number of Americans without health insurance had reached 38.9 million, an increase of 2.3 million over 1991. A major decline in health coverage occurred among workers in small companies. Some of these businesses dropped employee insurance as costs rose. However, 7.2 million of the uninsured were family members of workers in businesses with 1,000 or more personnel. The number of people with private health insurance and the number covered through employers have gradually declined. One indication of the strong relationship between health insurance and income is that among workers earning less than $10,000 a year, 50 percent lack coverage.

With the failure of the universal health coverage plan, politicians proposed more moderate and gradual reforms. One such measure, the insurance portability bill, allows people who change jobs to keep the insurance provided by their former employers. Sponsored by Senator Edward Kennedy and Senator Nancy Kassebaum, it was enacted in August, 1996. After a 12-month waiting period, insurers must now pay benefits to people with previously identified illnesses. The main advantage of this measure is to allow people who previously stayed in a job because it provided health insurance to move to more desirable work without a loss of coverage. Included in the bill is a Republican-backed experimental program that makes tax-deductible medical savings accounts (or MSAs) available to people who work for companies with fewer than 50 employees. These people can save limited sums in tax-deductible accounts to pay routine medical costs. However, the bill provides for only 750,000 MSAs. Other than the inclusion of the MSAs, it does nothing to make health care more affordable. People who take jobs without health coverage will have to pay for the insurance that they carry over from their former employers.

Health maintenance organizations (HMOs) have, to some extent, reduced the price of health care. Clinton had hoped that the use of these networks of doctors, hospitals, and insurers would make universal health care affordable. The number of people in HMOs climbed from about 38 million in 1990 to about 53 million in 1995. These organizations save money, but many people feel that they do not give members enough freedom to choose their doctors and sometimes discourage necessary procedures because of their cost.

1. *Explain why you AGREE or DISAGREE with the statement that there is a health care crisis in America.*
2. *Discuss the relationship between health care insurance and employment.*

The President's Health Care Plan

The plan introduced to Congress by President Clinton sought health insurance for all Americans (known as universal coverage). It would have guaranteed a generous basic package of coverage, negotiated separately in each state by alliances of consumers with insurance companies and medical groups. Most employers would have been required to pay 80 percent of average premiums. Employees and government subsidies would also have contributed to the payment of premiums. The plan also promised a new prescription drug benefit for the elderly. Most important of all, the President's plan was intended to provide health coverage to all citizens, employed or unemployed.

One of the major purposes of Clinton's desire to restructure the health care system was to control medical costs. He planned to use financial incentives to encourage consumers to join low-cost health maintenance organizations. Doctors, hospitals, and insurers were to be urged to join together in networks. By fostering competition among plans, the providers would have been forced to cut costs and offer better services.

1. *List the highlights of President Clinton's health care reform proposals.*
2. *Explain why health care reform would provide benefits to and require responsibilities from all Americans.*

The Battle for Health Care

Opposition to Clinton's health care reform proposals mounted in late 1993 and early 1994. The American Medical Association, the largest organization representing the nation's doctors, began a $1.6 million advertising campaign to make sure that doctors "keep primary responsibility for setting the standards of medical care." The AMA warned that the proposals pending in Congress would lead to "domination of America's health-care systems by giant profit-seeking corporations." The Health Insurance Association of America, whose 270 companies provide health insurance coverage for 55 million people, also began broadcasting advertisements critical of the Clinton plan. The National Association of Manufacturers, representing 12,500 large and small manufacturers, voted not to support the Clinton Administration's plan because it was too expensive.

President Clinton's proposals were not enacted into law by Congress. Legislative opposition was led by Senator Robert Dole, Republican of Kansas. In early 1994, Dole and other Republicans attacked the Clinton plan by claiming it was a new tax because it mandated that employers pay 80 percent of premium costs.

The health care reform effort was officially defeated in September, 1994. It was defeated in Congress because of the opposition of Republicans and well-financed interest groups. Those who continued to support health care reform reminded the nation that the problems of rising costs and the growing number of uninsured Americans would not go away.

♦ *Explain why you AGREE or DISAGREE with this statement:*

> If we let the health care system continue to drift in its present direction, Americans will have less care, fewer choices and higher bills.
>
> —*President Bill Clinton*

Section Review

1. *Complete the following sentences:*
   a. *Many Americans agreed on the need for health care reform because ______.*
   b. *A major goal of Clinton's plan was ______.*
   c. *Two organizations which opposed Clinton's health care plan are the ______ and the ______.*
   d. *In September, 1994, health care reform legislation ______.*
   e. *In 1996, the Senate passed the insurance portability bill, which allows employees ______.*
2. *Explain how health care reform became a topic of national debate in the 1990's.*

Human Rights: Progress and Problems

In February, 1994, Byron De La Beckwith, a white supremacist, was convicted in a Mississippi court for the murder of a black civil rights leader 31 years before. Medgar Evers was the Mississippi field secretary for the National Association for the Advancement of Colored People (NAACP). His death gained national attention and helped galvanize wide support in the North for the drive to secure basic civil rights for blacks in the South. Although De La Beckwith had bragged about killing Medgar Evers, all-white juries had failed to convict him in two previous trials in 1964. His unanimous conviction by a jury of eight blacks and four whites in 1994 was regarded by many as a positive ending to a violent chapter in the history of the civil rights movement.

White supremacy and segregation, against which Medgar Evers, Dr. Martin Luther King, Jr., and other martyrs fought, ended in Mississippi and other Southern states. Racism, however, did not. By the 1990's, it had taken different forms. When Minister Louis Farrakhan of the Nation of Islam and one of his senior aides made speeches attacking Jews and Catholics, the Anti-Defamation League of B'nai B'rith and other human rights organizations protested. So did the Reverend Jesse Jackson, the nation's foremost civil rights leader.

Tension between blacks and Jews increased in the 1990's. This was especially true in New York City. Riots exploded in the Crown Heights section of Brooklyn, in 1991, when a Jewish motorist struck and killed a black youngster. Subsequently, a Jewish scholar visiting from Australia was stabbed to death in a related incident in the same neighborhood. In January, 1994, New York police mistakenly raided a Nation of Islam mosque after a false robbery report. The violence that erupted between the police and those in the mosque was blamed by some on the city's "racist" policies.

The question of racism played a major role in the 1993 trial of four Los Angeles police officers for the arrest and beating of a black motorist in 1991. For violating the civil rights of Rodney King, two of the officers were sent to prison. The trial attracted national attention.

1. *Explain the importance of the murder conviction of Byron De La Beckwith in 1994.*
2. *Identify each of the following:*

   a. *Medgar Evers*
   b. *Louis Farrakhan*
   c. *Jesse Jackson*
   d. *Rodney King*

School Desegregation

Although the civil rights revolution of the 1960's helped end legal segregation, the struggle to fully integrate schools still continues. In early 1994, the schools of New York State were identified as among the most segregated in the nation. More than half of all black and Hispanic students in that state attend schools where at least 90 percent of the students are from minority groups. Illinois and Michigan were found to be even more segregated for black students, with 57.5 percent in minority-dominated schools. New Jersey and Connecticut were also among the ten states with the most segregated schools.

The Harvard Project on School Desegregation attributed the increasing concentration of black and Hispanic students to higher birth rates, immigration, and long-standing housing patterns. It also cited the 1974 ruling of the U.S. Supreme Court that desegregation plans need not require the busing of students across district lines.

The result has been the development of two different school systems in many states. One is urban, minority, poor, and failing. The other is suburban, white, affluent, and successful. The effort to correct this has involved a variety of actions. In Connecticut, a lawsuit was brought in state court to force the integration of the largely minority Hartford school district with its surrounding white suburban schools. Desegregation suits were also begun in the courts of Yonkers, New York, and Englewood, New Jersey.

Legal action in New York State has focused more on school financing than on desegregation. Rather than attempting to improve education by changing the racial mix of school populations, emphasis has been placed on increasing funding and setting higher standards. Also, federal aid has been given to schools to develop magnet programs which would attract white students and thus end "minority group isolation" in schools with segregated populations.

1. *Describe the school segregation problem of the 1990's.*
2. *State the steps taken to combat the effects of school segregation.*

Legal Rights of Illegal Aliens

The rising tide of illegal immigration into the United States has created another human rights issue: the status of aliens in American courts. The Amnesty Act of 1986 offered legal residency to all illegal aliens who had lived in the United States continuously since January 1, 1982. The one-year period of applying for amnesty expired on May 4, 1988. In November, 1993, U.S. Supreme Court Justice Sandra Day O'Connor ruled that the government could deport thousands of illegal aliens who had failed to apply for amnesty under the 1986 law.

Immigration rights groups attempted to obtain legal standing for these aliens. In June, 1993, however, the full Supreme Court denied legal status to 300,000 illegal aliens who were seeking it under the expired amnesty program.

Pending legal outcomes, deportations will be delayed. In September, 1996, the Senate passed the Illegal Immigration Reform and Immigrant Responsibility Act. It further penalized illegal entry by imposing fines on illegal immigrants and expanding the RICO (Racketeer Influenced and Corrupt Organizations) law to cover smuggling of illegal aliens.

♦ *Why do illegal aliens demand legal status in U.S. courts?*

Human Rights Abuses

Increased immigration has created the additional human rights problem of abuse of immigrant labor. Many goods marked "Made in the U.S.A." are made in illegal sweatshops.

In 1993, a three-month investigation by *U.S. News & World Report* found that as many as half of all women's garments made in America were produced in factories that pay below minimum wage, ignore federal safety laws, and require workers to spend 60 hours or more at their sewing machines each week. Overtime is not paid. Insurance benefits do not exist. Those who complain are fired. The investigation was based on visits to garment factories in the leading manufacturing centers of New York, Los Angeles, and Dallas.

In 1996, several celebrity-endorsed products were reported being made under sweatshop conditions. The celebrities denied knowledge of these conditions. Such findings have spurred more investigations into abuses of immigrant labor.

♦ *Define* sweatshop labor. *How has immigration increased it?*

Religion and the Law

Religious freedom is regarded as one of the most fundamental human rights. On November 16, 1993, President Clinton signed into law legislation requiring the government to meet stringent standards before instituting measures that might interfere with religious practices. The new law, the Religious Freedom Restoration Act, requires the government to demonstrate a "compelling state interest" to justify any measure restricting religious practices. Even in cases where government concerns like health or safety do justify infringements of religious practices, the new law requires the use of whatever means would be least restrictive to religion. Religious groups now have increased opportunities to apply for exemptions from routine legislation or regulations on the basis of the First Amendment's guarantee of religious freedom.

Among the types of government infringements of religious practices that would be more restricted by the new law are mandatory autopsies for those whose religion forbids autopsies; zoning laws that prevent the construction of churches close to the homes of their congregants; and local building codes that limit an architect's freedom to design places of worship.

The Religious Freedom Restoration Act was supported by an unusual coalition of liberal, conservative, and religious groups. Clinton praised the new law by stating that it held government "to a very high level of proof before it interferes with someone's free exercise of religion."

1. *Define the term* human rights.
2. *Describe a human rights problem or development in each of the following areas:*

   a. civil rights
   b. race relations
   c. education
   d. labor
   e. religion

Pro-Choice vs. Pro-Life

During her August, 1993, confirmation hearings before the U.S. Senate, Supreme Court Justice Ruth Bader Ginsburg strongly defended a woman's right to choose as a fundamental human right. She referred to the 1973 ruling of the Supreme Court in *Roe* vs. *Wade*. This landmark decision established that a state may not prevent a woman from having an abortion in the first three months of pregnancy, and could regulate but not prohibit abortion during the second trimester. In effect, the decision overturned abortion laws in 46 states. Since 1984, Justice Ginsburg has argued that abortion should be guaranteed under the 14th Amendment ban on discrimination. Many Americans, including President Clinton, are sympathetic to Justice Ginsburg's beliefs in a woman's right to choose whether she will carry a baby to term. But other Americans have religious and moral objections to the "pro-choice" position. Thus, a proposal prohibiting abortion was part of the GOP platform in 1980. Many Republicans were therefore angered in 1996 when Candidate Dole claimed that he favored a ban on abortion but would tolerate opposing views.

Polls have shown that most Americans believe abortion should remain legal, but subject to such restrictions as parental consent for minors or waiting periods. As an alternative to abortion, abstinence from sexual activity has been taught in schools and communities. In July, 1993, the House of Representatives voted to retain the Hyde Amendment prohibiting federal funding of abortion. However, exceptions to the ban were expanded to include rape and incest. This vote indicated how many members of Congress were sympathetic to the less extreme "right-to-life" arguments.

At times, the controversy has turned violent. In November, 1993, the Senate voted for a federal law to prohibit bombings, arson, and blockades at abortion clinics, and shootings and threats of violence against doctors and nurses who perform abortions. The bill offered protection to anti-abortion counseling centers as well as to abortion clinics. Senators opposed to abortion insisted that the bill interfered with free speech and the right to demonstrate. However, the Clinton Administration strongly supported the legislation.

A dramatic new development in the "pro-life vs. pro-choice" controversy occurred in January, 1994. The Supreme Court ruled unanimously that abortion clinics can sue violent anti-abortion protest groups for damages under the federal Racketeer Influenced and Corrupt Organizations (RICO) law. Aimed at organized crime, this law enables the conviction of all members of a criminal enterprise, not just those who actually commit the violent act. The Supreme Court decision was applied to a lawsuit brought by the National Organization for Women against Joseph Scheidler, leader of the Pro-Life Action Network. NOW accused Scheidler's group and several similar organizations of running a nationwide conspiracy to drive abortion clinics from business through a campaign of intimidation, bombings, and other violent acts. Abortion rights groups hailed the decision as a significant victory.

More attention was given to the violence problem when a doctor and his bodyguard were shot to death outside a Florida abortion clinic in July, 1994. Paul Hill, an abortion opponent, was convicted of the crime and sentenced to two life terms in prison. He described his deed as justifiable homicide.

Two abortion clinic workers near Boston were shot to death in December, 1994. John Salvi III was convicted of the murders and also given two consecutive life terms without parole. Attorney General Janet Reno examined the need for new laws to stop abortion clinic violence.

1. *Explain the connection of each to the "pro-life vs. pro-choice" controversy.*

   a. Ruth Bader Ginsburg
   b. Hyde Amendment
   c. RICO
   d. NOW
   e. Joseph Scheidler

2. *Explain why you AGREE or DISAGREE with each statement.*

   a. It is essential to a woman's equality with man that she be the decision maker.

   —*Justice Ruth Bader Ginsburg*

   b. This bill [prohibiting attacks on abortion clinics] raises the right of abortion above the Constitution, particularly the First Amendment right to assemble.

   —*Senator Strom Thurmond, Republican of South Carolina*

   c. American women have seen their doctors' offices transformed from safety zones into war zones.

   —*Senator Barbara Boxer, Democrat of California*

Gay Rights vs. Homophobia: The American Dilemma

By early 1994, large numbers of Americans were going to theaters to see the hit movie *Philadelphia,* starring Tom Hanks and Denzel Washington. The subject of the film is homophobia and AIDS. Tom Hanks plays a gay lawyer who loses his job when his firm learns he has AIDS. The only attorney he can find to represent him in his anti-discrimination suit against his former employers is a homophobic lawyer, played by Denzel Washington.

Homophobia is prejudice and discrimination directed against homosexuals. Homophobes are those who are verbally or physically abusive to gays, or who discriminate against them in housing and employment. Homophobia appears to be spreading. By November, 1993, five American cities had repealed laws banning discrimination against homosexuals.

As the gay rights struggle has attracted more public attention, gay people have found that increased visibility has its drawbacks. They have gained more political influence and social acceptance. However, they have also gained more unwelcome attention from the extreme right. Anti-gay harassment and violence have doubled in the 1990's.

The Clinton presidency began with an Administration attempt to protect the right of gays to serve in the military. The effort resulted in the "don't tell—don't ask" policy. This compromise policy did not please those who wanted a stronger pro-gay rights position from the President. In late 1993, a federal appeals court ordered the Navy to commission a dismissed midshipman and grant him his diploma. Joseph C. Steffan had been forced to resign from the United States Naval Academy six weeks before his graduation in 1987 because he had acknowledged under questioning by a disciplinary board that he was gay. The U.S. Court of Appeals for the District of Columbia ruled that the equal protection guarantee of the Fifth Amendment did not permit the government to remove members of the armed services merely because they say they are homosexuals. This decision cast doubt on the constitutionality of the Clinton Administration's new policy on homosexuals in the armed services. In 1996, Clinton further distanced himself from gay-rights activists by signing a bill banning marriage between people of the same sex.

Most Americans prefer to regard themselves as tolerant people. However, the national debate over gay rights has caused widespread division and conflict. By the 1990's, the controversy had become one of the great issues in American society.

1. *Define* homophobia *and explain its relationship to the film* Philadelphia.
2. *Write a brief paragraph to interpret this headline:*

   MILITARY REBUFFED BY APPEALS COURT OVER HOMOSEXUALS
3. *Explain why you AGREE or DISAGREE with this statement and how it relates to gays in the armed services:*

   > A cardinal principle of equal protection law holds that the government cannot discriminate against a certain class in order to give effect to the prejudices of others. Even if the government does not itself act out of prejudice it cannot discriminate in an effort to avoid the effects of others' prejudice. Such discrimination plays directly into the hands of the bigots; it ratifies and encourages their prejudice.
   >
   > —*Chief Judge Abner J. Mikva, U.S. Court of Appeals, District of Columbia*

The Difficulties of Welfare Reform

In December, 1993, Clinton's task force on welfare reform completed a tentative plan for changes in the welfare system.

The financing of the Clinton plan soon became a major political problem. A time limit on welfare payments was popular with many members of Congress, but it requires the government to provide expensive new services, such as job training and child care. Clinton insisted that the new services be paid for by cutting other programs.

The 1988 Family Support Act provides money for job training and education programs, and requires some welfare recipients to enroll in them. The tentative Clinton plan expanded those training programs and added tougher work requirements. It also required the spending of large, new sums of money on child care. The plan included Clinton's pledge to impose a two-year limit on welfare benefits, after which recipients would have to enroll in a work program or face financial penalties.

The plan also endorsed a national campaign to reduce teenage pregnancy. It called for dramatic improvements in the child-support enforcement system. The expanded job-training programs included one for absent fathers. Such an expansion could help fathers earn more, and therefore contribute more for child support. Implementing this part of the plan, however, would require a large increase in government spending.

Aid to Families with Dependent Children, the main federal welfare program, costs about $23 billion a year. A record five million families were receiving aid from this program in 1993. Food stamps and Medicaid for welfare families cost about $40 billion more. To reduce costs, it was proposed that the new plan be gradually phased in, either by starting in a limited number of states, or by extending the new requirements only to new welfare applicants.

In February, 1994, it was announced that the Clinton Administration was considering a plan to finance the new welfare system by taxing food stamps, welfare benefits, and housing assistance and by reducing aid to legal immigrants who are elderly and poor. Critics and opponents of the proposed taxes were quick to claim that this plan would hurt the very people the welfare reforms were designed to help—the poor.

However, the 1990 budget law requires the government to pay for any new spending increases with offsetting taxes or program reductions. The 1995 budget sent by the President to Congress in February, 1994, proposed cutting more than $30 billion from federal programs in order to pay for increases for crime prevention, homelessness, education, job training, and highway construction. Among the programs for which funding may be reduced are heating for the poor and housing for the elderly.

In 1996, Clinton angered many supporters by signing a Republican-sponsored welfare reform bill. It ended the guarantee of cash assistance to poor families with children and distributed welfare funding to the states in lump-sum payments. Many states considered this a hardship, because the grants were delayed until the states organized their own welfare programs. Moreover, a state could have its block grant reduced if fewer than half of its single mothers on welfare were working or training for work by the year 2002. Future legal immigrants would not be eligible for most welfare benefits for the first five years of their U.S. residence. Many Democratic leaders predicted an increase in homelessness and poverty.

◆ *List the goals of the Clinton welfare plan.*

Section Review

1. *Write a paragraph to link these headlines:*

   CLINTON'S WELFARE PLANNERS OUTLINE BIG PLANS TO BE FINANCED BY BIG SAVINGS

   DIFFICULT MATH OF WELFARE REFORM

   CLINTON CONSIDERS TAXING AID TO POOR TO PAY FOR REFORM

2. *Express your opinion of Clinton's 1996 welfare reform bill. Should it be changed? How?*

3. *Select two human rights issues of the 1990's. For each , summarize the issue and describe the Clinton Administration's response to it.*

Crime and Violence: The Public View

By early 1994, many Americans viewed crime as the single most important problem facing the country. The sharp rise in concern about crime assured its being a major political issue in local, state, and national elections. There was also a widespread sense that the country was powerless to deal with it. Most Americans polled have indicated that they do not expect violence to decline significantly in the next few years. In his State of the Union address in January, 1994, Clinton responded to this concern by stating his intention to introduce to the nation a "three strikes and you're out" plan. Such legislation would require mandatory life sentences for those convicted of a third violent crime.

Some experts attributed the increased worries about crime to the impact made by frequent media reports of violence. In 1995, however, the Federal Bureau of Investigation offered a rare gleam of hope in a report showing that overall serious crimes had decreased by 2 percent, compared with the incidence of crimes in 1994. It was the fourth consecutive year that serious crime had dropped. Experts warned against considering this drop a positive trend, however, and pointed to signs that the crime rate may rise again in the next decade. Most importantly, causes of crime were still present—joblessness, family disintegration, and drugs. A 1996 report, for example, showed a rise in teenage drug use.

The solution for crime proposed by most people—that is,

more prisons—has had little success in reducing crime. Both Congress and the state governments have searched for combinations of punishments and incentives that might have some beneficial effect.

♦ *State the reason(s) so many Americans have come to regard crime as the nation's foremost problem.*

The Search for Solutions

An omnibus crime bill passed by Congress in 1994 provided money to help the states pay for 100,000 additional police officers, provided for the construction of 10 federal prisons, and designated the death penalty for 52 more crimes, many of them the marginal ones covered by federal law. (Most violent crimes are violations of state laws.)

Also among its provisions was the "three strikes, you're out" measure. It mandates life imprisonment for anyone convicted of a federal crime who has two prior convictions for serious state or federal felonies. At least 30 states, including California and New York, are also considering this type of legislation. However, the number of felons convicted three times has been relatively small. For New York, a recent estimate was 300 a year. The 1994 law also expanded use of the federal death penalty.

In the view of police, prosecutors, and other experts, attempts to control crime through tougher sentences is unlikely to succeed. Roughly a fifth of all crimes result in arrests. Only about half of these lead to conviction in serious cases. Prisons are so overcrowded that the average convict serves only a third of his or her sentence. While prison does take criminals off the streets for a while, it does not stop new ones from appearing.

For most states, juvenile justice is the greatest challenge. Close to a fifth of all violent crime is committed by youngsters under the age of 18. Nearly all states are moving toward trying more juvenile offenders as adults. Some 30 states and the federal government are also experimenting with boot camps in which juvenile offenders are subject to a military-style shock program for three to six months. These programs feature military drill and hard work. Some also provide substance abuse treatment and job counseling. By 1994, however, such programs had not had much success in preventing repeated criminal offenses. A majority of their graduates are arrested within a year of returning to their old neighborhoods.

♦ *Describe some of the popular solutions to violent crime, and evaluate their success.*

A less popular approach to crime prevention has arisen among some legislators and community leaders. They favor social programs and reject the heavy emphasis on prisons and mandatory minimum sentences. Teen curfews, imposed in two dozen cities in 1993, have been challenged by the American Civil Liberties Union. The ACLU has warned against the willingness of people to trade freedom for law and order. This view has been supported by the influential Congressional Black Caucus. These members of Congress claimed that the imbalance in the omnibus crime bill in favor of penalties over social programs affects blacks disproportionately. Clinton responded to these sentiments by directing his Cabinet to develop a job-training initiative as part of the omnibus bill.

Concern about crime has also given renewed force to the gun control movement. After a 10-year debate, the Brady bill was passed by Congress in late 1993. It was named after James Brady, press secretary to President Ronald Reagan, who was seriously wounded during a 1981 assassination attempt on Mr. Reagan. The Brady bill sets a waiting period of five working days to give sellers and law enforcement officials time to check the backgrounds of prospective gun buyers for criminal records or mental instability. The waiting period will be lifted after five years, when an instant check of a buyer's background is supposed to be available nationwide by computer. The legislation also provides states with more than $200 million to upgrade their computerized records on criminals.

1. *List reasons why many Americans feel powerless to deal with violent crime.*

2. *Complete each sentence.*

   a. *From 1983 to 1993, violent crime ______.*
   b. *The federal omnibus crime bill provides for ______.*
   c. *Almost a fifth of all violent crime is committed by ______.*
   d. *An indication that teen boot camps are not very successful is ______.*
   e. *The ACLU has opposed teen curfews because ______.*

Section Review

1. *Describe the ways in which violent crime affects the quality of your life and your personal freedom.*
2. *Some Americans have claimed that law and order is more important than freedom. Do you agree? Explain your answer.*

Chapter 3 Review

A. *Write the letter of the correct response.*

1. *By the 1990's, many Americans had begun to lose faith in the idea of the United States as a (a) military superpower (b) melting pot (c) economic giant.*
2. *A 1986 law designed to stop illegal immigration was the (a) RICO bill (b) omnibus crime bill (c) IRCA.*
3. *Efforts to improve education have included (a) state takeover of local school systems (b) tax exempt voucher plans (c) both of these.*
4. *A major problem in American schools has been (a) lack of government monitoring (b) no financial support (c) student violence.*
5. *The health care plan introduced by President Clinton to Congress in September, 1993, included (a) a new prescription drug benefit for the elderly (b) a ban on health maintenance organizations (c) discouragement of networks of doctors, hospitals, and insurers.*

6. *In the struggle for human rights, frequent reference has been made to the (a) First and Fifth Amendments (b) Eighteenth Amendment (c) Sixth Amendment.*

7. *In the 1990's, homophobia has caused (a) an increase in gay marriages (b) court decisions barring gays from serving in the armed forces (c) a dramatic increase in the number of violent attacks on gay people.*

8. *A popular feature of President Clinton's 1993 plan for welfare reform was (a) time limits for welfare participation (b) elimination of job training programs (c) decreased child care.*

9. *An anti-crime measure proposed by President Clinton in his January, 1994, State of the Union address was (a) mandatory sentences for those convicted three times of violent crimes (b) increased parole opportunities for convicts (c) earlier retirement for law enforcement officials.*

10. *The Brady bill, passed by Congress in late 1993, provides for (a) the tax-free sale of automatic weapons (b) waiting periods and background checks for prospective gun buyers (c) funding for gun clubs.*

B. *Reread* Education: Successes and Failures *on pages 52–57. Then do the following:*

1. *List the major problems affecting the quality of education in American schools.*

2. *Select ONE of the problems you have listed. Explain why it is a problem and state some possible solutions.*

3. *Identify or define:*

   a. *Walter H. Annenberg*
   b. *"Adult Literacy in America"*
   c. *vouchers*
   d. *charter schools*
   e. *privatization*

C. *Study the graph on page 76 and indicate which statements are* true *and which are* false*. Then complete the concluding sentence.*

1. *Between 1988 and 1993, the number of juveniles arrested for violent crimes increased by approximately 50,000.*

2. *The largest increase in juvenile arrests for violent crimes occurred between 1988 and 1989.*

3. *The steepest one-year increase in juvenile arrests for violent crimes was between 1991 and 1992.*

4. *During the first part of the 1990's, there was a trend of increased juvenile arrests for violent crime.*

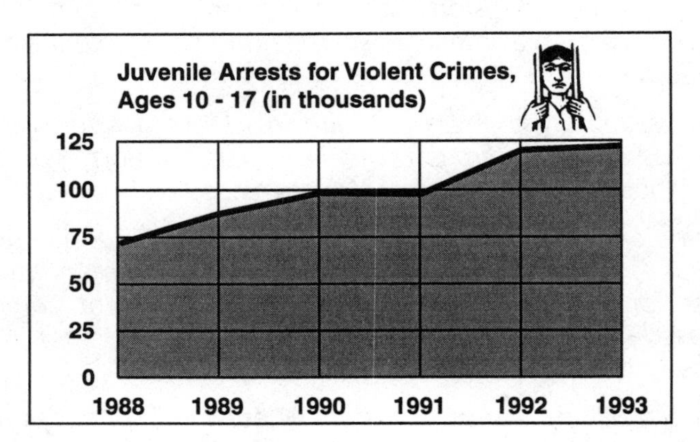

5. *A fact not indicated by the graph is that juvenile arrests for murder increased by 85 percent between 1987 and 1991.*

   A conclusion which might be drawn from this graph is ____ .

Chapter 4

Science and Technology

The 1990's have been a period of rapid growth for science and technology. The increasing use of computers, advances in telecommunications, and the development of interactive media have brought dramatic changes to American society. Continuing space exploration has provided the National Aeronautic and Space Administration (NASA) with much new information. Improvements in transportation have also bettered the ways we live and work.

The Continuing Computerization of America

Compact machines capable of processing and storing information rapidly were invented in the 1950's. With the development of the microchip in the 1970's, computers became faster and smaller, and increased their ability to store huge amounts of information. By the 1990's, computers had become important tools in every field of human activity. Computers guide space exploration flights. They record business activities and financial transactions.

Computers print books, magazines, newspapers, and a wide variety of other documents. They have helped to automate factories and are used in millions of offices. Computers are also used in schools for instruction and administration. By 1995, the global Internet had made international direct communication among millions of people possible.

Rapidly growing computer technology and dependence on computers is often called the "computer revolution." Information processing has become a major American industry. By 1990, production and sale of information made up half of the U.S. gross domestic product (GDP). They also employed about half of all American workers.

In the 1990's, more and more information has become electronic. People have learned to store information, or data, on computer disks and transmit it to other computers over telephone lines. Moreover, data in a computer can be relayed instantly via satellite to any place on Earth. Because of the speed and ease of computer applications, most businesses, schools, and government agencies have adopted computer technology. Computer literacy (knowledge of computer skills) has become a requirement for many types of employment.

1. *Define the terms* computer revolution *and* computer literacy.
2. *Why is information processing important to the economy?*

Computers in Homes and Workplaces

The computer revolution not only transformed the American workplace, it also reached into 25 million households by the early 1990's. Starting with the Apple II in 1977, low-cost personal computers began to appear in more and more homes. This trend continued as IBM and other firms competed with Apple to produce better and faster personal computers at lower prices. And as computers became cheaper and more "user-friendly" (easier to use), new software programs (instructions to computers) enabled consumers to do many daily chores effortlessly. Among software programs for personal computers in 1995 were E-mail—transmission of electronic messages from computer to distant computer—desktop publishing, home architectural design, medical and health guidance, money management, and travel arrangements.

The educational uses of computers were expanded by the placement of standard reference works on disks. Encyclopedias, almanacs, atlases, dictionaries, and periodical literature guides were placed on single CD-ROM (mass storage) disks. These gave students the ability to search through all the reference sources simultaneously for information on a single topic. Research was also made faster and easier by the availability in the 1990's of "online" computer services such as Compuserve and America Online. For a monthly fee, personal computer users in homes, libraries, offices, and classrooms have access to current news stories and historical backgrounds, financial reports, currency exchange rates, weather information, and a wide range of other informational sources.

Technological advances led to further improvements in the capabilities of computers. Animation and voice were added to the more expensive software programs. More powerful microprocessor chips, such as the RISC chip designed by MIPS Technologies and Intel's Pentium microprocessor, were introduced in 1993 and 1994. For the consumer, the new chips made software possible for presenting movie-style video and combinations of video, sound, and text, known as multimedia programs. Instruments called modems made computers compatible with telephones and enabled computers to "speak" to each other.

Other advances spurred the design of small, portable computers. Laptop, or notebook, computers became popular with students, business executives, and others for whom mobility was necessary. Even smaller "personal digital assistants" (PDA's), such as the Newton Message Pad and the Sharp Expert Pad, came into use by 1994. Some PDA's were offered with attached cellular telephones and wireless faxing. Such "personal communicators" were in the forefront of an ongoing process of computer improvement.

These innovations cause new problems. Replacing office personnel with computers speeds up corporate downsizing. Pornographers use online services to publish obscene material. Piracy of ideas is common because it is difficult to prevent copyright infringement. Some people fear that unscrupulous "hackers" will break computer codes and obtain data for using other people's credit and bank cards or accessing government secrets. Others feel that the average citizen's privacy is threatened by the information stored on the computers of government agencies and giant industries.

◆ *How have computers changed life and work in the United States? State two ways.*

Beyond personal computers and personal digital assistants are the mainframes. These are used by large organizations. In many business firms, several mainframe computers are located in a processing center that operates 24 hours a day, 7 days a week. Such centers often serve many users on terminals. In the 1990's, however, the use of mainframes began to decline. Reductions in the size of corporations and improvements in personal computers led to greater reliance on personal computer networks.

Finally, there are the supercomputers. These are used by giant industrial enterprises and government agencies for major research and development operations. In 1993, a group of American and German researchers drew up a list of the world's top 500 supercomputers.

The world's most powerful computer is located at the Los Alamos National Laboratory in New Mexico. The Thinking Machine CM-5 can perform 131 billion floating point calculations per second. It is used for calculations arising from fusion experiments.

America's growing involvement with computers is indicated by the marketing of software in increased numbers of programs for younger children. By 1994, programs were being designed for children 2 to 6 years of age. As more nursery schools invested in computers, the possibility arose that many children would become computer-literate before they were able to read and write.

◆ *Define each of the following:*

a. personal computer
b. CD-ROM
c. RISC
d. mainframe
e. supercomputer
f. software
g. PDA
h. user-friendly

Section Review

1. *List examples of improvements in computer technology.*
2. *PROVE or DISPROVE: In the last decade of the 20th century, the use of computers by Americans declined.*

The New Era of Multimedia and Interactive Technology

By late 1993, more than 1,000 multimedia programs were available to consumers. These programs combined computer technology with text, sound, animation, and video clips. For example, Multimedia Beethoven (Microsoft) enables the consumer to listen to the Ninth Symphony while reading synchronized commentary written by a college professor. The program also contains information about the composer's life and times.

Multimedia Mozart and Multimedia Stravinsky are also available. Twain's World (Bureau of Electronic Publishing) contains almost everything Mark Twain ever published—fiction, nonfiction, essays, speeches, letters—and material from critics and scholars. Some text is narrated. Some is coupled with specially created animations. Period music is scattered through the program. There are also photos of the writer and friends and the only known video clip of Twain, from a film reportedly made by Thomas Edison in 1909.

Art Gallery (Microsoft) provides the opportunity to view the 2,000 paintings in the permanent collection of London's National Gallery on a personal computer. Biographical information on 750 artists is provided, as is the opportunity to take an audio-guided tour.

The multimedia programs are reasonably priced. To use them, however, the consumer must transform an ordinary IBM-type personal computer into a multimedia computer. This can be done by adding a sound board, speakers, and a CD-ROM drive.

By mid-1993, a number of America's corporate giants had begun to invest in the development of multimedia services. In the forefront of this effort were Time Warner, Tele-Communications, News Corporation, and Walt Disney.

◆ *Explain why multimedia programs are expected to have a major effect on American business and education.*

Multimedia programs have been made possible by the development of digital technology. By converting words and pictures into digital form, programmers can send far more material by wire to computers and television sets. This enables TV viewers to receive many more channels.

Digital technology also allows viewers to send messages back through the TV lines. As a result, watching television may soon become a less passive activity. Instead, it will be an "interactive" process. As the technology develops, interactive TV services will include home shopping and banking, long-distance learning, video games, even telephone service. In order for this to happen, however, cable TV companies and telephone companies will have to spend large sums of money to upgrade their networks.

Sophisticated computer hardware and software are needed to make interactive services possible. To meet this need, cable companies began to form alliances with computer and telephone companies. In March, 1994, for example, the Microsoft Corporation and Tele-Communications, Inc. agreed to jointly test interactive cable television systems.

1. *Define* interactive services.
2. *Explain the connection between interactive services and digital technology.*

Section Review

1. *Explain why you AGREE or DISAGREE with each of the following statements:*
   a. *By the year 2000, multimedia programs and interactive services will have changed the ways in which Americans live and work.*
   b. *Corporations that invest in digital technology products in the 1990's will profit greatly in the upcoming century.*
   c. *Multimedia programs and interactive services are useful only for entertainment.*

2. *Give examples of multimedia programs and interactive services with which you are familiar.*

Advances in Telecommunications

The touchtone telephone has largely replaced the rotary dial. Call waiting enables a telephone user engaged in a conversation to be informed by a beep that someone else is attempting to reach him or her. Conference calls can involve more than two people in the same conversation. Mobile telephones and cellular telephones require no wires and can be used even in moving vehicles. These improvements in telecommunications have become standard in American homes and workplaces. In addition, the telecommunications industry has been in the forefront of the effort to develop an "electronic superhighway" (or "information superhighway") to bring increased amounts of information into every home.

In August, 1993, AT&T announced that it would acquire the largest cellular telephone company in the United States. Its takeover of McCaw Cellular Communications, which was formalized in 1994, gave AT&T control of a vast wireless network.

This acquisition was AT&T's response to the explosive growth in wireless communications, a field that includes cellular telephones, two-way paging devices, hand-held computers, and mobile fax machines. All of these devices use radio waves to send and receive information. By combining the computerized intelligence of its long-distance network with McCaw's wireless systems, AT&T hopes to develop a whole new line of customized services for consumers.

1. *Select ONE development in telecommunications and explain its importance to modern America.*
2. *Define* wireless communications.

Building the Information Superhighway

AT&T is expected to increase its role in the development of wireless computer networks and mobile computing. In 1993,

McCaw began to develop new data services that will allow people to send and receive large volumes of text on the same frequencies that now carry voice conversations.

Integrated Services Digital Network (ISDN) was invented at AT&T Bell Laboratories in 1978. It was designed to allow simultaneous voice and data services over a standard telephone line. But for years, most consumers saw no need for ISDN. In the 1990's, however, ISDN became important to the effort to build the information superhighway. For example, it has been used to gain access to the rapidly growing Internet. Internet is an international collection of computer networks that exchange mail, data, and a number of information services. In 1997, many millions of people were communicating over the Internet. It connects universities, private companies, and individual users throughout the world.

In early 1995, scientists began to use the Internet for remote control of advanced telescopes at the South Pole. At the same time, plans were made for the Microsoft Network to be linked to the Internet. Microsoft's entrance to the Internet is expected to stimulate a huge market for the online sale of goods and services. Congress also connected itself to the Internet in 1995 with arrangements to send bills, speeches, and debates to millions of computer users as electronic mail.

Business firms use ISDN to connect office computer networks to home computers via telephone lines at ten times the speed of the fastest modems. This has made it easier for employees to work at home by telecommuting.

Satellite telephone service is another recent advance in telecommunications. Motorola Corporation's Iridium service will depend on 66 low-orbit satellites and will provide telephone service which will be accessible worldwide from portable handsets. It will be available to customers in 1998.

Improvement of home banking by telephone has been the subject of recent experiments. Online Resources and Communications Corporation has developed the technology for a special telephone equipped with a miniature version of an automated teller machine's display. The phone can do anything an ATM can do, except dispense cash. The low cost of the special telephone and monthly charges makes this type of home banking cheaper than paying bills by check.

1. *Summarize the major advances or developments in telecommunications in the 1990's.*
2. *Explain the connection between telecommunications and the effort to build an information superhighway.*

Section Review

1. *Complete the following sentences:*
   a. *AT&T will change telecommunications in the United States by ______.*
   b. *A result of the merger of Bell Atlantic and Tele-Communications Inc. may be ______.*
   c. *ISDN has been used to ______.*
   d. *Motorola Corporation's Iridium service will provide ______.*
   e. *Home banking can be conducted cheaply by using a ______.*
2. *Make a list of ways in which advances in telecommunications can improve the quality of your life and work.*

The Exploration of Space

The age of space exploration began in 1957, when the Soviets launched *Sputnik,* an orbiting space satellite. As they developed the technology, the United States and other nations placed their own satellites in space. *Voyager 1,* launched in 1958, was the first U.S. satellite. This program resulted in improved television, radio, and telephone communication; more accurate weather forecasting; and the acquisition of important information about other planets. *Voyager 2*'s trip past Neptune in 1989 was one of the most important space exploration missions.

In the 1960's, scientists aimed to put people in space. In 1969, two U.S. astronauts landed on the Moon. In the 1970's and 1980's, the emphasis was on developing orbiting space stations, where astronauts could spend extended periods experimenting in a gravity-free environment. Experiments were also done in space shuttles. These small craft are a combination space capsule–airplane, designed for repeated voyages. The shuttle *Columbia* completed its first mission in 1981.

◆ *Explain how space shuttles differ from other types of space vehicles.*

NASA: An Uncertain Future

The American space exploration program has been administered by the National Aeronautic and Space Administration (NASA). In recent years, a series of difficulties has damaged NASA's reputation. In 1986, the shuttle craft *Challenger* exploded while being launched, killing its crew of scientists. Further shuttle missions were delayed until 1988 while the reasons for the disaster were investigated.

The exploration of Mars has been a major objective of the 1990s. In mid-1993, however, NASA's *Mars Observer* malfunctioned and was lost. This $1 billion robot probe was to have orbited and mapped Mars for up to six years. Another attempt was scheduled for late 1996. Earlier that year, scientists examining an ancient Martian meteorite were excited to find signs that life may once have existed there.

NASA also had trouble with the *GOES-Next* weather satellite project. By late 1993, it was three years behind schedule and had cost $1.7 billion. By 1996, however, two *GOES* satellites had been put into orbit. These satellites help forecasters make more accurate and timely weather observations.

And the Hubble Space Telescope, launched in 1990 at a cost of $1.6 billion, was semi-functional due to manufacturing errors and electronic problems. One consequence of this record was reductions in NASA's budget by both the Bush and Clinton administrations.

The flight of the space shuttle *Endeavor* in December, 1993, had two missions—to repair the Hubble telescope and to restore NASA's reputation. On five consecutive nights, the

Endeavor astronauts thrilled the world with a record number of space walks to replace faulty components of the Hubble Space Telescope. After being made fully operational, the telescope was placed back in orbit.

Additional shuttle flights included one by *Discovery* in February, 1994, and another by *Columbia* in March, 1994. The *Discovery* astronauts, five Americans and one Russian, carried out a number of medical experiments. The crew of *Columbia,* NASA's oldest shuttle, performed engineering and technology experiments and medical tests.

Remote controlled space flights provided valuable scientific information in the 1990's. Knowledge of solar dynamics was increased by the *Ulysses* spacecraft. It spent more than four years traveling in previously unexplored parts of the solar system. The *Magellan* spacecraft mapped 98 percent of the surface of Venus in 15,000 orbits of that planet between 1990 and 1994. Another *Discovery* flight, in September, 1994, demonstrated a new technology for gathering climate data.

Long-range exploration and improved long-distance telescope systems are being emphasized in the 1990's. In addition to the Hubble Space Telescope, the Very Long Baseline Array (VLBA) went into operation in 1993. It is the largest astronomical instrument ever built. The VLBA will enable scientists to examine long ago and far away space time. It will reveal the details of galaxies as they existed billions of years ago.

During the 1990s, NASA and Russia began to work together on an international space laboratory to orbit Earth. It should enable a shuttle to dock for a month of experiments and be large enough to contain U.S., European, and Japanese laboratories and facilities for a permanent crew.

The first phase of the joint project used a U.S. space shuttle and the Russian *Mir* space station as bases from which scientists and astronauts could learn to build and run the station.

In September, 1996, biochemist Shannon Lucid, the first American woman to live on *Mir,* broke the 115-day U.S. record for length of time in space. Her stay of 188 days not only made Lucid a hero but also let scientists further observe the effects on the human body of prolonged living in space.

♦ *List NASA's successes and failures in the 1990's.*

Section Review

1. *For each of the following dates, state an event or development in the U.S. space program.*

   a. 1958   *d. 1986*   *f. 1993*
   b. 1969   *e. 1990*   *g. 1994*
   c. 1981

2. *Explain the importance to NASA of the 1993* Endeavor *mission.*
3. *Describe the objectives of the U.S. space program in the 1990's.*

Transportation: Smart Roads and Other Innovations

In the field of transportation technology, American research and development in the 1990's has focused upon making air and road travel safer and faster. NASA has been involved in much of this effort.

In 1993, NASA began the High Speed Research Program. Its aim is to develop technology for an economically practical, environmentally safe U.S. supersonic airliner. At present, the British Airways Concorde is the only supersonic airliner in existence. A competing effort was begun by Aerospatiale, a French firm working on a European model. Supersonic transports (SSTs) are designed to fly faster than the speed of sound. The Concorde can get travelers from New York to London in three hours and fifteen minutes, instead of the six to seven hours required by a conventional jet aircraft. However, the higher cost of SST flights limits this form of travel to a small number of passengers.

Other NASA aeronautics programs were established to make future aircraft and the nation's air-traffic control system safer, more efficient, and more economical. Included are efforts to develop quieter, more fuel-efficient passenger-plane engines. Also being considered is the technology for controlled landings using engine power only, instead of normal flight controls. NASA and the Federal Aviation Agency (FAA) have also begun several new programs that will enable airports around the world to handle more planes with fewer weather and traffic delays while maintaining high safety standards.

For environmental and other reasons, American auto manufacturers have been attempting to develop a marketable electric car. In an unusual collaboration, Ford, General Motors, and Chrysler have been working on an electric battery. Size and weight have been the main design problems. Lead and acid batteries require 100 times the weight and 30 times the space of conventional gasoline tanks.

Ford and Chrysler began delivery, in 1993, of experimental electric power vans, mainly to public utility companies. In 1994, General Motors offered a limited number of utility customers around the country the opportunity to test-drive state-of-the-art electric vehicles. These vehicles were advertised as being cleaner and quieter than internal combustion vehicles. Utility companies informed their customers that the cars could be recharged at home using 120- or 240-volt electricity. Customers were also told that widespread use of electric vehicles could improve air quality and reduce dependence on imported oil. In 1995, another car manufacturer introduced an electric car made of lightweight composite materials. The Solectra Sunrise was designed for mass production in 1997.

1. *List the efforts made by NASA to improve transportation technology.*
2. *State an advantage and a disadvantage of an automobile powered by electricity.*

A Supercar for the 21st Century

In early 1994, Ford, General Motors, and Chrysler joined with the Administration of President Clinton to develop a prototype of a super fuel-efficient automobile by the year 2003. The government agreed to provide several hundred million dollars for research and a number of scientists to help the Big Three invent a car that achieves gas mileage of 82.5 miles per gallon. Defense researchers will be assigned to apply technology systems such as advanced energy storage to cars. The automakers will contribute their own money as well.

In January, 1994, the Chrysler Corporation displayed a race car it is developing that combines a clean-burning natural gas turbine engine with a flywheel battery. This combination provides 500 horsepower for extremely quick acceleration. The car could reach 200 miles an hour. Called the *Patriot,* this is a "concept" car. It is one of the kinds of cars envisioned by Clinton and Gore in the super-car program.

The Patriot's combination, or "hybrid," engine is being studied for possible use in the passenger cars of the future. However, it would not help Chrysler meet California's automobile rules. In 1998, California will require that at least 2 percent of the cars sold be electric.

The Big Three American auto manufacturers have also been examining ways to reduce automobile weight to improve fuel economy. In August, 1993, General Motors, Ford, and Chrysler began a cooperative research program to promote the use of aluminum, magnesium, and metal composites. If successful, this project could triple the amount of light metals used in cars. The use of plastics is also being investigated. Ford Motor Company revealed, in 1993, two concept cars that rely on light metals. The Synthesis 2010 uses aluminum for every major component and is a half-ton lighter than a Mercury Sable. The second is an "aluminized" Sable that is 400 pounds lighter.

- *Identify the Big Three and state the reason for their partnership with the Clinton Administration.*

"Smart" Cars and Roads

Computerized cars driving themselves on automated highways have been proposed by government planners to solve the nation's traffic problems. Government spending on the Intelligent Vehicle and Highway Systems (IVHS) program is expected to exceed $40 billion over the next 20 years. IVHS would put computers in charge of everything from timing traffic signals to deciding which route each car should take. It is also proposed to eventually have the computers do the actual driving.

In the early stages, a dashboard screen would display maps while a synthesized voice would give directions to the driver. Later, the Automated Highway System would become operational. Once passengers keyed in their destination, the computerized car would get them there without any effort by a human driver.

By 1993, IVHS had become a large-scale federal program with a budget of $218 million. "Smart" cars and highways have become the largest efforts in surface-transportation research and development of the 1990's. Clinton's Rebuild America proposal provided an extra $155 million for the Automated Highway System. The nation's primary transportation law, the Intermodal Surface Transportation Efficiency Act of 1991, gives approval for a fully automated highway by 1997.

Opponents of IVHS have argued that the technology proposed will merely increase the volume of traffic, the speed at which it moves, and the fuel consumed. They claim that the program will make worse the very traffic problems it seeks to solve.

◆ *List the possible advantages of computerized cars and highways.*

Section Review

1. *Explain the meaning of each of the following headlines:*

   THE ENDEAVOR MISSION: NASA'S DO OR DIE EFFORT

   TELESCOPES THAT SEE LONG AGO AND FAR AWAY

   RECHARGEABLE AUTOMOBILES

   THE BIG THREE TEAM UP TO TAKE THE WEIGHT OFF

   SMART ROADS END TRAFFIC JAMS

2. *Describe efforts made in the 1990's to improve automobiles. Which would you prefer to own—a "concept" car or a "smart" car? Explain your choice.*

Chapter 4 Review

A. *Write the letter of the correct response.*

1. *A major advance in computer technology in the 1970's was the development of the (a) monitor (b) microchip (c) laser printer.*
2. *An innovation of the 1990's was the appearance of (a) online computer services (b) mainframes (c) supercomputers.*
3. *The combination of computer technology with text, sound, animation, and video is called (a) high-definition television (b) CD-ROM (c) multimedia programming.*
4. *As interactive TV services develop, they are expected to include (a) home shopping and banking (b) long-distance learning (c) all of these.*
5. *Development of an ''information superhighway'' is dependent on improvements in (a) automobile design (b) telecommunications (c) word processing.*
6. *An important element of space exploration in the 1990's has been missions by (a) reusable space shuttles (b) astronauts landing on other planets (c) regulation of global weather patterns.*
7. *The task assigned to the crew of the* Endeavor, *in December, 1993, was to repair the (a) Very Long Baseline Array (b)* Mars Observer *(c) Hubble Space Telescope.*

8. *A joint U.S.–Russian project has been planned to build (a) an international space laboratory (b) a faster orbiting shuttle (c) a better space telescope.*
9. *A problem in the development of an electric car is the size and weight of its (a) carburetor (b) exhaust pipe (c) battery.*
10. *A goal of the Clinton Administration has been the development of a prototype of a (a) faster than the speed of light aircraft (b) super fuel-efficient automobile (c) solar-powered ship.*

B. *Reread* NASA: An Uncertain Future *on pages 86–87 and answer the questions which follow.*

1. *Which statements do you think reflect the facts which you have read?*
   a. *The* Mars Observer *mission was a success.*
   b. *The loss of $1 billion in federal funds was an embarrassment for NASA.*
   c. *By late 1993, NASA was in desperate need of an achievement which would capture the attention of the nation.*
   d. *From 1986 to 1993, NASA had experienced no problems in its space program.*
   e. *The purpose of the* Mars Observer *mission was to obtain photographs of the surface of the "red planet."*
2. *Write one or two paragraphs to state your opinion about the importance of the space exploration program to the United States.*

C. *Reread* Transportation: Smart Roads and Other Innovations *on pages 88–91 and study the graph below. Then write responses to the following questions:*

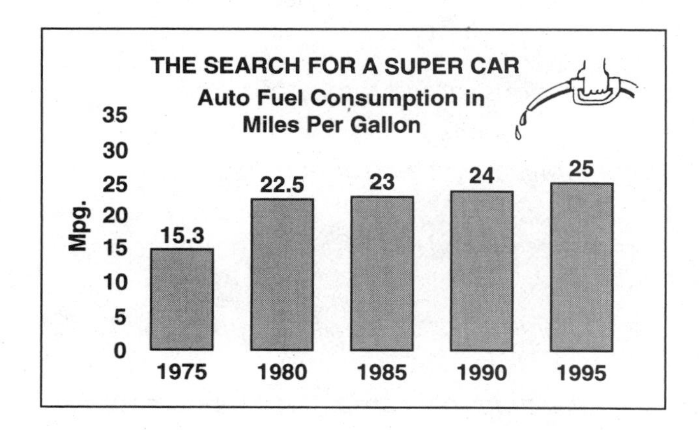

a. How has fuel consumption changed between 1975 and 1995?
b. Why do the Clinton Administration and the Big Three wish to build a "super car"?
c. How would concept cars and hybrid engines affect fuel consumption?

Unit 1 Review

A. *In a public opinion poll conducted by* U.S. News & World Report *and printed in its January 31, 1994, issue, the following information was provided:*

- 53 percent of those polled approved of the President. The approval rating for the First Lady was 57 percent.
- 63 percent of those polled agreed that Clinton would be a better president his second year in office.

1. *Use information from Unit 1 to evaluate the first year of the Clinton presidency. Be sure to discuss each of the following:*
   a. Clinton's major goals and programs.
   b. Crises or problems faced by the President.
   c. Relations with Congress and the federal courts.
2. *Explain why you AGREE or DISAGREE with the poll results stated above.*

B. *Review Chapter 2,* The Economy, *pages 24–46. Then answer the following questions:*

1. *What were the signs, or indicators, of economic improvement in 1993?*
2. *How has corporate downsizing affected employment opportunities in the 1990's?*
3. *As America moves toward the 21st century, where will the major job opportunities lie?*
4. *Why have labor unions lost some of their power and influence in the 1990's?*
5. *In what new directions has corporate America moved?*

C. *In the 1990's, a number of major problems affected American society. Use information in Unit I to help you do the following:*

1. *List the problems which caused significant stress across the nation.*
2. *Select TWO of these problems and describe them in detail. For each, indicate why it is a problem and what is being done to respond to the problem.*
3. *Identify the problem which you think is most destructive to American society. State the reasons for your choice.*

D. *American technology advanced dramatically during the 1990's. Use information from Unit I to help you write a brief essay on ONE of the following topics:*

The Computerization of America
Advances in Telecommunications
Space Exploration
Improvements in Transportation

UNIT II

AMERICA AND THE WORLD

For Americans, the late 20th century has been a time in which global changes have presented new challenges. The collapse of the Soviet Union in December, 1991, and the fall of Communist governments in East Europe ended the cold war. The United States has worked with its allies and former adversaries to create a new world order. American leaders were called upon to develop new policies that would respond to political, economic, and social problems in each of the world's regions. The highest priorities were placed on the promotion of democratic governments, free market economies, and human rights. Much attention was also given to the stimulation of business activity and the creation of new job opportunities.

Chapter 5

The United States and Europe

In developing a post-cold war European policy, the Administration of President Clinton emphasized support for the efforts of the governments of Russia and the other former Soviet republics to build new political and economic systems. Relations with the former Soviet satellite states of East Europe have been shaped by the desire of these nations to draw closer to the West by joining the North Atlantic Treaty Organization (NATO) and the European Union (EU). In the 1990's, these two organizations became the means by which the West European nations developed increased military, economic, and political unity. The rise of a "new Europe" presented American policymakers with new questions and problems. Among them were the formulation of responses to two great crises—the bloody civil war in Bosnia-Herzegovina and the continuing violence in Northern Ireland.

- *Explain why Europe in the 1990's required the development of new American policies.*

The Search for New Friends: Russia and Its Neighbors

The forming of a long-range policy toward Russia and the other 14 republics of the former Soviet Union has been a difficult task for the Clinton Administration. Following the collapse of the Soviet Union, Russia, Belarus, Ukraine, and some of the other republics formed a Commonwealth of Independent States (CIS). Russia is the largest of the republics and has the most military

EUROPE AND NEIGHBORING MEMBERS OF THE COMMONWEALTH OF INDEPENDENT STATES

power. By 1992, Russian President Boris Yeltsin had become the best-known political leader in the region. Agreements reached by Yeltsin and the leaders of the other republics provided for the creation of a central authority for the Commonwealth at Minsk, the capital of Belarus. They also decided to use the Soviet ruble as their common currency and to maintain neutrality in international affairs. Among the several matters causing anxiety for the United States and other nations was the presence in Russia, Belarus, Kazakhstan, and Ukraine of long-range nuclear weapons.

The United States, Germany, France, and the other industrialized nations of Europe were eagerly supporting the growth of democracy and free market economies in the newly independent republics. Urged by the United States, these nations gave substantial economic and humanitarian aid to the former Communist states. However, a number of problems soon arose.

In Russia, rapidly growing price inflation, shortages of food and consumer goods, unemployment, and a rising crime rate undermined public confidence in Yeltsin's government. Many Russians doubted their President's ability to reform the defective economy through *privatization* (placing state-controlled factories and businesses in the hands of private individuals and groups who would run them for profit). Criticism of Yeltsin's policies and challenges to his authority from his political opponents became louder and more frequent.

Among those who opposed Yeltsin's policies were Communists and ultra-nationalists. The Communists, led by Vice President Alexander Rutskoi and Ruslan Khasbulatov, leader of the Russian parliament, wanted to keep the power they held during the Soviet regime. The ultra-nationalists, such as Vladimir Zhirinovsky, demanded the use of Russian military power to dominate the other republics. This Communist-nationalist alliance caused a crisis in Russia in 1993.

1. *Describe conditions in the former Soviet Union in the early 1990's.*
2. *List the groups and individuals who opposed President Yeltsin.*

The Struggle in Russia

Determined to slow privatization and the growth of democracy, Yeltsin's opponents engaged in an open power struggle with the President. As economic conditions worsened, demonstrations and counter-demonstrations disrupted Moscow. In October, 1993, hard-line Communists and ultranationalists, led by Khasbulatov and Rutskoi, seized the Russian parliament building and appealed to the people to force Yeltsin to resign. When attempts to reason with the rebels failed, army and police forces loyal to the President stormed the parliament building. Along with many of their followers, Khasbulatov and Rutskoi were arrested and imprisoned for several months.

Throughout the crisis in Russia, the United States supported Yeltsin. Clinton proclaimed that the future of democracy and a free market economy in Russia depended on the political survival of Yeltsin. To assist Yeltsin's efforts to strengthen the economy of his country, increased aid was sent to Russia. Among the measures proposed by the American President were direct financial aid to stabilize the ruble, support for low interest loans, and sending Americans to Russia to help develop private business and democratic institutions. The leaders of the other industrialized nations were also persuaded to commit economic and technical aid to Russia.

American foreign-policy officials were startled by events in Russia in December, 1993. In a national referendum, Russian voters approved a new constitution. This document had been written by a commission formed by Yeltsin. It increased the powers of the President and reduced those of the parliament—provisions demanded by Yeltsin. He also called for a national election to choose a new parliament. The old legislature had been established under the Soviet government.

When the elections were held, however, the Communist and ultra-nationalist opponents of Yeltsin's reform programs captured a large number of parliamentary seats. Vladimir Zhirinovsky, the nationalist leader, emerged as a leading political figure and a possible future President. His Liberal Democratic Party became the single largest group in Russian politics.

The results of the 1993 election alarmed the Clinton Administration and raised doubts about Yeltsin's reforms and concern about the future of democracy in Russia. American fears focused upon Zhirinovsky. His preference for extending Russian power and domination by military means was viewed as a threat to the independence of the other republics. Some American officials urged Yeltsin to take steps to improve the daily lives of Russians by reducing unemployment and criminal violence.

1. *Identify each of the following:*

   a. *Boris Yeltsin*
   b. *Ruslan Khasbulatov*
   c. *Alexander Rutskoi*
   d. *Vladimir Zhirinovsky*

2. *Explain why developments in Russia in late 1993 worried the Clinton Administration.*

Concerns About Russia

By early 1994, Clinton and his advisers had additional worries about Russia. Yeltsin's economic reform efforts were slowing down. During a trip to Moscow in January, Clinton informed Yeltsin that no more American money would be given to Russia unless certain requirements were met. He urged the Russian President to restructure his budget in a way that would curb inflation and end subsidies (government payments) to unprofitable state industries. He suggested that American aid be used to reduce the Russian government's deficit and to provide jobless workers with pensions, unemployment insurance, and retraining programs. He also recommended that Yeltsin take steps to create a body of laws that would support and regulate a free market.

To implement such policies, however, Yeltsin would have to win cooperation from a hostile parliament.

While in Moscow, Clinton appeared on Russian television. He stated that Russia was still a great nation and offered political and moral support for its government and society.

However, he was also open about U.S. interests and indicated that there is a limit to what America can do for Russia. Many Russians appreciated his frankness and described the U.S. President as "a good muzhik" (a regular guy).

A 1994 spy scandal cast doubts on U.S. policy toward Russia. An official of the Central Intelligence Agency (CIA) had been giving U.S. security secrets to the Soviet Union and then to Russia. Congress was outraged that Russia would take billions in U.S. aid and engage in such subversion. Clinton expelled a senior Russian intelligence officer and stated that U.S. policy toward Russia was based "not on charity or blind faith, but on our clear American interests, clearly pursued."

Also unnerving to the Clinton Administration was Yeltsin's foreign policy, which was becoming more aggressive. Without informing the United States, Yeltsin sent Russian troops to war-torn Bosnia-Herzegovina to assist in peacekeeping efforts and to establish a Russian presence in the Balkans (Southeast Europe). Even more worrisome was Russia's use of its considerable military power to extend its influence into the other former Soviet republics. For example, Russian weapons were supplied to both sides in a civil war in Georgia. And economic pressure was used on Belarus, Moldova, and Ukraine when Russia reduced supplies of natural gas to them. Such actions appeared to be designed to make these neighboring states dependent on Russia for military and economic assistance. They were also intended as warnings to these countries not to mistreat their Russian-speaking inhabitants.

The outbreak of a deadly war inside Russia also alarmed U.S. officials in 1994. The people of the Chechnya region demanded separation from the rest of Russia. The Yeltsin government responded with military force. By 1995, the war had caused extensive damage to the region. The Clinton Administration urged Yeltsin to negotiate a peaceful solution.

Yeltsin, however, sent in more troops to enforce his control of Chechnya. The 20-month war ended in the summer of 1996, when Russian security chief Aleksandr Lebed announced a shaky peace agreement. A decision on Chechnya's secession from Russia was postponed until 2001. As of now, Chechnya seems autonomous (self-governing), but Yeltsin has repeatedly asserted that Chechnya should remain part of Russia.

The peace negotiations and Lebed's popularity with the Russian army focused world attention to him as a potential political power. Yeltsin had just been reelected president, but his heart condition caused speculation about possible successors. Polls showed Lebed to be the Russians' first choice.

Some U.S. leaders distrusted Lebed. His statements about NATO were veiled threats. Moreover, during Clinton's visit to Moscow, he and Yeltsin had agreed that U.S. and Russian nuclear weapons would no longer be aimed at each other. A hostile Russian leader might go back on this agreement.

Many in the West viewed Russia's aggressive foreign policy as a return to imperialism as practiced by the Soviet Union and by the czars of old Russia. For the Clinton Administration, a reexamination of U.S. policies toward Russia and the other republics was necessary.

In October, 1996, Yeltsin fired Lebed. Lebed, referring to his support by the Russian military, announced that he would use only "democratic means" to regain political status.

- *State the Russian problems which concerned President Clinton in early 1994.*

Section Review

1. *Explain each of the following headlines:*

   ELECTION RESULTS IN RUSSIA SHAKE WASHINGTON

   WHY RUSSIA CONTINUES TO TORMENT AMERICA

   WHAT HAPPENS IF THE BIG BAD BEAR AWAKES?

2. *PROVE or DISPROVE: A change in America's policy toward Russia became necessary in 1994.*

Relations With the Other Former Soviet Republics

Seeking to disprove criticisms that U.S. policy toward the former Soviet Union favored Russia over the other 14 republics, Clinton's administrators announced that countries other than Russia would receive more than half the $2.5 billion in aid authorized in 1993 for former Soviet republics.

After his visit to Moscow, Clinton traveled to Minsk, the capital of Belarus (see map, page 103). To the Soviet-style government of this republic, run by former Communists, Clinton pledged at least $50 million in additional economic aid, including $25 million to help the government eliminate the 81 Soviet nuclear missiles left on its soil. Clinton praised Belarus for being the first former Soviet republic to plan a nuclear-free future. Clinton also attempted to persuade Prime Minister Vyacheslav F. Kebich (head of the government from 1990 to 1994) to hold free elections and to press ahead with economic reforms.

Opposition to Kebich's Communist regime was led by Stanislav Shukevich, chairman of Belarus's parliament. While in Belarus, Clinton met with Shukevich and other opposition leaders. They urged him to cut off all aid to Belarus, claiming that the money would not be used for reform.

In 1994, voters, unhappy with the Kebich government, elected Aleksandr Lukashenko, a crusader against corruption, as the first President of Belarus. He carried out economic reforms but made no move toward nuclear disarmament, even though Western nations threatened to cut off aid.

1. *Name the two cities visited by President Clinton during his visit to the former Soviet Union in January, 1994.*
2. *Identify the foreign policy goal pursued by President Clinton in each city.*

Reduction of Nuclear Weapons

A major goal of American policy in the former Soviet Union has been the reduction of nuclear weapons in the region. Clinton's visit to Belarus had been for the purpose of thanking the government for its decision to give up its nuclear weapons and to draw attention to the refusal of Ukraine to do the same. Ukraine, however, changed its mind the week before Clinton's visit and agreed to surrender its 176 nuclear missiles and 1,800 warheads over a period of seven years.

In March, 1994, Clinton met with Ukraine's President, Leonid M. Kravchuk, in Washington. To reward the Ukrainian leader for his decision to destroy his nuclear weapons and to encourage him to bring about economic reforms leading to privatization of state-owned businesses and the development of capitalism, American aid to Ukraine was doubled to about $700 million a year.

In November, 1994, the Ukrainian parliament agreed to sign the nuclear non-proliferation treaty. This agreement pledges the signers, with exception of the United States, Britain, France, and Russia, to rid themselves of all nuclear weapons. It was a move eagerly sought by the United States.

Ukraine's decision to join the nuclear non-proliferation treaty encouraged Russia to move toward ratification of the Strategic Arms Reduction Treaties (START). START I and START II provided for deep cuts in both American and Russian long-range nuclear weapons. Under START I, Kazakhstan also agreed to eliminate its nuclear weapons.

◆ *Evaluate the success of the Clinton Administration in reducing nuclear weapons in the former Soviet Union.*

Elsewhere in the Former Soviet Union

To assist efforts at political reform in Kazakhstan, Clinton pledged, in early 1994, to triple aid to that republic. The American funds were also intended to help the Kazakhs dismantle their nuclear weapons and to provide support for the dozens of American businesses involved in an oil boom there.

President Nursultan Nazarbayev signed a number of agreements with the United States. One concerned Kazakhstan's participation in the treaty banning the spread of nuclear weapons.

Clinton acknowledged the strategic importance to the United States of both Kazakhstan and its President. Kazakhstan borders Russia, China, the Caspian Sea, and three other former Soviet republics: Kyrgyzstan, Turkmenistan, and Uzbekistan. Kazakhstan has large deposits of gold, silver, chrome, zinc, and iron ore and is an exporter of wheat and coal. Since the discovery of 25 billion tons of oil and gas reserves, this country has become a valuable strategic ally of the United States. And Nazarbayev has made a strong commitment to the economic reform programs necessary to maintain foreign investment.

Few other nations offer such impressive opportunities for American trade and investments. Seventy American firms were doing business in Kazakhstan in 1995. A major concern of the Clinton Administration is that the Kazakhs might build a pipeline to transport their oil to the Mediterranean Sea or the Persian Gulf through Iran, a nation not friendly to the United States.

American relations with the former Soviet republics have been conditioned by the strong desire of Russia to remain the dominant power in the region. Some experts contend that it is unrealistic of the United States to encourage the other republics to assume that they can have real independence. However, some of the world's biggest reserves of oil and gas are in Azerbaijan, Kazakhstan, and Turkmenistan; and Russia has demanded a share of their oil development projects. American business interests may require that the United States take a firmer stand to oppose Russian interference in the affairs of its neighbors.

Russia has sent "peacekeeping" forces into Tajikistan, where they imposed a pro-Russian government. It also dispatched secret military advisers to Azerbaijan, which is at war with Armenia.

In Georgia, a civil war was caused by the demands of its province of Abkhazia for independence. After sending weapons to both the government forces and the rebels, Russia played the role of peacemaker. To gain Russian support, President Eduard Shevardnadze agreed to bring Georgia into the Commonwealth of Independent States. This decision increased Russian influence in Georgia.

Russia claims that the purpose of its military activities is to protect the interests of the Russian-speaking population living outside of Russia.

When he was in Moscow, President Clinton said that he would support the idea that Russian-speaking people in the Baltic nations (Latvia, Lithuania, and Estonia) be respected. His statement alarmed officials in Latvia, who were at that time negotiating for the removal of 12,500 Russian troops. In response, Clinton notified the Latvian President that it was not his intention to link the question of troop withdrawals with the treatment of Russian-speaking inhabitants of the country.

The question of a future American policy toward the growth of Russian imperialism will affect the amount of influence the United States will have in the region.

1. *Review* Relations With the Other Former Soviet Republics. *Then indicate which of the following statements are* true *and which are* false.

   a. *Russia received all of the economic aid given by the United States to the former Soviet Union in the 1990's.*
   b. *In early 1994, Clinton visited Minsk and met with the leaders of Belarus.*
   c. *The republic with the most strategic significance to the United States is Turkmenistan.*
   d. *Statements made by Clinton about respecting Russian-speakers in the Baltic nations worried the President of Latvia.*
   e. *The presence of large oil resources has attracted American businesses to Azerbaijan, Kazakhstan, and Turkmenistan.*

Section Review

1. *State three goals of American foreign policy in the former Soviet Union in the 1990's.*
2. *Explain why you AGREE or DISAGREE with the following statement:*

   Since the United States will not commit its military forces anywhere in the former Soviet Union, it must recognize that the Russians can do what they like in the region.

Dealing With the New East Europe

At the end of the cold war, the "satellite" nations of East Europe replaced their Communist leaders with democratically elected governments. They dissolved the Soviet-dominated Warsaw Pact military alliance and began to develop capitalism and closer relations with the West.

American foreign policy goals for East Europe included encouraging the growth of democracy and free-market economies. In addition, the United States supported the insistence of the new governments on the rapid withdrawal from their countries of the military forces of the former Soviet Union. However, the great diplomatic question of the 1990's was that of how best to ensure the security of the East Europeans.

Distrusting the ambitions of Russia, the East European nations wanted to join the North Atlantic Treaty Organization (NATO). NATO was organized in 1949 as a military alliance of the United States and its allies in Western Europe. Its mission was to defend the West against attack by the Soviet Union and its Warsaw Pact allies. After the cold war, the East Europeans wanted to ensure that they would not again fall under the domination of Russia. But membership in NATO would require American and West European troops to fight in the defense of any former Warsaw Pact member threatened by Russia. In 1995, the NATO allies were not prepared to make this commitment. And the Clinton Administration was not prepared to offend Russia, whose foreign minister had warned the East European governments not to apply for NATO membership.

During his January, 1994, tour of Europe, Clinton expressed support for the growth of democracy and capitalism in East Europe. He urged the NATO allies to integrate the security of East and West with strong American backing. His priority, however, was the success of democracy in Russia. This required that he avoid inflaming Russian nationalist feelings.

In Prague, the capital of the Czech Republic, Clinton met with many of the East European leaders. He told them to be patient about NATO membership and to work toward that goal by joining a "Partnership for Peace." Poland, the Czech Republic, Hungary, and the other former satellite nations were offered the opportunity to participate in NATO military exercises and planning without becoming full members of the alliance. Some Europeans and Americans called that "appeasement" and urged a tougher stand against possible Russian bullying of the East Europeans. Clinton expressed the opinion that the NATO allies would defend the East Europeans if they were attacked.

1. *List the nations that would be in greatest danger from Russia if it became aggressive.*
2. *List the nations which would have to defend Eastern Europe from Russia, and explain why you think they were reluctant to do this in 1994 and 1995.*

Section Review

1. *Define the term "Partnership for Peace."*
2. *PROVE or DISPROVE: The Partnership for Peace will weaken the government of President Yeltsin and will encourage extreme nationalists in Russia.*
3. *Evaluate the policies of the Clinton Administration toward Eastern Europe. How effective have they been in improving the security of this region?*

The Crisis in Bosnia-Herzegovina

A bloody civil war in the former Yugoslavia became a foreign policy dilemma for the Clinton Administration. From 1945 to 1990, Yugoslavia was a Communist nation but not a Soviet satellite. In 1992, Croatia, Bosnia-Herzegovina, Slovenia, and Macedonia declared independence from Yugoslavia. Serbia, the largest, most powerful Yugoslav republic, opposed their decision, and Serbian President Slobodan Milosevic decided to use military force to end their independence. Focusing on Bosnia, an ethnic mix of Muslims, Serbs, and Croats, Serbia armed the Bosnian Serbs and encouraged them to revolt. Similarly, Croatia supported Bosnian Croats. By the end of 1992, a brutal war was raging among the three ethnic groups.

As atrocities mounted, especially against Bosnian Muslims, public opinion in the United States, Europe, and Muslim nations demanded action by the West to stop the killing. The Western governments, however, were willing to commit military forces only as part of small U.N. peacekeeping units. By September, 1992, Serbian forces occupied 70 percent of Bosnia. A smaller area was under Croatian control. The population of Sarajevo, the Bosnian capital, endured a continuing siege and suffered enormously.

Clinton received U.N. approval for an airlift of food and medical supplies to Bosnia but was unable to persuade the NATO allies to take military action. U.S. military aircraft were sent to Italy, and U.S. troops joined U.N. units in Macedonia. In early 1994, a U.S. fighter plane shot down two Serb fighters that had violated the "no-fly zone" set up by the U.N. Clinton also arranged a NATO ultimatum threatening to bomb Serb forces if they did not stop shelling Sarajevo.

In March, 1994, as a result of an economic embargo and a "peace offensive" launched by the Clinton Administration, Bosnian Croatians agreed to form a federation with the Muslims. The Administration tried to persuade the Bosnian Serbs to do the same, but despite a U.S. pledge of $10 million to aid postwar recovery, the Bosnian Serbs continued the war.

As Russian influence in the Balkans grew, U.S. peacemaking efforts became increasingly dependent on Russian diplomacy. When the Serbs in Croatia rebelled against that government and established an independent republic, Russia persuaded them to negotiate with Croatia. For Serbs in both Bosnia and Croatia, the United States was the enemy, whereas the Russians, fellow Slavs, were regarded as sympathetic to their objectives. U.S. and Russian diplomats, therefore, worked together to achieve a general peace.

As the war dragged on, the Clinton Administration urged that the international arms embargo against Bosnia be lifted to permit the Bosnian government to buy weapons for its defense. In June of 1996, Croatia, Serbian-led Yugoslavia, and the three conflicting ethnic factions of Bosnia signed an arms control agreement that limited the size of their arsenals. In recognition of this pact, the U.N. Security Council lifted its 1991 weapons embargo on the former Yugoslavian republics. The agreement included $100 million in arms sales by the United States to the Muslim-Croat federation.

In November, 1995, the stricter U.S. economic sanctions against Bosnia were lifted. Bosnian Serbs, along with representatives from Croatia, Serbia, and Bosnia, then met in Dayton, Ohio, and signed a peace agreement. The Bosnian Serb leaders resigned from office, although they continued to govern through their successors. Sarajevo was named capital of the central government, and various territories within Bosnia became sub-states of the new Muslim-Croat Federation or of the Bosnian Serbs. U.S. leaders expected renewed violence during the Bosnian elections in September, 1996. None took place, however. Voters elected a Muslim, a Croat, and a Serb to a three-part presidency. Nevertheless, the situation remained fragile. Foreign policy experts predicted that international troops would have to remain in Bosnia for years.

◆ *Review* The Crisis in Bosnia-Herzegovina. *Then complete the following sentences:*

a. In 1992, Bosnia-Herzegovina declared its independence from _______.
b. The Bosnian Serbs received assistance from the _______ government, led by _______.
c. The peace offensive of the Clinton Administration included a warning to the Serbs to stop _______.
d. The Clinton Administration persuaded the Bosnian Croatians to _______.
e. In September, 1996, Bosnians elected _______ to a three-part presidency.

Section Review

1. *State the policy of the Clinton Administration in the Balkans, and list some of the steps taken by the United States.*

2. *Explain why American diplomacy in the Balkans became linked with Russian influence by 1994.*
3. *Express your opinion of U.S. efforts to bring peace to the former Yugoslavia. What do you think should have been done that was not done?*

Relations With Western Europe: The Search for a New Security

American policy in the 1990's has been directed toward helping Europeans build a new security system based on their increasing economic and political unity. With the end of the cold war came the question of how much American involvement in the problems of Europe was necessary or desirable.

In mid-1992, President George Bush turned his attention to his reelection campaign. A period of weak American leadership in Europe began. As the Clinton Administration took office, West Europeans understood the American President's need to deal with domestic problems first. Some thought that this would strengthen the 12-nation European Union's influence and independence in world affairs.

The growth of the European Union (EU) had become a foundation of the "new world order" of the 1990's. Starting in 1957, Belgium, Denmark, France, Germany, Greece, Ireland, Italy, Luxembourg, Netherlands, Portugal, Spain, and the United Kingdom had gradually formed the European Community (EC) to reduce trade barriers and increase economic cooperation among members. The *Maastricht Treaty* of 1991 committed the EC member nations to develop a common currency and create a political union of the European democracies. By 1992, the EC had become a common market, or trading bloc, of 300 million people. In 1993, the EC renamed itself the European Union (EU). On January 1, 1995, Austria, Finland, and Sweden joined the EU. This made the EU the world's richest commercial and political grouping of nations.

Nevertheless, by late 1993, the governments of Western Europe were concerned about the possibility of a future without strong American leadership. The Clinton Administration was showing increased interest in stronger ties with the rapidly growing economies of Asia and Latin America. And the

United States' failure to end the bloodshed and starvation in Somalia, Africa, had left Americans with little enthusiasm for involvement in foreign problems.

1. *State the reasons for the lack of strong American leadership in Europe in the early 1990's.*
2. *Describe the growth of the European Union.*

To reassure Western Europe that it was still America's main ally, Clinton called for a meeting of NATO leaders in Brussels in early 1994. His stated purpose was to join Europe in building a new security for the 21st century by binding Europe together through "military cooperation, prosperous market economies, and vital democracies."

The West European leaders wanted a post–cold war alliance system that would give Eastern Europe security without causing an ultra-nationalistic reaction in Russia. They wanted the United States to play a central role in this effort, while Russian nationalists opposed Western intrusion in former Russian satellites.

Even France was eager for strong U.S. involvement. In 1966, France had left NATO, resenting American leadership. It led a drive to give Europe an independent defense force in the 1990's. By 1994, however, France had drawn closer to NATO and supported the retention of a U.S. military presence in Europe. (U.S. troop strength on the continent had dropped from 314,000 in 1990 to 150,000 in 1994.)

West Europeans had suffered a long economic recession and had failed to stop the war in Bosnia. As their sense of danger increased, they looked to the United States for the reassurance and direction it had provided during the cold war.

Accordingly, France called upon the United States to play a bigger role in Bosnia. It asked for American air support to relieve Muslim communities besieged by the Serbs and suggested that American ground troops participate. It also warned the United States that France might have to withdraw its peacekeeping forces from Bosnia. Britain, Spain, and Canada issued similar warnings.

Clinton, however, preferred a leadership role for the United States in the new Europe without deeper involvement in the

Bosnian crisis. In the spring of 1993, the Europeans rejected a U.S. proposal to lift a weapons embargo that had been imposed on Bosnia's Muslim-led government and launch air strikes against Bosnian Serb artillery positions near Sarajevo. Subsequently, the Clinton Administration made it clear that Bosnia was a problem that the Europeans would have to solve. However, as the crisis worsened in 1995, Clinton stated that U.S. ground forces could assist in the evacuation of U.N. peacekeepers.

At the 1994 NATO conference, Clinton defended his "Partnership for Peace" plan, which seeks to connect Eastern Europe to NATO through limited military cooperation. The plan stopped short of making the United States and Western Europe responsible for the security of countries formerly under Soviet domination. Finally, the President promised to keep approximately 100,000 American troops in Western Europe.

In 1995, Russia joined the Partnership for Peace. NATO leaders welcomed Russia's participation and tried to calm the former enemy's fears about the desire of the Eastern Europeans to join NATO.

◆ *Decide which of the following statements are correct:*

a. *In early 1994, President Clinton called a NATO conference in Belgium. His purpose was to assure Europeans that America's leadership would continue.*
b. *France wanted a stronger U.S. military presence in Bosnia.*
c. *The "Partnership for Peace" plan would require the United States to defend Poland, Hungry, and Romania.*
d. *To join NATO, a nation needs the approval of all current NATO nations.*

Section Review

1. *Read the statement below, and explain what it tells you about the policy of the United States toward Europe in the 1990's.*

> We must build a new security based not on the cold-war formulation of one bloc against the other, but on the new mandate for consolidating the gains of democracy and integrating the historic democracies

with the emerging new ones. The purpose of my trip is to help lead the movement to that integration and to assure you that America will be a strong partner in it.

—*President Bill Clinton*

2. *Write a letter to an imaginary friend in a European country. Tell your friend why you think the United States should or should not do more to settle European crises such as that in Bosnia.*

U.S. Reactions to the Crisis in Northern Ireland

Since 1969, approximately 1,600 people have been killed as a result of violence between Catholic and Protestant extremists in Northern Ireland. The crisis began with demonstrations by the Catholic minority against discrimination in education, housing, and employment. As it continued, the outlawed Irish Republican Army (IRA) demanded Northern Ireland's independence from the United Kingdom and its union with the mainly Roman Catholic Republic of Ireland. To achieve this goal, the IRA has carried out kidnappings, assassinations, and bombings in England, as well as in Northern Ireland. To keep the province British, Protestant extremists have committed similar acts of violence. Although British troops have been sent to Northern Ireland to keep the peace, the bloodshed has continued.

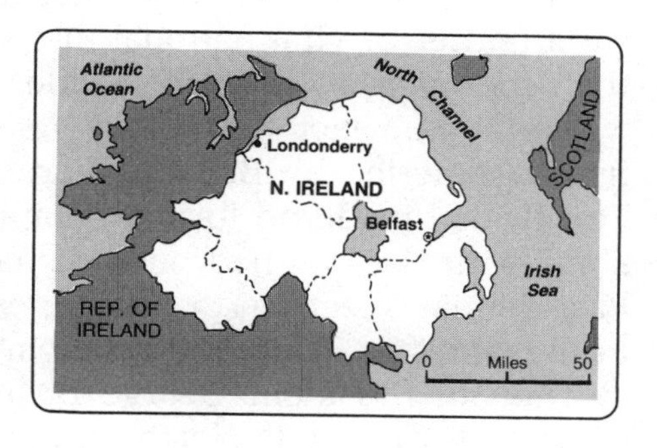

In February, 1994, Gerry Adams, President of Sinn Fein, the political party representing the outlawed IRA, visited the United States. During his two-day stay in New York City, Adams charmed Americans by proclaiming his willingness to compromise with both the British government and the Protestant extremists to achieve peace. He stated his desire to see a unified Irish state and a British withdrawal from Northern Ireland.

The crisis in Northern Ireland is the longest endured by any Western democracy. The United States has always condemned the violence of both the IRA and the Protestant extremists as terrorism. Also, the American and British governments have long had a "special relationship" as the two closest NATO allies. One result of this has been close cooperation between American and British law enforcement agencies in the arrest and detention of suspected IRA terrorists in the United States.

Since December, 1993, the Clinton Administration has supported the *Downing Street Declaration*. This document was issued by British Prime Minister John Major and Albert Reynolds, the Irish Prime Minister. The statement affirmed that both countries would abide by any settlement democratically agreed upon by the people of Ireland, north and south. It also declared that full-scale peace talks would begin if the IRA would make a statement denouncing violence. At the time of Adams's visit to New York, that statement had not been made. In March, 1994, the IRA dropped 12 unexploded mortar shells on London's Heathrow Airport.

Clinton issued a visa to Adams despite objections by Britain, as well as the U.S. Attorney General and the FBI Director. Forty members of Congress, including two powerful Democratic senators, supported the Sinn Fein leader's visit. Many of them represented large Irish-American communities concerned for the future of Northern Ireland.

For the British, Clinton's decision was an embarrassment. On a matter of vital national interest, they could not persuade the Americans to take their side. Their discomfort was made worse by the fact that Gerry Adams's visit coincided with a trip to America by Britain's Foreign Secretary, Douglas Hurd. The British made no formal complaint. Their "special relationship" with the U.S. had been damaged enough during the 1992 Presidential election campaign, when the administration of Prime Minister Major had shown strong support for the reelection of President George Bush.

Hope for peace in Northern Ireland rose on August 31, 1994. The IRA decided to abandon its 25-year campaign of terror and violence and to enter peace talks over the future of the province. The Protestant militant groups joined the cease-fire in October.

In early 1995, the governments of Britain and Ireland developed a Framework Document. This set of proposals for settling the future of Northern Ireland stressed the right of the people of the province to decide their future.

In the summer of 1996, the IRA broke the cease-fire. The Protestant-Catholic violence halted peace talks. Nevertheless, former U.S. Senator George Mitchell, chairman of the talks, felt that real progress toward peace was still possible. As IRA bombings continued through October, British and Irish leaders resumed talks but denied participation to Sinn Fein until the cease-fire was observed.

1. *Identify or define each of the following:*

   a. Gerry Adams
   b. Sinn Fein
   c. IRA
   d. John Major
   e. Downing Street Declaration
   f. Framework Document

2. *Explain why you AGREE or DISAGREE that the United States should send peacekeeping troops to Northern Ireland.*

Chapter 5 Review

A. *Write the letter of the correct response.*

1. *A goal of American foreign-policy makers in the 1990's has been (a) supporting the growth of democracy and free-market economies in the former Soviet Union and Eastern Europe (b) gaining NATO approval for the use of American ground forces in Bosnia-Herzegovina (c) ensuring an IRA victory in Northern Ireland.*
2. *The Clinton Administration has supported the Russian reform program of (a) Zhirinovsky (b) Yeltsin (c) Ruskoi.*
3. *One development in the former Soviet Union that worried Americans in the 1990's was (a) oil development in Kazakhstan (b) Belarus's decision to eliminate its nuclear weapons (c) Russia's increasingly aggressive foreign policy.*
4. *The former Soviet republic that offered the most investment opportunities to American businesses in the 1990's is (a) Kazakhstan (b) Belarus (c) Ukraine.*
5. *Supporting the insistence of newly elected governments that Soviet troops withdraw was a U.S. policy pursued in (a) Western Europe (b) Eastern Europe (c) Southern Europe.*
6. *The "Partnership for Peace" plan offered former Warsaw Pact members the opportunity to (a) join NATO (b) form a new East European military alliance supported by the United States (c) participate in NATO military exercises.*

7. *The Bosnian Serbs agreed to sign a peace accord in 1995 after President Clinton (a) threatened to bomb Serb forces (b) pledged $10 million to aid recovery after the peace agreement (c) lifted some economic sanctions.*
8. *The September, 1996, Bosnian election resulted in (a) bloodshed (b) withdrawal of international troops from Bosnia (c) a three-part presidency composed of one Muslim, one Croat, and one Serb.*
9. *Which of the following statements best describes the role of the United States in Europe in the 1990's? (a) The United States provided strong leadership. (b) The United States preferred to avoid deep involvement in European problems. (c) The United States became isolationist.*
10. *In 1996, talks on how to govern Northern Ireland were (a) chaired by Gerry Adams (b) successfully concluded (c) interrupted when the IRA broke a cease-fire.*

B. *Base your answers to the questions below on the cartoon on page 110, and on what you have read.*

1. *What did President Clinton mean when he pledged to build a "new security" in Europe?*
2. *Why have some Europeans expressed a desire for deeper American involvement in their affairs in the 1990's?*
3. *What European nation did not want strong American leadership in the 1990's? How did its history and present ambitions affect its attitude toward the United States?*

C. *Select TWO European leaders. For each, identify the country he leads or has led and explain how American policies have either helped him or posed a problem.*

Boris Yeltsin	*John Major*
Eduard Shevardnadze	*Slobodan Milosevic*

D. *Identify the two crises of Europe in the 1990's. For each, do the following:*

1. *Explain how the crisis developed.*
2. *Describe the role of the United States.*
3. *Explain what you think of the actions taken by the United States to help resolve the crisis.*

Chapter 6

The United States and Asia

In November, 1993, President Clinton hosted the first-ever summit conference of Asian leaders. At this historic meeting in Seattle, Washington, the American President pursued his vision of a new "Pacific community." He received an enthusiastic response to his promise that the United States would take a stronger and more creative interest in Asia. Clinton was the first U.S. President since the Vietnam War to recognize the importance of dealing with China, Japan, and the other expanding economies of Asia. By the spring of 1994, however, the talk of harmony between Asia and the United States had given way to growing criticism of the policies of the Clinton Administration. Asian leaders claimed that the American government was arrogant and interested mainly in imposing its own rules on Asia.

After the Seattle Conference, Clinton's Asian policy had three goals: to open Japan's markets to American products; to use trade threats to force China to respect human rights; and to prevent North Korea from developing nuclear weapons. The American policies on China and Japan came under heavy attack from other Asian governments. They feared that Amer-

EAST ASIA

ican pressure on Japan would lessen their ability to sell their own products to that country. They also objected to American efforts to link trade to human rights, claiming that the United States had no right to impose its standards on Asian governments. These unfavorable reactions threatened to limit Asian support for the Clinton Administration's efforts to halt North Korea's rise as a nuclear power.

For many Asians and Americans, the efforts of the United States to pursue conflicting goals in the areas of security, human rights, and economic opportunity have caused confusion and resentment. Experts urged the Clinton Administration to decide which policy is of greatest importance to American national interests.

1. *List the goals of the Clinton Administration's Asian policy.*
2. *Explain why the Asian policy of the United States has been criticized by Asian leaders.*

Trade War with Japan

Meeting with the Japanese Prime Minister in early 1994, President Clinton warned that an agreement to allow the sale in Japan of American-made cellular telephones must be honored. Otherwise, he would impose restrictions on the importation of Japanese products by the United States. To avoid a trade war, the Japanese Prime Minister agreed to comply with Clinton's demands. He also ordered his government to develop a plan to limit Japanese exports to the United States.

A major goal of the Clinton Administration has been to reduce America's trade deficit with Japan. In the United States, demand for Japanese products, especially for automobiles, computer technology, and other electronic products, has created a severe imbalance between the sale of Japanese goods in the United States and the sale of American products in Japan. The result of Japan's restrictions on American imports has caused the U.S. a loss of wealth. In 1995, this trade deficit reached almost $60 billion.

Japan's rise as an economic superpower was assisted by the United States. At the end of World War II, Japan's industries were in ruin. The United States had contributed to the destruction by wartime bombings of Japanese cities, including the dropping of atomic bombs on Hiroshima and Nagasaki in August, 1945. Following this action, Japan surrendered and was occupied by American military forces. With American help, Japan developed democratic government and rebuilt its industries. By the 1990's, Japanese products dominated Asian and other markets around the world. Japan's economic expansion included the building of manufacturing plants and other businesses in the United States and the purchase by Japanese investors of American companies.

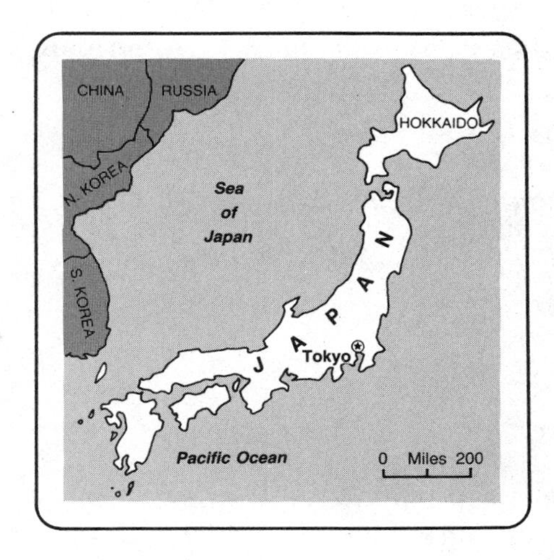

However, while American markets and investment opportunities were open to Japan, its markets were largely closed to American products and investors. The resulting trade deficit was economically damaging to the United States. American efforts to reduce this deficit by economic and diplomatic means have included threats of a trade war. It would involve the imposition of hundreds of millions of dollars of *tariffs* (taxes on imports) on Japanese products. Such a step would destabilize the Japanese economy; deprive American industries and consumers of Japanese products; and hurt American employees of Japanese-owned businesses. To avoid a trade war with America's second-largest trading partner, the United States government has attempted other measures to reduce the trade deficit.

1. *Define* trade deficit *and* tariff.
2. *Explain why the United States and Japanese governments would like to avoid a trade war.*

Reducing the Trade Deficit

In 1993, the Administration of newly elected President Clinton took steps to reduce the trade deficit by forcing an increase in the value of the Japanese yen. This raised the prices of Japanese goods and reduced their appeal to American consumers. The Clinton Administration also pressed for numerical goals for the export of particular American products to Japan. The Japanese resisted what they called "managed trade."

A slowdown in the Japanese economy began in 1992 and continued into 1994. During this recession, Japan purchased fewer American goods. The United States urged Japan to cut taxes and thus increase Japanese purchasing power. The government failed to do so but lowered gas and electricity rates and promoted lower import prices.

In late 1993, Japan eliminated or eased 475 legal and economic regulations. Japan's trading partners had long urged such reductions to increase competition, lower prices, and remove obstacles to the sale of foreign goods in Japan.

Economists contend that the real answer to the American trade deficit is to reduce the demand in the United States for Japanese goods by making American products more competitive. Nevertheless, American policies continue to focus on pressuring Japan to reduce exports and increase imports. In mid-1995, these policies led to a threat to impose a 100 percent tariff increase on Japanese car imports if provisions were not made for the sale of more U.S. cars in Japan.

Japan's slow recovery from recession hurt Japanese buying power, especially for American goods. The U.S. trade deficit with Japan continued to be high in 1996.

1. *Describe Japan's economic problem.*
2. *List the measures demanded of Japan by the United States.*
3. *State the actions taken by Japan in response to American demands.*

Missiles for Technology

For many years, the United States had given Japan specialized data about the construction of military aircraft, ships, and other weapons. The Japanese built them under a U.S. license. Japan, however, had not turned over any technological information to the United States.

In 1993, the Japanese wanted to create a missile defense system able to detect and intercept missiles from Communist North Korea. To correct the imbalance in technological trade with Japan, the Clinton Administration proposed to help construct such a system in exchange for commercial technology that could help American industry. The proposed project would take considerable time to negotiate.

Despite difficulties with the United States over trade, Japan has remained committed to an American military presence in

Asia. Like other Asian countries, Japan regards the United States as the nation best able to ensure stability in the region.

During the Persian Gulf War, in 1991, Japan gave financial support to the U.S.-led coalition fighting against Iraq. However, no Japanese troops joined the allied forces, despite Japan's heavy reliance on Persian Gulf oil. The Japanese constitution prohibits the use of Japanese military forces outside of Japan.

1. *Describe the Clinton Administration's 1993 technological exchange proposal.*
2. *State the Japanese view on defense arrangements with the United States.*

A Change in Government

Japan's economic recession was blamed, in part, on public exposure of corruption in government circles. The leaders of the Liberal Democratic Party, which had ruled Japan for 38 years, were discredited. As a result, Morohiro Hosokawa, a reformer, was chosen as Prime Minister. He stated his intention to clean up Japanese politics and reduce tensions with the United States. In April, 1994, however, he was accused of having accepted a questionable loan in 1982. Although extremely popular, and responsible for the passage of a landmark political reform bill, Hosokawa resigned.

For Clinton, this development was a disappointment. His efforts to reduce trade tensions with Japan had been based on his good relations with fellow reformer Hosokawa.

For more than two years, voters rejected the Liberal Democrats in favor of two opposition parties. Then, in October of 1996, a Liberal Democrat, Ryutaro Hashimoto, was elected Prime Minister. He owed his victory to support by a coalition (temporary alliance) of political parties. Hashimoto's party had always been friendly to the United States, and American leaders expected it to be sympathetic to requests that Japan follow fairer trade procedures. It was clear, however, that Hashimoto would first have to speed up the recovery of his own country's economy.

Section Review

1. *Correct each incorrect statement:*
   a. *During World War II, Japan and the United States were allies.*
   b. *Hiroshima and Nagasaki were destroyed by the Soviet Union in 1945.*
   c. *By the 1990's, Japan was in political control of most of Asia.*
   d. *The United States exports more goods to Japan than it imports from that country.*
   e. *Numerical goals for the sale of American products in Japan were accepted by the Japanese government in 1993.*
2. *Explain why you AGREE or DISAGREE with the belief of some economists that the United States must reduce the American demand for Japanese products in order to lower its trade deficit with Japan.*
3. *Write one or two paragraphs on the topic of U.S.-Japanese relations in the 1990's.*

China: Economic Opportunity vs. Human Rights

By 1994, one of the main concerns of American foreign policy was how to deal with China. The growth rate of China's economy in the 1990's has been extraordinary. For American businesses and investors, opportunities for profitable investment in that country have steadily increased. The importance of this situation has been noted by Clinton, who wishes to base his foreign policy on the principle of "economic security" for the United States. This means increasing American exports to Asia, especially to the growing market in China. However, Clinton has also committed himself to the improvement of human rights in Asia, and China's human rights record has been poor. American insistence on better treatment of Chinese dissidents (those who criticize the government) and greater freedom for the Chinese people has irritated China's leaders. Tension between the two governments has troubled American businesses.

Since 1949, when the Chinese Communist Party took control of China, and during the cold war, the United States and China were adversaries. During the Korean War (1950–53), Chinese and American military forces fought each other. Successive American Presidents opposed the dictatorship and state-

controlled economy introduced by Mao Zedong, China's first Communist leader.

In 1972, U.S. President Richard Nixon visited China, the first American leader to do so. Discussions between the two governments led to the establishment of full diplomatic relations in 1979.

Following the death of Mao Zedong in 1976, China's new leaders began to make changes in education, culture, and industry and sought better relations with non-Communist countries. By the mid-1980's, China had made major economic reforms, moving away from rigid state control and toward a market-oriented economy. In the 1990's, China opened its economy to the outside world. To speed economic development, private enterprise and foreign investment were encouraged. As its economy expanded, the standard of living of many Chinese, especially in the industrial cities, began to rise. American and other Western business firms moved quickly to take advantage of new opportunities in a market with more than one billion consumers.

Economic progress was not matched by the growth of democracy and human rights in China. In 1989, pro-democracy demonstrations by a million people in Beijing, and demonstrations in other cities, were put down by Chinese army troops. It is estimated that 5,000 died, 10,000 were injured, and hundreds of students and workers were arrested. The United States and other Western nations protested the harsh treatment of China's dissidents.

1. *For each of the following years, state an event which was significant in Chinese-American relations:*

   a. 1949
   b. 1950–53
   c. 1972
   d. 1979
   e. 1989

2. *Describe the economic changes which occurred in China in the 1990's.*

The Human Rights Dilemma

The United States had for years used the threat of trade sanctions to promote free immigration and human rights in Communist countries, including China. In May, 1993, Clinton signed an executive order stating the steps that he wanted China to take to win renewal of its trade benefits. Since the 1970's, China has enjoyed "most favored nation" (MFN) status. This has allowed China to send its products to the United States at the lowest available tariff. MFN status must be renewed annually.

Tiananmen Square, 1989

Clinton's order called for China to begin putting into effect an agreement made in early 1993 to end its practice of using prison labor to make goods exported to the United States. It also required China to allow certain dissidents and their families to leave the country. Additional conditions for renewal of China's MFN status included "significant progress" in China's handling of and accounting for political prisoners; increased freedom for Tibet, which China conquered in 1951; and less jamming of foreign radio programs.

In early 1994, Secretary of State Warren Christopher visited China to press the human rights issue and persuade Chinese leaders to comply with Clinton's order. The trip was a diplomatic disaster. The Chinese government made clear its resentment of American interference in China's internal affairs.

The Presidential order touched off a debate within the Clinton Administration and in Congress. In March, 1994, Secretary of State Christopher and Anthony Lake, the President's National Security Adviser, asked that Clinton issue a public statement reaffirming his commitment to the executive order. The President was also asked to state his approval of Christopher's handling of the human rights effort. However, Secretary of the Treasury Lloyd Bentsen and other members of the Clinton economic team wanted to ensure that their views be heard when policy toward China was discussed.

The Administration's economic officials argued that withdrawal of China's trade benefits would cost thousands of American jobs and billions of dollars in contracts. They also claimed that trade had become an important instrument for opening up Chinese society and for promoting the rule of law and freedom of movement in that country. Trade was also viewed as a means of encouraging the Chinese government to allow its citizens to acquire a wide variety of products, including satellite dishes and foreign newspapers.

This view was supported by some members of Congress. They urged Clinton to consider ways of pressuring China to improve human rights without revoking its MFN status. Among the alternatives recommended were limited trade sanctions which would target, for example, only products made by China's state-controlled industries, rather than goods produced by privately owned companies. Some lawmakers recommended the use of the Super 301 trade law. This law empowers the President to impose trade sanctions on a country, or on a specific category of that country's exports, or on a particular product, if the country is engaged in an "unreasonable denial of worker rights."

Other members of Congress recommended non-trade sanctions to try to win human rights in China. These might include using diplomatic pressure to link China's loans from the World Bank to its human rights behavior.

For the Clinton Administration, the development of a trade policy toward China had become a dilemma. As more Americans did business in China, they saw their economic interests endangered by an ideological fight about human rights.

In May, 1994, President Clinton decided to unconditionally renew China's MFN status. However, a new trade dispute developed in 1995. To end Chinese piracy of American films, computer software, and other "intellectual property," the United States threatened to impose trade sanctions on more than $1 billion of Chinese goods. A trade war was avoided when China agreed to take steps to find and punish copyright violators. The Chinese also agreed to remove quotas on imports of American films. The agreement was viewed as a victory for both the Clinton Administration and American business.

By 1996, the Chinese government seemed to be making a greater effort to crack down on businesspeople who pirate U.S. intellectual property. In June, China entered into a new copyright agreement with the United States. Nevertheless, because of mutual suspicions and differing ideologies, U.S.–Chinese relations remained uneasy, especially after the Chinese, in the fall of 1996, sentenced a young dissident to long-term imprisonment for his democratic views.

1. *Define* MFN status *and* Super 301.
2. *Explain why the development of a China policy became a puzzlement for President Clinton in 1994.*

China's Changing Global Role

The end of the cold war and the lessening of the Russian military threat have required the Clinton Administration to reexamine China's role in the world. It is no longer being viewed as a barrier to Soviet expansionism in Asia, but as an emerging world power in its own right.

China's growing military strength worries its neighbors. The Chinese government has modernized its armed forces in an effort to make China the dominant military power in Asia. It has also laid claim to the Spratley Islands (also claimed by

Vietnam, Malaysia, the Philippines, and Taiwan) and some islands in the East China Sea belonging to Japan.

Most Asians think that U.S. military might will prevent conflict between China and Japan. The Administration has extended the U.S. military alliance with Japan and also encouraged U.S.–Chinese discussions on regional security.

China's role as a world power rests upon its nuclear weapons, its U.N. Security Council seat, and its flourishing economy. It has not, however, acted like a partner to other world powers. For example, it did not participate in the 1991 war to liberate Kuwait. For the United States, it is critical to know whether China will support its efforts to prevent North Korea's production of nuclear weapons.

China's leaders have resented American efforts to make Chinese society more open and more liberal. Nevertheless, they have been forced to recognize the effects of global communications and rising demands for more freedom in their increasingly prosperous cities.

In 1997, the British colony of Hong Kong reverted to Chinese rule. Prior to the takeover, China claimed it would not interfere with Hong Kong's economic system or civil rights policies. Western leaders closely monitored the new rule of this democratic territory, viewing it as a test of China's pledge to honor the human rights of Hong Kong citizens.

The Clinton Administration must find a way to foster American interests in China while maintaining the security of Asia. This will depend upon the development of new methods of pressing for improved human rights without destroying American trade and creating a hostile, anti-American China.

Section Review

1. *Complete the following sentences:*
   a. *Despite movement to capitalism and a market economy, China's leaders have refused to permit ______.*
   b. *In May, 1994, the Clinton Administration had to decide whether or not to renew China's ______.*
   c. *A goal of the United States has been improvement of China's performance in the area of ______.*

d. Two U.S. government departments which have had opposing views on policy toward China in the 1990's are _______.
e. In the 1990's, American businesses have regarded China as a place to _______.

2. Write a letter to President Clinton. State your views on the policies of his Administration toward China.

3. PROVE or DISPROVE:

a. China and the United States have been friends and allies since 1949.
b. By 1994, all disagreements between China and the United States had been resolved.
c. American interest in China decreased in the 1990's.

Concerns About North and South Korea

To discourage North Korea from developing nuclear weapons, the United States developed a strategy which combined diplomatic efforts with threats of United Nations economic sanctions. Such sanctions might include a ban on trade with North Korea to withhold oil and other vital resources. In May, 1994, however, Clinton's administrators admitted that their strategy was failing. Despite American protests, North Korea continued to build a new, larger nuclear reactor and sought to expand its capacity to reprocess plutonium, an element needed for nuclear bombs.

Critics of the Administration's policy pointed out that economic sanctions would require a vote of the U.N. Security Council. Such a measure might be vetoed by China, a permanent member of the Security Council and a traditional ally of North Korea. Even worse, the Communist government of North Korea announced that it would regard economic sanctions as an act of war and would react accordingly.

As a Communist dictatorship, North Korea regards itself as an enemy of the United States. During the Korean War (1950–53), United Nations forces, led by the United States, forced North Korean and Chinese troops to withdraw from South Korea. The Communist government in the north had attempted to unify Korea by force, invading the non-Communist south in June, 1950. Following the failure of this attempt, the two Koreas remained divided at the 38th parallel with a heavily guarded demilitarized zone between them.

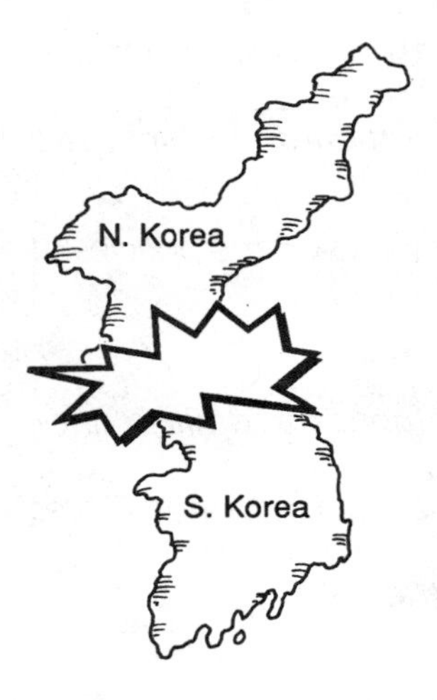

North Korea continued as a Communist dictatorship. Kim Il Sung, one of the founders of the nation, ruled it for more than 40 years. Upon his death in 1994, his son, Kim Jong Il, took power. Despite abundant mineral and hydroelectric resources, the North Korean economy faltered in the 1990's. Although industrial output was limited and crop failures touched off food riots, North Korea spent a great deal of money to build and maintain an army of 1.1 million soldiers and, at the same time, develop missile technology. Such military expansion worried South Korea, Japan, and the United States.

From 1961 to 1987, South Korea was a military dictatorship. Following a period of public protest, direct election of presidents and other constitutional reforms were enacted by 1990. President Kim Young Sam was elected in 1993 as the country's first civilian leader. By the 1990's, South Korea's rapid economic growth had made it a lucrative field for American and Western investment. Along with Hong Kong, Singapore, and Taiwan, South Korea became one of the "Asian tigers" of international trade.

The United States has remained an ally of South Korea. It maintains a force of 37,000 troops there.

1. *List the differences between North and South Korea.*
2. *Explain why the relationship between the United States and South Korea differs from America's relationship with North Korea.*

The Development of a Crisis

In 1993, North Korea declared its intention to become the first nation to withdraw from the Nuclear Nonproliferation Treaty (NPT). This 1968 agreement was negotiated to prevent the spread of nuclear weapons. North Korea and other nations that signed the treaty agreed not to develop nuclear weapons. They also agreed to allow periodic inspection of their nuclear power plants and storage facilities by the International Atomic Energy Agency (IAEA). President Kim Il Sung's government decided to withdraw North Korea from the NPT rather than permit IAEA inspections.

The Clinton Administration began a diplomatic campaign to keep North Korea in the NPT. As an inducement, the United States agreed to cancel its *Team Spirit* military exercises. Held annually in South Korea, these have involved American and South Korean troops in joint training operations. The North Korean government has regarded these exercises as an indication that the United States and South Korea have been planning an invasion of the north. Another inducement was offered by the South Korean government, which held out the possibility of investments in North Korea.

North Korea postponed its withdrawal from the NPT. IAEA inspectors then visited seven sites at the Yongbyon nuclear complex. Six passed inspection. At the seventh, however, inspectors discovered that plutonium capable of being used for bombs might have been extracted from nuclear fuel rods. Since they could take no samples for analysis, no conclusions were possible. The matter was referred to the U.N.

Clinton warned that the United States would not permit North Korea to develop a nuclear weapon. In April, 1994, however, North Korea added to the U.S.'s woes. It shut down its Yongbyon reactor and announced plans to discharge its fuel. This step could add to its supply of bomb-grade material. The North Korean government stated that IAEA inspectors could monitor the removal of the fuel. But it rejected the agency's demands that its inspectors be permitted to take measurements of the fuel rods. The inspectors wanted to determine how much plutonium North Korea might have diverted to weapons programs in past years. North Korea also refused to allow inspectors to visit two nuclear-waste-disposal sites or to complete inspections at a nuclear reprocessing plant at Yongbyon.

By May, 1994, the Clinton Administration realized that its ability to change the policies of Kim Il Sung's government was quite limited. It also faced up to the fact that it could not stop the North Korean nuclear arms program without starting a war. In July, 1994, Kim Il Sung died. His son, Kim Jong Il, became leader of North Korea. The nation's nuclear weapons program continued.

In answer to the growing tension, North Korea placed its armed forces on alert and declared that the Korean peninsula was on "the brink of war." The United States was reminded that 56,246 American soldiers had died in the Korean War. South Korean officials at a conference were threatened by North Korean officials.

In March, 1994, South Korea put its 633,000 troops on alert. It also accepted an American offer to deploy 48 Patriot missile launchers to defend South Korea against North Korean Scud missiles. In addition, planning was resumed for the *Team Spirit* military exercises with the United States.

For President Clinton and his Administration, the long-range task became one of persuading the Communist government of North Korea to trade away its nuclear arms program for diplomatic recognition and reasonable financial aid. At the same time, it hoped to prevent the outbreak of a war in Korea. In early 1994, two-thirds of the Communist military forces were deployed at the demilitarized zone, only 25 miles from Seoul, the capital of South Korea. Although American military power is sufficient to stop a North Korean invasion of the south, the casualties and destruction would be high.

Later in 1994, North Korea agreed to freeze, and ultimately dismantle, its nuclear weapons program. In return, the United States promised to help North Korea to build a modern, non-military nuclear reactor. The United States also offered $500 million in oil.

In the summer of 1995, floods worsened North Korea's already desperate economic situation. Fearing that the country's hardship might lead it to threaten South Korea, Clinton and other Western leaders encouraged North Korea to bid for foreign aid and investment. In July, the United States, in recognition of North Korea's commitment to freeze its nuclear weapons program, increased funding of oil shipments to the country. North Korea, however, had continued to build up its military arsenal. In October, Japanese and U.S. experts reported signs that North Korea had the capability of reaching Japan with missiles.

1. *Explain how a crisis developed in Korea in 1993 and 1994.*
2. *Describe the efforts of the Clinton Administration to deal with this crisis.*

The Danger of Nuclear Proliferation

The possible sale to other nations of North Korean nuclear technology became a major concern of the Clinton Administration in 1993 and 1994. In the past three decades, North Korea has developed chemical and biological weapons and, more recently, the ballistic missiles needed to deliver them to targets hundreds of miles away. With its economy depressed, North Korea needs hard currency. To get this money, it has become a major arms supplier for countries that can no longer buy all the weapons they want from Russia or China.

North Korea is suspected of sharing chemical and biological weapons technology with Syria, Iran, and Libya—nations that have been hostile to the United States. But it is North Korea's growing trade in ballistic missiles that concerns the Clinton Administration. Starting in 1989, North Korea has sold Scud missiles to Syria and Iran. Fired from Syria, these missiles have the range to hit any target in neighboring Israel.

In the 1990's, North Korea developed the Redong and Nodong missiles. The latter has a range of 600 miles. Developed with Iranian financial support and cooperation, the Nodong is capable of carrying nuclear warheads. By 1994, two newer missiles, with ranges of 1,200 and 2,200 miles, were also being built.

American officials worry that sales of North Korean nuclear weapons technology and material could follow the missiles, with Iran the most probable customer. In early 1994, North Korea and Iran agreed to increase military and nuclear cooperation. North Korean nuclear scientists are believed to be working in Iran. In time, North Korean nuclear technology might enable Iran to produce its own nuclear weapons. The Clinton Administration viewed its 1994 agreement with North Korea as an essential part of the effort to stop nuclear proliferation.

1. *Define* nuclear proliferation.
2. *Explain why the Clinton Administration has searched for a way to prevent the development of nuclear weapons by North Korea.*

Section Review

1. *Evaluate the efforts of the United States to resolve problems with North Korea. Include responses to these questions:*
   a. *Why have the actions of the North Korean government in the 1990's worried the United States?*
   b. *How has the United States responded?*
2. *Explain why you AGREE or DISAGREE with the following statement:*

   The United States must stop the North Korean nuclear weapons program by any means, even if the effort causes a war in Korea.
3. *Indicate which statements are correct:*
   a. *Kim Young Sam is one of Clinton's Asian allies.*
   b. *North Korea has been selling weapons technology to countries unfriendly to the United States.*
   c. *American forces have never fought in Korea.*
   d. *Kim Jong Il will work with President Clinton to plan* Team Spirit *exercises.*
   e. *A goal of the Clinton Administration in 1993 was to persuade North Korea to remain in the NPT.*

A New Look at Vietnam

In February, 1994, President Clinton made a major foreign policy decision. He ended the embargo on trade with Vietnam. This embargo, which prohibited trade with the Communist nation, had been in effect since 1975. Together with the damage caused by American involvement in the Vietnam War (1965–73), the embargo had retarded the country's economic recovery from two decades of war and destruction.

Prior to World War II, Vietnam was a French colony, in the area known as French Indo-China. After the conquest of France by Nazi Germany in 1940, Japanese forces took control of the area. Vietnamese resistance to the Japanese occupation was led by Ho Chi Minh, a Communist. Following the defeat of Japan, the French tried to reestablish control over Vietnam. Again Ho and his Communist troops fought a war of national liberation, defeating the French in 1954. By international agreement, Vietnam and the other former French colonies—Laos and Cambodia—acquired independence. The Communists retained control only of the northern portion of Vietnam, with

Hanoi its capital city. South Vietnam became a non-Communist country with its capital at Saigon.

Dominated by wealthy landowners and business interests, the South Vietnamese government was corrupt and inefficient. Starting in the 1960's, a group of rebels, called the Viet Cong, attempted to overthrow this regime and appealed to the Communist government in the north for aid. Seeking to prevent the spread of Communism throughout Southeast Asia, the United States sent military advisers, weapons, and equipment to South Vietnam in ever-increasing numbers. In response, the government of Ho Chi Minh committed North Vietnamese troops to the civil war in the south.

After 1965, the United States became involved in a full-scale war against the Viet Cong and their North Vietnamese allies. Despite the loss of more than 50,000 Americans, the United States was unable to win. American forces were withdrawn from Vietnam in 1973. The South Vietnamese continued to fight until April, 1975, when Saigon fell to the victorious Communist forces. Vietnam became a unified country with its capital at Hanoi, and Saigon was renamed Ho Chi Minh City.

The Vietnam War had caused terrible divisions in American society. Those in favor of American involvement and those opposed to it were in conflict throughout the country. Many young men refused to serve in the armed forces and left the United States rather than be drafted into military service. Among those who opposed the war was an Arkansas student named Bill Clinton. While attending college in England, the future President organized war protest activities in that country.

1. *Identify the policy decision made by President Clinton in February, 1994.*
2. *Explain why the Vietnamese were at war for more than 20 years.*

New Opportunities

In the view of many, the lifting of the trade embargo by President Clinton finally ended the Vietnam War. For the President, though, the decision involved some political risk. Many people wanted the embargo maintained until the Vietnamese government had accounted for the Americans who had never returned from the war and whose fates are still unknown. Families of the personnel listed as "Missing in Action" (MIA) have exerted political pressure on both the American and Vietnamese governments to solve the mystery of the MIA's.

To improve relations with the United States, the Vietnamese government has found and returned to the United States the remains of some Americans killed during the war. In addition, American search teams have been permitted to come to Vietnam. The President's announcement of the lifting of the embargo was accompanied by his solemn promise to continue pursuing "the fullest possible accounting for our prisoners of war and our missing in action."

For some American business firms, the ending of the embargo represented a new investment opportunity. PepsiCo moved into Vietnam within hours of Clinton's announcement. It placed a giant can of soda in the middle of a square in Ho Chi Minh City and distributed 40,000 bottles of soft drinks, free of charge. It was PepsiCo's way of telling Vietnam that it was open for business.

More than 30 other American corporate giants have expressed an interest in doing business in Vietnam. Most will have to compete with European and Asian firms that had been operating in Vietnam during the years of the embargo. The Vietnamese have been buying Japanese and South Korean electronic products and cheap Chinese imports for a long time. The U.S. firms will also have to wait before realizing significant profits, as Vietnam is one of the world's poorest countries. Most of its 69 million people are only potential customers for American goods.

Despite these factors, Vietnam is viewed as an investment opportunity. In 1994, Microsoft made plans to invest in Vietnam's growing personal computer business. Digital Equipment anticipated about $100 million in consulting work to link incompatible computer systems; also in 1994, the Vietnamese government granted Mobil Oil Company a 50 percent share of the exploration rights in the Blue Dragon oil field in the South China Sea.

By the 1990's, the Vietnamese had become eager for American investment and trade. New capital and technology would improve the lives of millions of farmers and city dwellers. Also, a strong U.S. economic presence would give the Vietnamese some protection against China, its traditional enemy. China's economic power hangs heavily over developing nations. Vietnam is concerned about China's heavy sales of cheap consumer goods in Vietnam and its building of airstrips on the Spratley Islands, claimed by both the Chinese and the Vietnamese.

A Vietnamese trade delegation visited the United States in May, 1994, the first to do so following the lifting of the trade embargo. The purpose of the delegation was to encourage American business firms to finance new ports, bridges, airfields, telecommunications, natural resource development, and roads in Vietnam.

In July, 1995, President Clinton declared that the United States would officially recognize the government of Vietnam and exchange ambassadors. While MIA families and some veterans' organizations protested bitterly, most Americans welcomed the opportunity for normal relations between the two nations. U.S. allies around the world supported Clinton's decision.

Section Review

1. *Correct each incorrect statement:*
   a. *The United States and Vietnam have been allies since 1965.*
   b. *Starting in 1973, the American and Vietnamese governments negotiated a series of trade agreements.*
   c. *As a democratic nation, Vietnam has received much American foreign aid.*
   d. *In 1994, American businesses expected to make immediate profits in Vietnam from the heavy sales of their products.*
   e. *General Motors was the first American firm to do business in Vietnam in the 1990's.*
2. *Complete the following sentences:*
   a. *In 1994, President Clinton ended ______.*
   b. *One of the resources in Vietnam that interests U.S. investors is ______.*
   c. *The Vietnamese want an American economic presence to ______.*

3. PROVE or DISPROVE: *President Clinton's decision to end the embargo on trade with Vietnam was a good way to finally end a terrible chapter in American and Asian history.*

Chapter 6 Review

A. *For each question, indicate the correct response.*

1. *An American goal in the 1990's has been to (a) open Japan's markets to American trade (b) reward China for its progress in the field of human rights (c) sell nuclear weapons to Korea.*
2. *Asian governments have objected to American efforts to (a) sell weapons technology to Japan (b) link human rights to trade (c) expand investment activity in China.*
3. *A disappointment for President Clinton in 1994 was (a) the resignation of Japan's Prime Minister Hosokawa (b) the movement of PepsiCo into Vietnam (c) the visit of South Korean President Kim Young Sam to China.*
4. *A foreign policy question for Clinton in 1994 was to (a) continue diplomatic relations with Taiwan (b) retain U.S. military forces in East Asia (c) renew China's MFN status.*
5. *The Super 301 trade law empowers the President of the United States to (a) impose trade sanctions on a country (b) send troops to a country (c) bar a country's diplomats from the United States.*
6. *Asian governments in the 1990's have been concerned about the growing military strength of (a) Japan and South Korea (b) China and North Korea (c) Vietnam and Japan.*
7. *In the 1990's, the United States has had difficulty persuading (a) China not to acquire Hong Kong (b) North Korea not to build nuclear weapons (c) Japan not to trade with Vietnam.*
8. *An "Asian Tiger" in which Americans have invested heavily is (a) Laos (b) South Korea (c) Cambodia.*
9. *From 1975 to 1994, the United States maintained a trade embargo on (a) Thailand (b) Hong Kong (c) Vietnam.*
10. *In the 1990's, Vietnam became eager for a (a) strong American economic presence (b) military alliance with China (c) trade war with Japan.*

B. *Write a letter to President Clinton explaining your views about his Asian policy. State your opinion about his priorities and how he should respond to the problems he has had in dealing with Asian leaders.*

C. *Explain how each of the following has been important to the United States in the 1990's:*

Morohiro Hosokawa
Kim Jong Il
Kim Young Sam

D. *Explain each of the following newspaper headlines:*

TRADE WAR WITH JAPAN FEARED

CHINA'S MFN STATUS IN PERIL

NORTH KOREA SELLS WEAPONS TECHNOLOGY

VIETNAM WAR FINALLY ENDS

Chapter 7

The United States and the Middle East

In April, 1994, Secretary of State Warren Christopher made a quick trip to the Middle East to try to arrange a peace between Israel and Syria, and to persuade the Palestine Liberation Organization (PLO) and Israel to conclude a peace agreement. They had been negotiating one for months. He visited Israel, Saudi Arabia, Syria, and Egypt, meeting with the leaders of those nations and with Yasir Arafat, the PLO Chairman. Christopher also went to London to consult with King Hussein of Jordan, who was in Britain for medical treatment.

It was necessary for the Secretary of State to have talks with Arab leaders at the highest levels to ensure the resumption of American-backed peace talks between Israel and Jordan, Lebanon, and Syria. These talks had been suspended since February, 1994, when an Israeli fanatic killed 29 Arabs in a mosque in the Israeli-ruled West Bank territory. Terrorism remained an obstacle to peace. In January, 1995, a suicide bombing claimed 21 Israeli lives. Shortly after, President Clinton and Mr. Christopher took steps to renew peace talks by meeting with the foreign ministers of Egypt, Israel, and Jordan and a Palestinian diplomat. In a statement issued by Christopher, the Palestinians committed themselves to a crackdown on terrorists in return for economic benefits.

In addition, Christopher wished to impress upon the Arab nations the intention of the United States to maintain international economic sanctions against Iraq. Preventing a resumption of aggression by Saddam Hussein, Iraq's dictator, has been a key part of American policy in the Middle East in the 1990's.

Other American concerns in the region included the efforts

ISRAEL AND NEIGHBORING ARAB STATES

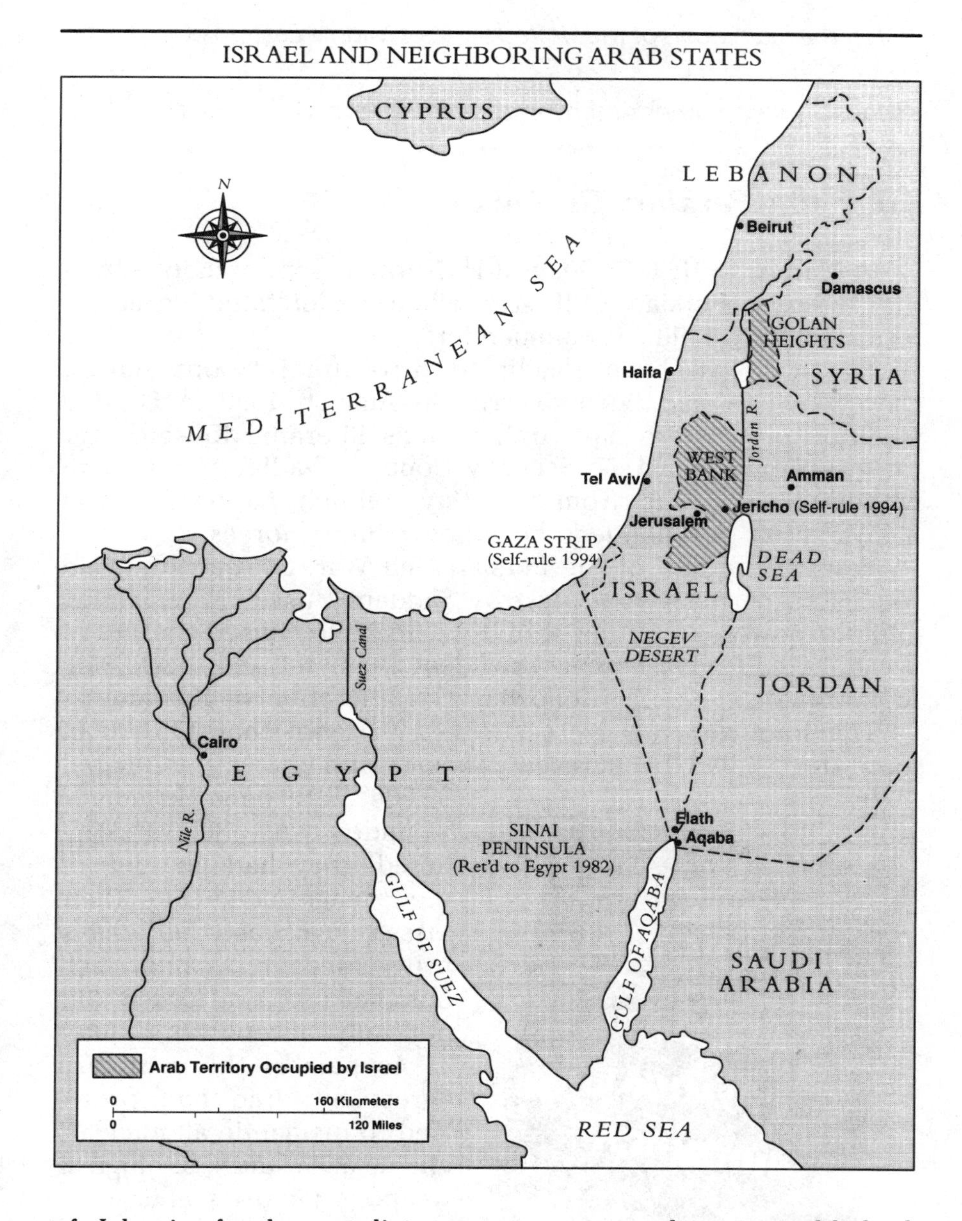

of Islamic fundamentalist groups to overthrow established Arab governments; the continuing hostility of Iran; the problems of Turkey, a major ally; and the crisis in Yemen.

1. *Explain why the Secretary of State of the United States went to the Middle East in April, 1994.*

2. *List the main goals of the United States's Middle Eastern policy in the 1990's.*
3. *Identify some other American concerns in the Middle East.*

After the Persian Gulf War

In March, 1991, U.S. General H. Norman Schwarzkopf ended the six-week Persian Gulf War when he dictated cease-fire terms to Iraqi military commanders.

The war had been fought to drive Iraqi troops out of Kuwait, which had been overrun in August, 1990. A U.S.-led coalition of Western and Arab nations liberated Kuwait after the expiration of a U.N. Security Council deadline for Iraq to withdraw its forces from the tiny, oil-rich nation. General Schwarzkopf commanded the Allied military forces.

Toward the end of the Persian Gulf War, Schwarzkopf had requested permission to destroy Saddam Hussein's remaining military power, an action which would have caused the fall of the dictator's government. President Bush refused, preferring to terminate hostilities following the liberation of Kuwait.

The Iraqi generals were shocked to learn that 175,000 of their troops had been taken prisoner and that an estimated 85,000 had been killed or wounded. As Schwarzkopf noted, they had no idea of the magnitude of their losses. Yet, as the 1990's progressed, it became obvious that Saddam Hussein did not fully accept his defeat.

As part of the cease-fire agreement, Iraq had promised to dismantle all nuclear, chemical, and biological weapons factories and allow U.N. observers to inspect and verify that this had been done. The Iraqi government had been warned that U.N. trade sanctions would remain in effect until it complied with this requirement.

In July, 1992, tensions rose when a U.N. inspection team

was denied entrance to a government site in Baghdad, the capital. When the United States threatened military action, the U.N. team was allowed to enter but found no evidence of prohibited weapons.

In January, 1993, Allied naval vessels launched missile attacks on an Iraqi industrial center. It had been identified by the International Atomic Energy Agency (IAEA) as the location of advanced computer-controlled machinery used by Iraq in its nuclear weapons program.

Evidence was uncovered that Iraq had tried to assassinate former President Bush during his April, 1993, visit to Kuwait. In June, therefore, President Clinton ordered another missile attack on Iraq's intelligence headquarters in Baghdad.

After the war, there had been revolts against Saddam Hussein throughout Iraq. In early 1993, Iraqi troops drove Kurdish rebels and civilians into mountainous northern Iraq, near Turkey and Iran. To prevent the extermination of the Kurds, a long-persecuted minority seeking to establish an independent nation in Iran, Turkey, and northern Iraq, the United States began Operation Provide Comfort. Safe havens for the Kurds were set up in northern Iraq and initially protected from Iraqi troops by U.S. air patrols.

The United States, however, did not follow through with this operation. In mid-1996, Turkey, which also has a Kurdish minority to deal with, began to set the several Kurdish factions against one another. Saddam Hussein then intervened to assert his authority in northern Iraq. The United States responded by attacking sites in southern Iraq, which allowed Kurd-against-Kurd fighting in the north to continue. This seemed to leave open the possibility of future interventions in Kurdish affairs by Turkey, Iran, and Iraq.

1. *Identify the problems which caused conflict between the United States and Iraq after the Persian Gulf War.*
2. *Explain the role of the IAEA in Iraq after the war.*

Rebuilding Iraqi Power

By the spring of 1994, it had become obvious to American officials that Saddam Hussein had gone back to business as usual. In defiance of U.N. sanctions that banned nonhumanitarian trade and placed an embargo on weapons sales to Iraq, he has worked to rebuild his military and industrial might. The Iraqi dictator has had the help of neighboring countries as well as Western business firms. These firms are eager to build commercial contacts with a big potential customer who also possesses the world's second-largest oil reserves. They have demonstrated a greater interest in profits than in supporting American or U.N. peacekeeping efforts.

To achieve his goals, Saddam Hussein does not always have to defy the U.N. Although Security Council resolutions prohibit Iraq from possessing or developing weapons of mass destruction, they place no such ban on its conventional arms industry. Using a secret technology procurement network never fully dismantled, despite American efforts, Saddam has been able to buy spare parts for his tanks from China and Russia, and antitank and air defense missiles from Bulgaria. He has also begun to look to Western European firms for electronics needed by his air force. At the same time, he has pressed forward with ballistic missile research at newly built laboratories in Iraq. Although his armed forces have been reduced to about 400,000 troops, Saddam Hussein still has the largest army in the Persian Gulf region.

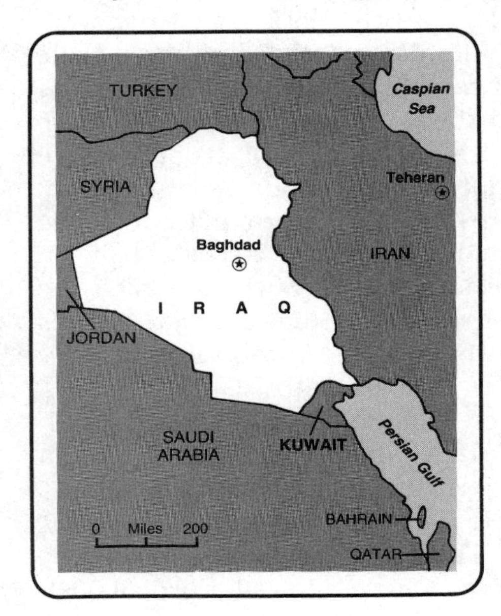

Hopeful that U.N. trade sanctions would be lifted, Iraq negotiated trade agreements with France, Turkey, and Russia in early 1994. Discussions with American companies were also held. A loophole in the sanctions allowed foreign companies to enter into deals with Iraq that would take effect after the U.N. embargo is lifted. Despite U.S. government objections, the French, Russians, Turks, and others interpreted this to mean that they could sign contracts with Iraq for participation in its reconstruction.

The United States has strongly opposed even limited oil sales by Iraq. Nevertheless, Turkey, in 1994, requested U.N. approval for a partial reopening of the Iraqi oil pipeline running through Turkey. This would permit the Iraqis to periodically "flush" the pipeline of old oil, which the Turks claim has been corroding the pipe, and fill it with fresh oil. Each flush would provide Iraq with approximately $50 million in income. There could be several such operations each year.

Turkish officials claimed an annual loss of $250 million from lost pipeline fees while the U.N. sanctions remained in effect. They promised that Iraq would get only humanitarian aid, and not cash, in exchange for its oil. The Security Council reacted favorably to Turkey's request. The United States reluctantly went along with the Security Council plan because the Clinton Administration did not want to offend Turkey, an important ally. Turkey allows American jets based within its borders to patrol the skies over Iraq.

The U.N. trade sanctions hit Iraq hard. The nation's economy was crippled. By 1994, price inflation in Iraq had soared to 250 percent of prewar levels, while living standards dropped to half of what they had been before the war. To save money, Baghdad closed fifteen of its embassies in foreign capitals.

Until 1994, Iraq's frequent arguments for an end to the embargo were rejected by the U.N. sanctions committee in New York. New support for the easing of the trade bans, however, came from three of the five permanent members of the committee—France, Russia, and China. All three wanted to profit from contracts to help rebuild Iraq. France and Russia were among Iraq's major prewar trading partners. They would benefit if a loosening of trade sanctions enabled Iraq to pay its large debts to them.

The United States and Britain have insisted that trade bans remain in effect until Iraq has complied with every condition in the U.N. resolutions that ended the Persian Gulf War. U.S. officials stated their doubts that Saddam has given up his dreams of dominating the Persian Gulf region. They declared that he continued to violate the U.N. resolutions by refusing to acknowledge Kuwait's independence and by committing human rights violations against Iraq's Kurds. They also pointed to the growing evidence that Iraq is rebuilding its long-range missile and nuclear weapons development programs.

Although some American firms would like to renew trade

with Iraq, Clinton administrators and U.N. weapons inspectors argue against a hasty return to doing business with Iraq. They seek assurances that Saddam Hussein's military and industrial capability to pursue conquest in the Persian Gulf region does not come back to life. However, an increasing number of Western allies appear more concerned with the prospect of the profits to be gained from ending trade sanctions.

By 1995, Iraq was bypassing U.N. sanctions and selling oil illegally, especially to French companies. France's government felt that only Britain and the United States had emerged from the Gulf War as major Western oil-trading partners in the region. The French wanted a larger share of this trade.

Thus, the sanctions lost much of their power to keep Saddam under control. This situation, in turn, encouraged Saddam's defiant intervention into the Kurdish safe havens in northern Iraq and the retaliatory U.S. air attacks on Saddam's air defense network in the south.

1. *Describe the steps taken by the government of Saddam Hussein to rebuild Iraq's military and industrial power.*
2. *Explain why some Western nations have urged a lessening of U.N. trade sanctions on Iraq.*
3. *State the policy of the United States government on the resumption of trade with Iraq.*

Section Review

1. *Explain why you AGREE or DISAGREE with the following statements:*
   a. *The Persian Gulf War accomplished little of importance for the United States.*
   b. *Kuwait and Iraq are important to the United States only because of their oil resources.*
2. *Write a letter to former President George Bush and offer your opinion of his decision to stop the Persian Gulf War after the liberation of Kuwait. State the alternatives that were open to him.*
3. *List the arguments for and against the ending of U.N. sanctions on trade with Iraq and the renewal of full business relations between the United States and Iraq.*

Peacemaker to Israel and the Arabs

On the White House lawn, in September, 1993, President Clinton brought two men together for a historic handshake. They were Yitzhak Rabin, Prime Minister of Israel, and Yasir Arafat, Chairman of the Palestine Liberation Organization (PLO). They had met to sign a Declaration of Principle (DOP), which provided for Palestinian self-government in Gaza and the West Bank city of Jericho.

The Arab-inhabited territories of Gaza and the West Bank were taken by Israeli troops during the Six-Day War of 1967. The United States supported Israel in this war, as well as in most other Arab-Israeli conflicts.

Created in 1948 by a United Nations vote, Israel is a democracy surrounded by traditionally undemocratic nations. Arab leaders, opposed to a Jewish state in their midst, went to war with Israel in 1948, 1956, 1967, and 1973. These wars resulted in victory for Israel and an increase in the territory it controlled. See map on page 145.

The Arab population of Palestine, as Israel was known before independence, also opposed the creation of a Jewish state. When the first Arab-Israeli war began, in 1948, many Palestinian Arabs fled to neighboring countries. The host nations kept them in refugee camps, where they depended on international agencies and charities for food, clothing, and other essentials. Their condition has been an obstacle to peace in the Middle East. Arab demands for Israel's withdrawal from Gaza and the West Bank have also been a source of conflict in the region. In the late 1980's, a Palestinian rebellion, or "intifada," against Israeli rule of the territories began.

Formed in 1964, the PLO has used terrorism in its long effort to destroy Israel and gain control of Palestine. To the Israeli conquest of Gaza and the West Bank, the PLO reacted with a campaign of bombings inside Israel. Many Israelis have regarded Yasir Arafat as one of their principal enemies.

In 1983, however, the PLO abandoned terrorism in favor of political discussion. It accepted the right of Israel to exist. Its goal in the 1990's has been the establishment of a Palestinian state in Gaza and the West Bank. Most governments, including the United States, have been willing to negotiate with the PLO.

The establishment of a lasting peace in the Middle East has been a long-standing foreign-policy goal of the United

States. In 1978, President Carter negotiated a "Framework for Peace in the Middle East" with Egypt and Israel. A peace treaty between them was signed in 1979.

Clinton negotiators have sponsored Israeli peace talks with Syria, Lebanon, and Jordan. The DOP signed in Washington in 1993, and co-signed by many Arab governments, was a signal step toward a general Middle Eastern peace. Another step was taken in July, 1994, when Israel and Jordan agreed to end the 46-year-old state of war between them.

The United States has attempted to use the DOP to spur a resumption of peace talks and encourage increased cooperation with the peace process.

For the United States, the role of peacemaker arises from a need to support Israeli democracy while maintaining good relations with the oil-rich Arab nations. The victory of the American-led coalition in the Persian Gulf War increased American prestige and strengthened its peacemaking efforts.

1. *Identify or define each of the following:*
   a. *Gaza and the West Bank*
   b. *PLO*
   c. *Framework for Peace*
   d. *Intifada*
   e. *DOP*
2. *Describe the American peacemaking effort in the Middle East.*

The Peace Process Continues

Secretary of State Christopher returned to the Middle East in May, 1994. In Cairo, he attended the signing of the finalized agreement on self-rule for the Palestinians of Gaza and the West Bank city of Jericho. Following the withdrawal of Israeli troops from these areas, he visited Jericho, where he met with Palestinian officials.

Christopher's visit to Jericho was made to draw world attention to the Palestinians' exercise of self-rule over their own territory. U.S. officials accompanying him, however, were quick to say that the Administration was not in favor of establishing a Palestinian state. Many Israelis remain strongly opposed to such a development.

Another city visited by the Secretary of State was Damascus, the capital of Syria. Here, too, the American diplomat attempted to restart peace talks with Israel. Syria's President Hafez Assad had given cautious approval to the DOP. Assad's main concern, however, was recovery for Syria of the strategic border area known as the Golan Heights. Like Gaza and the West Bank, this territory had been captured by Israel during the Six-Day War of 1967.

To encourage Syrian cooperation with the peace process, the Israeli government offered to withdraw its forces from Golan. As a reward for this decision, the United States promised the Israeli government increased military assistance, including early warning devices. The Israelis were especially eager to obtain early warning AWACS aircraft and super-enhanced F-15 fighter-bombers.

Christopher was able to bring from Damascus some hopeful news. President Assad responded to the Israeli offer by abandoning his long-standing demand for an immediate and total withdrawal of Israeli forces from the Golan Heights as a condition for normal relations. Instead, the Syrian leader accepted the idea of a phased withdrawal over a period of years. Other matters, however, remained in dispute. These included security arrangements for Golan, the length of the withdrawal period, and the pace of normalization of relations. During the remainder of 1994 and early 1995, there was little progress toward a Syrian-Israeli peace agreement.

In November, 1995, Prime Minister Yitzhak Rabin was assassinated by a militant Jewish nationalist. Benjamin Netanyahu, elected Prime Minister in 1996, was less willing than Rabin to restore contested territory to the Palestinians. Israel expanded its settlements in Arab areas and delayed withdrawing troops from the West Bank city of Hebron. Palestinian extremists responded with suicide bombings. A general uprising followed when the Israelis opened an archaeological tunnel near a sacred Muslim site in Jerusalem. Netanyahu refused to close the tunnel and continued plans for expanding Israeli settlements. Such plans, said Arafat, broke an agreement made by Rabin's government. After much U.S. guidance and some concessions from Israel, talks resumed in October, 1996. Israel's refusal to withdraw from Hebron, however, once more halted the peace process.

1. *State the reasons for Warren Christopher's visits to Cairo, Jericho, and Damascus.*
2. *Explain the importance of the Golan Heights to the peace process.*

Section Review

1. *Complete the following sentences:*
   a. *A long-standing goal of American policy in the Middle East has been _______.*
   b. *Traditionally, the United States has supported Israel because _______.*
   c. *In 1979, the United States helped to negotiate a peace treaty between _______.*
   d. *Good relations between the United States and the Arab nations are necessary because _______.*
   e. *American prestige in the Middle East was increased by _______.*
2. *Describe the efforts of the Clinton Administration to bring peace to the Middle East.*
3. *Identify each of the following:*
   a. *Yitzhak Rabin*
   b. *Yasir Arafat*
   c. *Warren Christopher*
   d. *Hafez Assad*

The United States and Islamic Fundamentalism

In early 1993, Americans experienced the kind of terrorism to which other countries have been exposed. The explosion of a powerful car bomb in a garage under the World Trade Center in New York City caused six deaths and considerable damage. A few months later, authorities forestalled a plot to blow up the United Nations building in New York City and to assassinate some prominent political leaders, including the U.N. Secretary General.

An FBI investigation led to the arrest of Sheik Omar Abdel Rahman, an Egyptian Islamic fundamentalist living in the United States, and some of his followers. The sheik was accused of urging them to commit the bombings. Islamic militants responded with threats to attack other U.S. targets.

Nevertheless, four of those indicted for the Trade Center bombing were given life sentences. Egypt requested, in vain, that the sheik be extradited to stand trial for terrorist acts in Egypt. Then, in 1996, three men were convicted of plotting to blow up 12 U.S. airliners. One of the men, Ramzi Ahmed Yousef, was alleged to be the mastermind of the World Trade Center bombing.

Islamic terrorists target the United States because of its support for Israel and moderate Arab governments. Such terrorists are supported by such hostile regimes as Iraq, Iran, and Libya.

1. *Complete the following sentences:*
   a. *The 1993 attack on the World Trade Center was the first time _______.*
   b. *This attack was carried out by _______.*
   c. *The United States was targeted because _______.*
2. *Give your opinion as to whether foreign terrorists should be tried in the United States or extradited to their own countries.*

The International Scene

The activities of militant Islamic organizations in other countries have troubled the United States government. These groups seek to replace secular Arab governments with religious regimes run in accordance with the Islamic teachings of the Koran. Their efforts have led to violence and disruption in Egypt, Pakistan, Algeria, and Turkey. Strong fundamentalist movements are also underway in Kuwait and Jordan. Since these countries are friendly to the United States, their stability is important to the conduct of American foreign policy in the Middle East.

Events in Egypt in the 1990's have been of particular

concern to the United States. Egypt has supported American peacemaking efforts and has been a center of U.S. intelligence operations in the region. The country is also the second-highest recipient of American aid.

Efforts of the fundamentalist al-Jama al Islamiya organization to overthrow the government of President Hosni Mubarak have included the assassination of government officials and repeated attacks on Western tourists. By mid-1994, the severity of these attacks had devastated the country's multi-million-dollar tourist industry. The fundamentalists have sworn to rid their country of political corruption and evil Western influences. In retaliation, Egyptian security forces have carried out extensive arrests and executions.

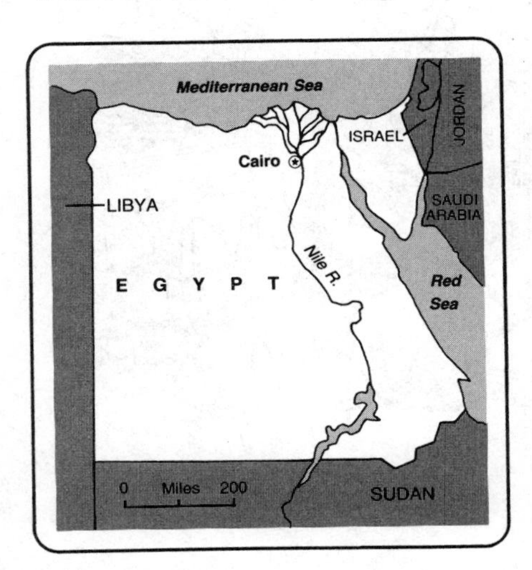

A harsh armed crackdown on the fundamentalists came in April, 1994. Egyptian security forces rounded up thousands of militants and killed dozens in raids. Thirty-six were hanged on the orders of special military courts.

These actions drew strong criticism from human rights groups in the United States and elsewhere. They repeatedly accused the Egyptian government of torturing political prisoners. The death of a well-known militant Muslim lawyer, while in police custody, in 1994, further focused attention on human rights violations in Egypt. The United States urged the Egyptian government to make public an investigation into the death of the lawyer, Abdel Harith Madani. Madani was a member of the Muslim Brotherhood, a group which opposes the Mubarak government, but rejects violence.

Egypt has prided itself on being the most democratic country in the Arab world. Although the survival of the Mubarak government is vital to the conduct of American foreign policy in the region, concerns about Egypt's human rights record has troubled Clinton administrators. Their quiet, private diplomacy failed, by 1994, to persuade Mubarak to combat militant fundamentalism by introducing economic and social reforms, increasing housing and employment opportunities, and reducing government corruption.

1. *Explain why Egypt's struggle with Islamic fundamentalism is of concern to the United States.*
2. *State the criticism directed at Egypt by human rights groups.*

Section Review

1. *In early 1994, an article in* The New York Times *described the rise of militant Islam as a threat to world peace and security. Write a letter to the* Times *to explain why you AGREE or DISAGREE with that opinion.*
2. *The Egyptian newspaper* Al Ahram *warned the West not to confuse the great religion of Islam with fundamentalist terrorism. It said, "Terrorism is not Islam, and Muslims are not terrorists." Give your reaction to this point of view.*
3. *Identify:*

   a. *Sheik Omar Abdel Rahman*
   b. *Hosni Mubarak*
   c. *al-Jama al Islamiya*
   d. *Muslim Brotherhood*

The Hostility of Iran

To the people of Iran, the United States is the "Great Satan," an evil nation and the enemy of Islam. This has been the official position of the Iranian government since 1979, when an Islamic Revolution brought to power the Ayatollah Khomeini. A fanatical religious leader, Khomeini made Iran the sole Islamic religious state in the Middle East.

Khomeini was hostile to the United States. America had given support to the Shah (king) of Iran, whose government Khomeini's followers had overthrown. In November, 1979, Iranian militants seized the U.S. Embassy in Teheran and took 62 Americans hostage. Despite international condemnation of this action, the crisis continued until January, 1981. At that time, Iran agreed to release the hostages in return for the unfreezing of its financial assets in the United States.

Diplomatic relations between the two countries were broken in April, 1980. During Iran's war with Iraq (1980–88), the United States gave assistance to Iraq. Also, the U.S. Navy protected shipping in the Persian Gulf against Iranian attack. In 1988, an American warship shot down an Iranian commercial airliner after mistaking it for an Iranian fighter. The plane's 290 passengers were killed.

Despite mutual distrust, a U.S. offer of assistance was accepted after a major earthquake caused extensive death and destruction in northern Iran in June, 1990. Nevertheless, Iran's hostility to the United States and to other Western nations continued in the 1990's. During the Persian Gulf War, Iran offered safety to Iraqi military aircraft, thus preventing their destruction by the Allied forces and helping Saddam Hussein preserve some of his air power. Disregarding Clinton's efforts to have NATO protect Muslim havens endangered by the fighting in Bosnia, Iran accused the West of supporting the Serbs against the Bosnian Muslims.

Of greatest concern to the United States has been Iran's support of terrorism. Islamic militants seeking to destabilize secular Arab governments in Egypt and elsewhere have received Iranian funding. So have other terrorist groups. In mid-1994, the American and British governments became aware of Iranian contacts with the Irish Republican Army and the Greek November 17th terrorist movement.

In early 1995, Iran increased its military forces on three islands at the mouth of the Persian Gulf. This alarmed the United States and its allies in the region. Fears arose that Iran could cut off shipping in the Strait of Hormuz. Through this waterway flows 20 percent of the world's oil production.

Also of concern to the United States is Iran's effort to acquire nuclear reactors and long-range missiles.

◆ *Identify the sources of tension between Iran and the United States.*

Section Review

1. *PROVE or DISPROVE: The actions and policies of the government of Iran has meant little to the United States.*

2. *Write a brief composition in which you give your ideas for improving relations between Iran and the United States.*

The Troubles in Turkey

A NATO ally and a strong supporter of American policy during the Persian Gulf War, Turkey's political stability is important to the United States. However, Tansu Ciller, the nation's American-educated Prime Minister, and the first woman to hold that position, faced a number of problems in 1994 and 1995. Chief among them was the threat to the tourist industry. The PKK, a Kurdish rebel group, wants an autonomous Kurdish region in southern Turkey. To force the government to negotiate, PKK terrorists bombed hotels and other tourist centers. As a result, hotels in Istanbul, a city favored by foreign visitors, suffered a 20 percent fall in occupancy rates by June, 1994. The decline of the tourist trade threatened to destroy a number of business enterprises across the nation.

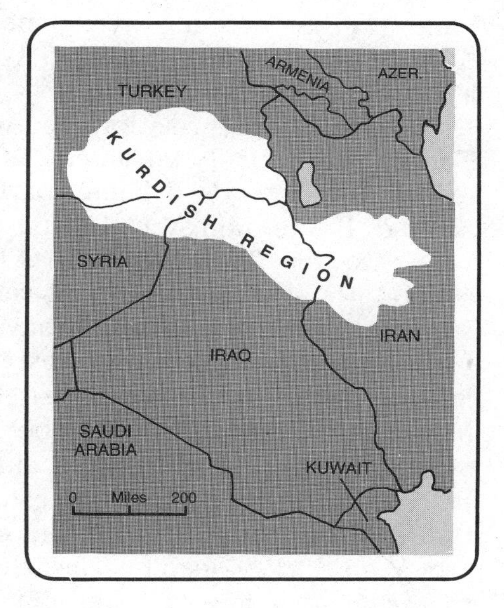

Prime Minister Ciller responded by abandoning her promise to address the Kurdish problem by democratic means. Instead, she allowed the Turkish military to use any means necessary to crush the ten-year PKK rebellion. This resulted in the bombing, burning, and forced evacuation of Kurdish villages. In addition, some members of parliament, journalists, and others favoring the Kurdish cause were imprisoned. These measures were successful in forcing PKK fighters and their families to flee to northern Iraq. However, Turkey's Western allies sharply criticized Ciller's government for human rights abuses.

An economic crisis also threatened Turkey. An inflation rate of 50 to 70 percent, an overvalued currency, a foreign debt of

$68 billion, rising unemployment, and bank failures undermined confidence in the government. As a result, Rafah, an Islamic fundamentalist political party, gained support in 1994 and 1995. Rafah is especially popular in the Kurdish-inhabited region of southeastern Turkey and in the rural villages. The Muslim militant surge has been described as a serious, long-term danger to any pro-American regime.

To deal with the economic crisis, the Ciller government sought $1 billion in loans from the International Monetary Fund (IMF). Such an arrangement would have granted this huge lending agency, based in Washington, D.C., control over Turkey's economic affairs.

By July, 1996, relations between the United States and Turkey were badly strained and became worse when the leader of Turkey's Islamic party, Necmettin Erbakan, was elected Prime Minister. During his campaign, Erbakan had vowed to take Turkey out of NATO and create a new "Islamic NATO." He also planned to disassociate Turkey from American support of the Kurdish safe havens in northern Iraq.

To assert his intention of establishing closer ties to radical Islamic countries, Erbakan visited the Libyan leader, Colonel Muammar el-Qaddafi, in October, 1996. The visit upset Turks as well as their Western allies, since Qaddafi used the occasion to criticize Turkey's pro-Western stance and its repression of the Kurds. Because Erbakan did not repudiate Qaddafi's verbal attack on Turkey, leading Turkish politicians called for Erbakan to resign as Prime Minister, but he chose to ignore then.

1. *Describe the crisis in Turkey and explain why it is of concern to the United States.*
2. *Compare Turkey's problems in the 1990s with those of Egypt.*

Section Review

1. *Decide which of the following statements are correct:*
   a. *An Islamic fundamentalist victory in Turkey would be unwelcome to the United States.*

b. Before her election as Prime Minister, Tansu Ciller had no knowledge of the United States.
c. The Turkish government has been criticized by the United States and other Western nations for human rights abuses.
d. The United States has supported the PKK.
e. Rafah is a pro-American political party.

2. Why did the United States support the government of Tansu Ciller?

3. Explain why you AGREE or DISAGREE with the recommendation of some human rights advocates that President Clinton should discourage IMF aid to Turkey until it improves its human rights record.

The Crisis in Yemen

In May, 1994, Assistant Secretary of State Robert Pelletreau arrived in Sana, the capital of Yemen. His mission was to negotiate a settlement of the civil war which had begun the month before.

North and South Yemen had united in 1990. The decision of the northern and southern leaders to form a single nation was based on mutual need. The north was troubled by the growth of a tribal Islamic movement. The south was bankrupt. Together, they had the resources to deal with their problems. General Ali Abdullah Saleh, the northern leader, became President of Yemen. The southern leader, Ali Salem al-Baidh, was made Vice President. Arguments over power sharing soon developed.

The southern region had provided 40 percent of the oil which is Yemen's most valuable product. Recent discoveries of even more oil in the south raised questions about how the revenues should be shared. Mr. al-Baidh wanted a lion's share of the south's oil money, but President Saleh objected on the grounds that the south has only a quarter of the population of the north.

Angered by this dispute and by an assassination campaign against southern politicians by unknown terrorists, al-Baidh and his followers moved back to Aden, the southern capital, in August, 1993. After the failure of mediation attempts by King Hussein of Jordan and other Arab leaders, President Saleh decided to use military force to keep Yemen united. In July,

1994, northern troops captured Aden. The southern rebellion ended soon after.

The decision of the United States to extend its peacemaking role to Yemen was motivated by the country's rising oil production and by its location. Yemen lies along the southern border of Saudi Arabia, a strong ally of the United States and a supporter of American policies in the Middle East. Like Turkey, Saudi Arabia has long enjoyed a special relationship with the United States. Military conflict and potential destabilization in that area are not in the interests of either the Saudis or the Americans. Across the Gulf of Aden from Yemen is Somalia and the Horn of Africa, a region in which the United States has labored to bring peace. The United States supported a June, 1994, U.N. resolution calling for an immediate cease-fire in Yemen and a cutoff in arms shipments to the country.

1. *State the causes of the civil war in Yemen.*
2. *Explain the American role.*

Section Review

1. *Complete the following sentences:*
   a. *The United States wants peace in Yemen in order to protect ______.*
   b. *In the 1990's, Yemen's importance has increased because ______.*
   c. *The capital of Yemen is ______.*
   d. *Another important city in Yemen is ______.*
   e. *In June, 1994, the United States supported a U.N. resolution calling for ______.*
2. *PROVE or DISPROVE: The Clinton Administration was right to be concerned about the civil war in Yemen.*
3. *Identify:*
   a. *Robert Pelletreau*
   b. *Ali Abdullah Saleh*
   c. *Ali Salem al-Baidh*

Chapter 7 Review

A. *For each question, indicate the correct response.*

1. *The United States's main goal in the Middle East in the 1990's has been (a) peace between Israel and its Arab neighbors (b) the destruction of Iraq (c) establishment of independent Kurdistan.*

2. *The Clinton Administration has demanded that trade sanctions on Iraq be maintained until (a) Saddam Hussein is overthrown (b) the Kurds are liberated (c) all conditions of the Persian Gulf War cease-fire agreement have been met.*

3. *In June, 1993, a U.S. missile attack on Baghdad was a response to (a) Iraqi weapons purchasing (b) an attempt to assassinate former President George Bush (c) Iraq's demands for a lifting of trade sanctions.*

4. *The Declaration of Principle signed in Washington in 1993 was an agreement between (a) the U.S. and Israel (b) Israel and the Palestine Liberation Organization (c) the U.S. and the Muslim Brotherhood.*

5. *In 1994, the United States attempted to negotiate an understanding about the Golan Heights between (a) Israel and Syria (b) Iraq and Yemen (c) Iran and Israel.*

6. *Islamic fundamentalists were blamed for (a) the bombing of the World Trade Center in New York City in 1993 (b) the civil war in Yemen in 1994 (c) the defeat of Iraq in the Gulf War.*

7. *A nation vital to the conduct of American foreign policy in the Middle East is (a) Syria (b) Iran (c) Egypt.*

8. *Iranian hostility to the United States stems from (a) American opposition to the efforts of Islamic fundamentalists to destabilize governments in the Middle East and North Africa (b) U.S. assistance to the Shah of Iran (c) both of these.*

9. *A U.S. ally threatened by economic crisis and Kurdish rebels in the 1990's was (a) Yemen (b) Saudi Arabia (c) Turkey.*

10. *American interest in ending Yemen's civil war stemmed from that country's proximity to (a) Lebanon (b) Saudi Arabia (c) Jordan.*

B. *Select TWO of the leaders listed. Explain why each is important to the United States and how each has helped or hindered American policies in the Middle East.*

Benjamin Netanyahu
Yasir Arafat
Hafez Assad
Hosni Mubarak
Necmettin Erbakan

C. *Compare developments in Egypt and Turkey in the 1990's by answering the following questions:*

1. *Why are these countries important to the United States?*
2. *How has a conflict between human rights and national security developed in each?*
3. *How has the United States responded to their problems?*
4. *Should their leaders fail to resolve their national crises, what problems might be created for the American government?*

D. *Explain why you AGREE or DISAGREE with each of these statements:*

1. *American peacemaking in the Middle East has been effective.*
2. *The United States should support Islamic fundamentalism.*
3. *American business firms should be allowed to do business with Iraq.*
4. *Closer relations between the United States and Iran should be developed.*
5. *Civil wars in Middle Eastern nations are not the concern of the United States.*

Chapter 8

The United States and Africa

Torn by wars, ethnic violence, political upheaval, and banditry, Africa has become a continent of crises. To make matters worse, African turmoil has been accompanied by drought and crop destruction. Starvation and disease have afflicted millions.

In the 1990's, the United States has responded to Africa's problems with aid from public and private agencies and support for those attempting to promote democracy and human rights. Of special concern to Americans have been the rise of multiracial government in South Africa and the efforts to stabilize Angola, Zaire, Somalia, and Rwanda.

South Africa: The Triumph of Democracy

On May 10, 1994, Nelson Mandela became the first black President of South Africa and the first one elected with the participation of a black majority. Among the 45 international leaders observing the historic event was an American delegation led by Vice President Al Gore and First Lady Hillary Rodham Clinton. Their presence demonstrated American support for the process by which white minority rule and the apartheid system of racial separation had been ended. It was a process which had begun in 1990. At that time, Mr. Mandela was serving a life sentence in prison for trying to overthrow the government of South Africa.

◆ *State the reason for the presence of Vice President Gore and First Lady Hillary Clinton in South Africa on May 10, 1994.*

AFRICA

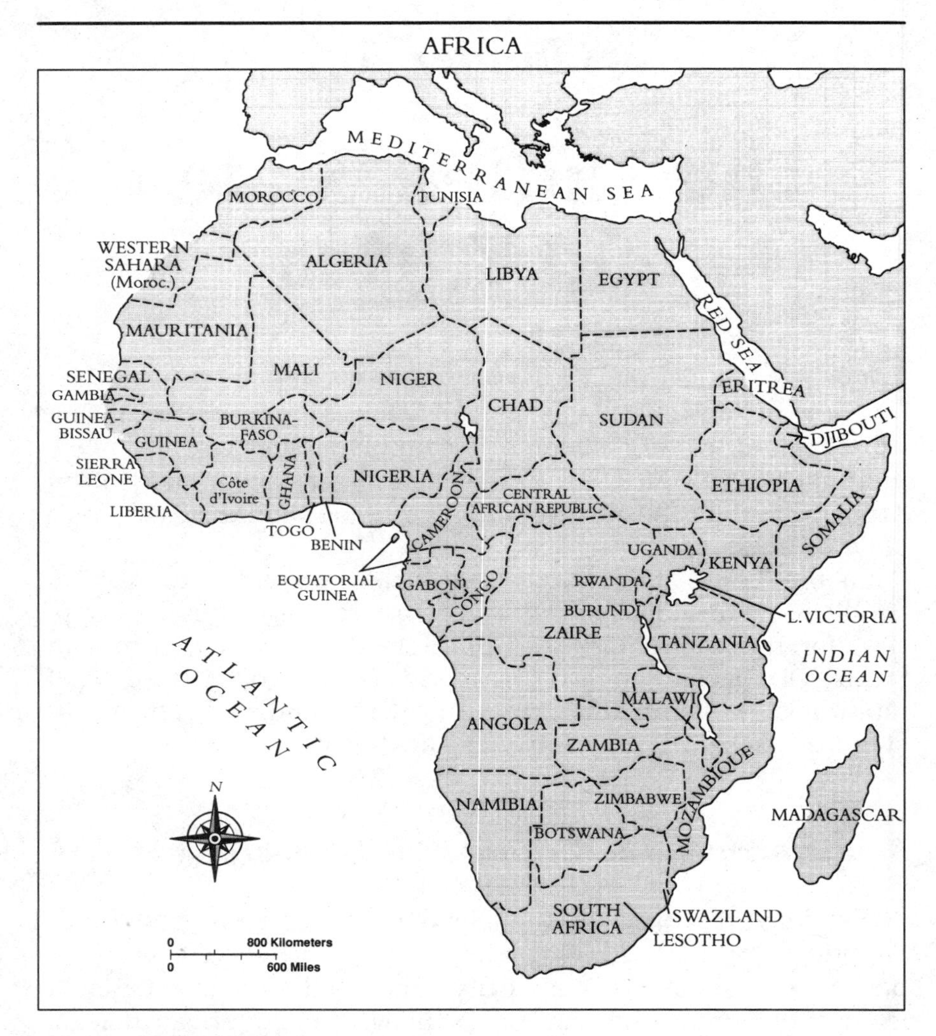

The End of Apartheid

The United States opposed *apartheid,* a system of rigid separation of the races and denial to blacks of political rights, education, and economic opportunity. Apartheid also involved the creation of ten black "homelands," in which blacks could live separately. The homelands, however, had no economic opportunities and few job possibilities. As citizens of the homelands, blacks could not work or travel in white-populated areas without "passbooks."

Apartheid began after World War II. It was designed to

ensure the continued rule of South Africa by a white minority constituting only 13 percent of the total population. The system was the policy of the National Party, which had governed the country for most of the 20th century. Many of the supporters of the National Party were Afrikaners—descendants of Dutch, French, and Germans who began settling in South Africa in the 17th century. Among the white inhabitants, the Afrikaners were more numerous than the English, whose presence dates back to the 19th century.

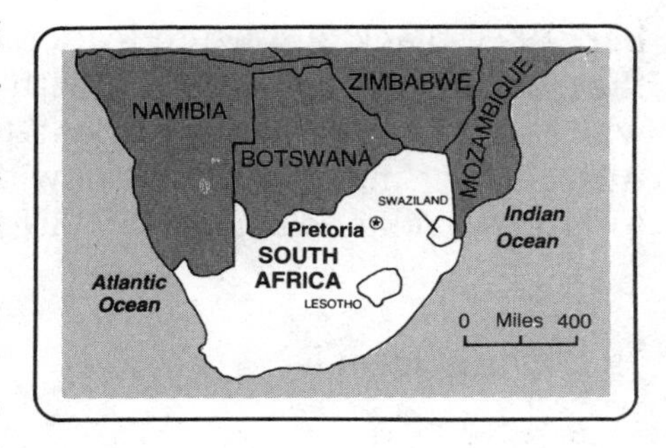

Between 1984 and 1986, demonstrations against apartheid caused an eruption of violence in South Africa. Declaring a state of emergency, the government used the police and army to maintain order. In opposition to South Africa's harsh apartheid policies, the United States supported an international trade embargo of that country. Starting in 1987, the Western nations refused to do business with South Africa until it granted democracy and human rights to its black majority.

Change came in 1990. F.W. de Klerk, South Africa's President, took steps to ensure a new future for his country. He lifted the ban on the African National Congress (ANC), the main group fighting for majority rule, and released Nelson Mandela, the ANC leader, from prison. The following year, de Klerk sponsored the repeal of a hated law which required South Africans to register with the government by race.

De Klerk and Mandela worked together to plan a process of political change. Periodic violence between the ANC and its political rivals failed to stop the movement toward multiracial democracy. In November, 1993, black and white leaders approved a new constitution that balanced majority rule with safeguards for the rights of whites and other minorities. At the end of April, 1994, South Africa's first multiracial, nationwide election resulted in victory for Nelson Mandela and the ANC.

1. *Define or identify:*

   a. *apartheid*
   b. *white minority rule*
   c. *Afrikaners*
   d. *National Party*
   e. *F.W. de Klerk*
   f. *Nelson Mandela*

2. *Describe the action taken by the United States to support the struggle to end apartheid and white minority rule in South Africa.*

Building Democracy and Prosperity

President Mandela formed a cabinet which reflected South Africa's racial and political diversity. It included the defeated National Party and the mainly Zulu Inkatha Freedom Party, which had opposed the ANC. F.W. de Klerk became one of two vice presidents. Mandela stated his immediate goals to create jobs, provide housing, expand education, and assure peace and security for all. He also indicated the need to reduce the government deficit, contain inflation, lower interest rates, and maintain a stable currency.

To fulfill these aims and maintain Africa's richest economy, Mandela must attract private international investment and foreign aid. Before taking office, he visited the United States. Meeting with its businesspeople, Mandela stressed the advantages of investing in the new South Africa's economy.

Following the end of trade sanctions by the United States and other nations, the South African economy began to expand once again. A growing black middle class provided a larger market for goods and services. To obtain the skills and education needed to meet new demands, the ANC sought help from black Americans. In 1993, nearly 300 black Americans, seeking to start their own firms, moved to South Africa. The ANC expects that number to triple in the 1990's.

For large African-American-owned firms, South Africa represents an untapped market of 45 million consumers. Sloan Financial, one of the largest black-owned investment management firms in the United States, transferred $500 million to South Africa in 1994. Other American-owned firms and investors moved rapidly to buy up South African businesses. By mid-1994, the country's largest clothing manufacturer was American.

These developments, and support offered by the Clinton Administration, reflected a strengthening relationship between the United States and the new South Africa.

In May, 1996, de Klerk's National Party endorsed a new constitution and withdrew from the coalition. The constitution completed the change from white minority rule to democracy. It established a strong presidency, ensured civil rights, and restored land taken by the government under apartheid.

1. *Explain why many Americans have regarded South Africa as a land of opportunity in the 1990's.*
2. *State the reasons for the desire of the ANC to attract African Americans to South Africa.*

Section Review

1. *Indicate which of the following statements are correct:*
   a. *The United States did little to oppose apartheid in South Africa.*
   b. *The establishment of a multiracial democracy in South Africa in 1994 was approved by the United States.*
   c. *The United States refused to do business with South Africa from 1987 to 1993.*
   d. *Mandela sought military aid from the United States.*
   e. *African-American businesses have begun to seek investment opportunities in South Africa.*
2. *Explain the meaning of a 1994 South African newspaper headline which said, "THE YANKS ARE COMING."*
3. *Why do you AGREE or DISAGREE with the demand by human rights groups for U.S. support of the Mandela government.*

Somalia: America's Noble Effort

Upon taking office in January, 1993, President Clinton inherited the involvement of the outgoing Bush Administration in the Horn of Africa. During the last weeks of his presidency, George Bush had decided to send American troops to Somalia, a nation destroyed by civil war, government collapse, and starvation. Their mission was to keep the peace and protect relief workers as they distributed food and other supplies. The Americans—and the British, French, Italian, and other troops who joined them—were carrying out a peacekeeping mission planned by the United States and approved by the United Nations.

The trouble in Somalia stemmed from political rivalries among local warlords. These leaders equipped their personal forces with weapons brought to Somalia by Russia, Cuba, and the United States during the cold war. The warlords used their firepower to fight each other and the government for power.

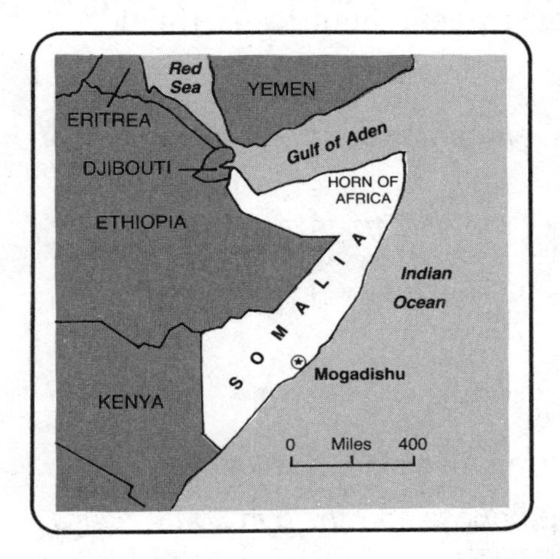

By late 1992, Somalia had almost ceased to exist as a nation. All government had been destroyed. Drought and famine had caused the deaths of several hundred thousand people. Distribution of food, fuel, and medicine by the Red Cross and other relief agencies was disrupted by the rival militias. The armed gangs attacked the relief workers and looted their convoys and warehouses.

◆ *Explain how and why American troops were sent to Somalia in 1993.*

Peacekeepers Under Attack

The military effort to assure the distribution of relief aid and to stop factional fighting was led by U.S. envoy Robert B. Oakley and General Robert Johnston, the American military commander in Somalia. To stabilize the country, Oakley and Johnston concentrated on disarming the warlords and persuading them to switch from military to political competition.

Oakley convinced fourteen major faction leaders to attend a national reconciliation conference in March, 1993. It resulted in a pact among the rival groups to disarm, to establish a transitional government, and to hold national elections in two years. At the same time, plans were made for an expanded United Nations military force to assume responsibility eventually for bringing peace to Somalia.

American and U.N. efforts were opposed by General Mohammed Farah Aidid, the strongest Somali warlord. Aidid's supporters made anti-American radio broadcasts and launched attacks on U.N. troops. In response, U.S. and U.N. forces carried out attacks against his followers and attempted to capture him. However, this policy was abandoned in November, 1993, after 17 American soldiers were killed in a fight with Aidid's forces. Instead, efforts were made to persuade the clan leader to join negotiations to plan the future of Somalia.

The loss of American lives reduced popular support for the peacekeeping mission. In the United States, a clamor arose for President Clinton to set a date for the withdrawal of American troops. His Administration assured the public that plans were underway for an expanded U.N. military force to assume full responsibility for the mission.

In March, 1994, rival factions signed a pact to stop fighting in the southern port of Kismayu and its surrounding territory. At this time, too, American forces departed from Somalia.

By early 1995, both the Clinton Administration and the U.N. were forced to admit that their policies in Somalia had failed. During the two-year U.N. mission, many Somalis had been saved from starvation. Peace, stable government, and democracy, however, were not established. The last U.N. forces were withdrawn from Somalia in March, 1995.

◆ *Explain why American enthusiasm for the peacekeeping mission in Somalia declined.*

Section Review

1. *Complete the following sentences:*

   a. *The mission of U.S. troops in Somalia was _______.*
   b. *The U.S. mission was approved by _______.*

c. *American troops were killed in Somalia during an effort to ______.*
d. *In 1994, the American forces in Somalia were replaced by ______.*

2. *Identify each of the following:*
   a. *Robert B. Oakley*
   b. *Robert Johnston*
   c. *Mohammed Farah Aidid*
3. *Write a letter to President Clinton. Tell him why you AGREE or DISAGREE with his decision to withdraw American troops from Somalia.*

The Slaughter in Rwanda

In June, 1994, the Clinton Administration sponsored a conference about Africa. Among those attending were African officials, experts on Africa, and business executives involved there. The President's National Security Adviser, Anthony Lake, stated his hope that the conference would help the Administration redefine its policies on Africa. Mr. Lake promised an increase in attention and assistance to the troubled continent.

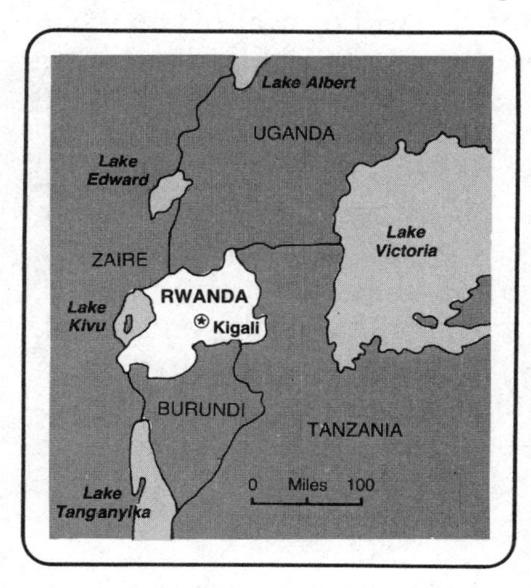

Nevertheless, the conference was boycotted by members of the Congressional Black Caucus (an influential group of African-American members of Congress). A spokesperson for the legislators faulted the Administration for its lack of focus on Africa. In particular, he criticized its failure to condemn the killings in Rwanda as genocide during the previous two months.

The bloodletting began in early April, 1994, when a mysterious plane crash killed the President of Rwanda. This event set off a cycle of mass ethnic and political killings that claimed over 200,000 lives by June. Members of the majority Hutu tribe, which controlled the government, blamed the destruction of their President's plane on the Tutsis, a minority. After being driven out of Rwanda years before, many of the Tutsis had become exiles, living in poverty in neighboring countries. Some had formed a military organization, the Rwandan Patriotic Front (RPF). To force the Hutu government to readmit them, RPF guerrillas invaded Rwanda in October, 1990. The tribal warfare that followed the death of the Rwandan President was accompanied by a full-scale offensive by the RPF against government forces. The result was killing on a massive scale, panicky flight by thousands of refugees, and the spread of chaos throughout the country.

♦ *Explain how a major crisis developed in Rwanda in 1994.*

The American Response

As rebel forces closed in on Kigali, the Rwandan capital, U.N. workers tried to distribute food to thousands of trapped civilians, but the small force lacked personnel and equipment to rescue refugees. In desperation, the U.N. commander in Rwanda asked for U.S. military equipment.

The recent experience in Somalia had made the Clinton Administration wary of peacekeeping missions. Nevertheless, international treaty obligations required U.S. intervention in situations involving mass ethnic killing, or *genocide*. Administration spokespersons, therefore, were instructed not to describe the deaths in Rwanda as genocide. They were told to say that "acts of genocide may have occurred."

U.N. Secretary General Boutros Boutros-Ghali opposed this decision. He insisted that Hutu majority violence against the Tutsi minority involved the deliberate, widespread extermination of an ethnic group. However, in the absence of historic or economic U.S. ties to Rwanda, the Administration reasoned that military intervention would be too costly in lives and dollars.

In addition to refusing to send U.S. troops, the Administration also objected to a U.N. plan to move an African peacekeeping force of 5,500 soldiers to Rwanda.

These decisions drew heavy criticism at home and abroad. The Senate Foreign Relations Committee sent a letter to Clinton urging him to acknowledge formally that genocide was occurring in Rwanda.

In response to the criticism, the White House speeded up plans to equip United Nations peacekeepers in Rwanda with armored personnel carriers. In addition, Secretary of State Warren Christopher publicly stated that acts of genocide had been committed in the African nation. In June, 1994, the United States also expressed approval of France's offer to send its troops to Rwanda to stop the ethnic massacres.

By July, 1994, the RPF had taken control of all of Rwanda and had installed a new government. Although the fighting had ended, the refugee problem had grown enormously. Over four million Rwandans who had fled into neighboring countries were dying of disease and starvation. To assist U.N. efforts to distribute food, water, fuel, and medicine, the Clinton Administration sent specialized troops and emergency supplies to Rwanda, Zaire, and Uganda. Despite these efforts, the ethnic violence continued. In April, 1995, Tutsi soldiers killed over 2,000 Hutu refugees.

In 1996, the violence spread to Zaire, where a Tutsi minority, complaining of government harassment, rebelled. Zaire, charging the Tutsi governments of Rwanda and Burundi with aiding the rebels, shelled Rwanda. The hostilities further displaced Hutu refugees and added to their suffering. War again seemed imminent. Late in the year, U.S. personnel were sent to join an international peacekeeping force in Zaire.

1. *Describe the response of the United States government to the crisis in Rwanda and state the reasoning of the Clinton Administration.*
2. *Explain how a change in U.S. policy was effected in June, 1994.*

Section Review

1. *PROVE or DISPROVE: The United States had a responsibility to take action in Rwanda.*
2. *Explain the role in the Rwandan crisis of each of the following:*
   a. *Clinton Administration*

b. Senate Foreign Relations Committee
c. United Nations

3. Write an editorial for your school newspaper about the American response to the crisis in Rwanda. React critically to the decisions of the U.S. government.

Angola: A Cold War Legacy

In June, 1994, a delegation from the United States, Portugal, Russia, and the U.N. urged President Mandela of South Africa to become involved in efforts to end Angola's long civil war. They believed that Mandela might be able to persuade the warring Angola factions to agree on a power-sharing plan not too different from the one that had brought multiracial democracy to South Africa.

The Angolan civil war began in 1975, as the former Portuguese colony was gaining independence. At that time, the United States and the Soviet Union were competing for influence in Africa. Intervention by the superpowers in the affairs of African nations was common. In Angola, rival anticolonial forces became involved in the worst cold war confrontation in Africa.

The Marxist Popular Front for the Liberation of Angola (MPLA), led by Jose Eduardo dos Santos, was able to take control of most of the country with Soviet aid and the direct support of Cuban troops. Dos Santos was opposed by Jonas Savimbi, leader of the National Union for the Total Independence of Angola (UNITA). Savimbi received assistance from both the United States and South Africa. During the Administration of President Ronald Reagan (1981–89), UNITA was considered to be of major importance in the war against Soviet expansionism in Africa. And the white minority government in South Africa sent troops to Angola to support UNITA because it hoped to destabilize a Communist neighbor that was providing a haven for ANC guerrilla forces trying to overthrow apartheid.

1. *Explain how the United States, Portugal, the Soviet Union, and South Africa were involved in the civil war in Angola.*
2. *Identify Jose Eduardo dos Santos and Jonas Savimbi.*

Efforts to Make Peace

In 1989, American diplomacy led the way in negotiating an agreement that resulted in the withdrawal of all foreign troops from Angola. However, genuine reconciliation within the country did not take place. Although UNITA signed a peace agreement with the MPLA government in May, 1991, violence continued. In 1992, national elections, supervised by the United Nations, confirmed dos Santos as president. Savimbi refused to accept this outcome. To enforce the election results, the dos Santos government attacked Savimbi's forces and killed or captured many UNITA leaders. Also, Savimbi lost the support of his main backers, the United States and South Africa.

Despite these setbacks, UNITA was not defeated. Jonas Savimbi's troops counterattacked and took control of nearly two-thirds of Angola by April, 1993. Their capture of the country's diamond and oil-producing regions provided UNITA with substantial financial resources. They also acquired large stores of weapons, including tanks, artillery, and antiaircraft guns, thus enabling them to continue the war for a long time.

New U.N.-sponsored peace talks began in April, 1993. The United States, Russia, and Portugal sent observers to the peace conference. In May, 1993, the United States formally recognized the MPLA administration as the official government of Angola. In addition, the United States and other Western countries donated nearly $200 million in food aid to prevent a war-induced famine.

A resurgence in fighting forced a suspension of U.N. World Food Program airlifts in May, 1994, thereby threatening Angola with starvation once again. By mid-1994, Africa's longest civil war had claimed more than 500,000 lives.

In June, 1994, the international delegation at the Angolan

peace talks proposed a power-sharing arrangement that would give UNITA a share of seats in national, provincial, and local governments. Since this agreement did not originate with the representatives of UNITA or the Angolan government, it was viewed with distrust by both sides. The American, Russian, and Portuguese diplomats, therefore, turned to Nelson Mandela to persuade Angola's warring factions to accept the power-sharing plan.

Representatives of Angola and UNITA agreed to a cease-fire in November, 1994. In early 1995, the U.N. Security Council approved sending several thousand troops to Angola to aid the peace process. In February, 1996, the Council extended the mission by only three months, hoping to pressure Angolans to accept responsibility for maintaining the peace.

1. *Describe the effort to bring peace to Angola.*
2. *Explain why Angola was on the brink of disaster by 1994, and list the actions taken by the United States to prevent it.*

Section Review

1. *Explain why you AGREE or DISAGREE with the following statements:*
   a. *The war in Angola began as a cold war confrontation.*
   b. *American diplomacy in Angola has been successful.*
   c. *South Africa has played a role in the Angola conflict.*
2. *Write letters to President dos Santos and UNITA leader Savimbi giving recommendations for bringing peace to Angola.*
3. *Develop arguments for and against:*
   a. *U.S. military intervention in Angola.*
   b. *U.S. withdrawal from the Angolan crisis.*

Zaire: A Nation in Chaos

In office since 1965, President Mobutu Sese Seko of Zaire has been one of Africa's longest surviving dictators. His repressive policies have resulted in military mutinies, destructive riots in the larger cities and towns, and economic ruination. By mid-1994, Zaire was in chaos. Epidemics of AIDS and bubonic plague were sweeping the country. Crime and violence were rampant. The government was bankrupt, lacking even the money to pay the European printers of its worthless currency. Mobutu, however, was wealthy. Diamonds smuggled out of the country provided the dictator with a guaranteed source of income. He has also been accused of laundering drug money for Latin American narcoterrorists.

For much of his time in office, Mobutu was supported by Western nations. Chief among his patrons were the United States, France, and Belgium. During the cold war, the Zairian dictator was regarded as an anti-Communist ally. After the cold war, when the American policy in Angola changed, Mobutu was seen as having outlived his strategic usefulness to the United States. Zairian territory was no longer needed as a staging area for Americans to supply Jonas Savimbi and his National Union for the Total Independence of Angola (UNITA). As promotion of democracy became the American policy in Africa, the United States, Belgium, and France began putting pressure on Mobutu. To qualify for continued foreign aid, the dictator would have to introduce democratic reforms and improve his government's poor human rights record.

These steps were not taken. Instead, repression and disorder worsened. As a result, the Clinton Administration began to take an increasingly tough stance toward Mobutu. In a 1993 statement, a State Department official said the United States held President Mobutu responsible for a situation that put at risk the lives and welfare of millions of Zairians and the stability of the entire region. Mobutu was urged to resign.

1. *Explain why President Mobutu Sese Seko was supported by the United States for much of his long career.*
2. *Describe the relationship between Mobutu and the Clinton Administration.*

An Appeal to Washington

In early 1994, Mobutu sent a conciliatory letter to President Clinton. The dictator promised to end years of political turmoil and asked for American help in organizing Zaire's first multiparty elections.

The American response was cautious. State Department officials said they welcomed any solid steps toward resolving Zaire's social and political crisis. However, they doubted Mobutu's sincerity.

In Zaire, the opposition to Mobutu has been led by Etienne Tshisekedi, who was part of the Mobutu regime in the 1960's and 1970's. Political parties hostile to Mobutu elected Tshisekedi Prime Minister in 1992. They also elected their own parliament to oppose the one elected by parties loyal to Mobutu. In addition to two parliaments, Zaire also had two Prime Ministers. Mobutu and those loyal to him appointed Faustin Birindwa to that post. In January, 1994, Mobutu dismissed Birindwa and ordered the two parliaments to merge. Multiparty elections were scheduled for the end of the year. Mobutu took these steps to avoid the loss of Western aid.

By 1994, Western support for Tshisekedi as the democratic replacement for Mobutu had faded. The Prime Minister's commitment to democracy was doubted.

The United States and the other Western nations have avoided involvement in Zaire's current problems. There are no vital American interests at stake in that country. However, the Clinton Administration has looked for ways to shift away from cold war politics and to aim for constructive foreign policy achievements. The creation of a democratic system to enable the Zairian people to choose their leadership could be a major advance.

1. *Describe the reaction of the Clinton Administration to Mobutu's 1994 appeal.*
2. *Identify Etienne Tshisekedi and Faustin Birindwa.*

Section Review

1. *Complete the following sentences:*
   a. *In 1994, Zaire's problems included _______.*
   b. *Mobutu Sese Seko has been accused of _______.*

c. The United States stopped supporting Mobutu in the 1990's because ______.
d. To avoid the loss of U.S. aid, Mobutu ______.
e. The United States avoided involvement in Zaire because ______.

2. *In 1994, the Clinton Administration considered Mobutu Sese Seko's request for technical assistance with the organizing of elections. What do you think the response should have been? Give reasons for your opinion.*
3. *Explain why you AGREE or DISAGREE with the belief that the United States has a humanitarian responsibility to solve the problems of Zaire and other nations with similar difficulties.*

Chapter 8 Review

A. *For each question, indicate the correct response.*

1. *A foreign policy concern of Americans in the 1990's has been (a) the establishment of multiracial democracy in South Africa (b) the victory of Mobutu Sese Seko over his political opponents (c) maintenance of a permanent U.S. military presence in Somalia.*
2. *An action taken by the United States to assist the government of President Nelson Mandela was (a) the sale of military equipment to South Africa (b) loans to the National Party and Inkatha (c) agreement on the ending of trade sanctions.*
3. *To stabilize Somalia, U.S. envoy Robert Oakley and General Robert Johnston attempted to (a) use military force to conquer the whole country (b) disarm warlords and persuade them to compete in non-military ways (c) establish a puppet government under American control.*
4. *When American troops departed from Somalia in March, 1994, their peacekeeping mission (a) had been turned over to the U.N. forces (b) had succeeded in stabilizing the whole country (c) had resulted in the establishment of an elected government.*
5. *The Clinton Administration responded to the 1994 crisis in Rwanda by (a) taking military action to stop acts of genocide (b) sending armored personnel carriers to U.N. peacekeeping forces in the country (c) offering financial support to any and all U.N. operations in Rwanda.*

6. *The Angolan anti-colonial group supported by the United States during the cold war was (a) UNITA (b) MPLA (c) Inkatha Freedom Party.*

7. *In 1994, the United States, Russia, and Portugal asked President Nelson Mandela of South Africa to (a) send South African troops to Angola (b) persuade Angola's warring factions to accept a power-sharing plan (c) approve a plan to return Angola to Portuguese rule.*

8. *The nations which joined the United States in supporting the dictatorship of Mobutu Sese Seko during the cold war were (a) Belgium and France (b) Britain and Russia (c) Germany and Portugal.*

9. *In 1994, Mobutu Sese Seko asked President Clinton for American assistance in (a) driving Belgian troops out of Zaire (b) organizing Zaire's first multiparty elections (c) reducing Zaire's dependence on foreign aid.*

10. *An African nation in which the United States has no vital interests at stake is (a) Egypt (b) South Africa (c) Zaire.*

B. *Base your answers to the questions below on the cartoon and on what you have read.*

1. *Explain why you AGREE or DISAGREE with the opinion of the cartoonist.*

2. *Review American actions in each of the following countries: Angola, Rwanda, Somalia, South Africa, Zaire. To what extent do they support the opinion of the cartoonist?*

C. *Select TWO of the leaders below. Explain why each is important to the United States and how each has helped or hindered American policies in Africa.*

Nelson Mandela
Mohammed Farah Aidid
Jose Eduardo dos Santos
Jonas Savimbi
Mobutu Sese Seko

D. *Write a newspaper article to accompany ONE of these headlines.*

VICE PRESIDENT AND FIRST LADY ATTEND HISTORIC EVENT
AMERICAN FORCES LEAVE SOMALIA
CLINTON ADMINISTRATION DRAGS FEET ON RWANDA
UNITA FIGHTS ON WITHOUT U.S. HELP
MOBUTU REQUESTS AMERICAN AID

Chapter 9

The United States and Latin America

Declaring Latin America to be the world's fastest-growing buyer of American exports, U.S. Secretary of Commerce Ronald H. Brown toured the region in June, 1994. Accompanying him were executives from 22 United States corporations. Latin America is the only region where the United States has consistently enjoyed a trade surplus. Imports of American products doubled between 1987 and 1994, reaching $80 billion in 1993. Among the matters discussed by Brown with Latin American leaders was the admission of more countries to an expanded North American Free Trade Association (NAFTA). The association includes Canada, Mexico, and the United States.

Along with the opportunities offered to U.S. businesses by the expanding free-market economies of Latin America, other developments posed serious problems for the United States. Chief among them were the political crisis in Haiti and the continuing effort to stop the flow of illegal drugs into the United States from Colombia and other nations. Also, a plebiscite on the future of Puerto Rico, demands for increased human rights in Mexico and elsewhere, and speculation about the future of Cuba were high on the U.S. policy agenda for the 1990's.

- ♦ *List reasons for the special interest of the United States in Latin America.*

NAFTA and Beyond

In 1991, the governments of Canada, the United States, and Mexico negotiated an agreement to eliminate, within fifteen

years, tariffs and other trade barriers among the three nations. This North American Free Trade Association will eventually create a single market of 370 million people, producing and consuming $6 trillion a year in goods and services.

The approval of NAFTA by the U.S. Congress in November, 1993, was an act of great symbolic importance. By establishing a free-trade pact with Mexico, the United States opened the way to closer economic relations with all Latin American and Caribbean nations and an eventual hemisphere-wide free-trade system.

Argentina, Costa Rica, and Chile have been considered leading candidates for admission to an expanded NAFTA. These countries have been successful in developing free-market economies, balancing budgets, reducing inflation, and selling state-owned industries to private investors. Trailing closely as a candidate for NAFTA membership is Colombia, regarded by the Clinton Administration as having implemented significant economic reforms. From 1991 to 1994, United States exports to Colombia doubled. After Brazil and Venezuela, Colombia is the third-largest Latin American importer of United States goods. These have included a wide range of products, from American automobiles to Häagen Dazs ice cream in the supermarkets.

Brazil, however, has the potential for an even more profitable economic relationship with the United States. It has 40 percent of Latin America's population and produces 40 percent of the continent's economic output. If Brazil matches the economic reforms of its neighbors, it is expected to become a booming market for the products and capital investments of the United States in the 1990's.

Critics of NAFTA again questioned the wisdom of the trade agreement in early 1995. A severe drop in the value of the Mexican peso caused an economic crisis in that country. The Clinton Administration responded with massive financial aid to fight Mexico's recession. For some Americans, NAFTA had linked the U.S. and Mexican economies too closely. Others continued to believe in the need for economic interdependence and free trade in the Americas.

1. *List the nations which are candidates for NAFTA membership.*
2. *State the reasons for the special interest of the United States in Brazil and Colombia.*

The Pursuit of Free Trade

Latin America responded to NAFTA by forming regional free-trade agreements. Argentina, Brazil, Paraguay, and Uruguay are linked in the Southern Cone Common Market; the Andean Pact provided for free trade among Bolivia, Colombia, Ecuador, Peru, and Venezuela; and the Central American Common Market has eliminated trade barriers among Costa Rica, Nicaragua, Honduras, and El Salvador. The governments of these countries have discussed an extension of their free-trade pact to include monetary union and a single currency. Discussions also began in 1994 for establishing a free-trade agreement between Colombia and the eight-nation Caribbean Community.

Some of these arrangements arose from a fear that NAFTA would reduce the flow of Latin American goods to the United States, especially from Central America and the Caribbean. President Clinton promised to protect these nations from any damage from NAFTA. The Caribbean nations, for example, were offered temporary NAFTA trade benefits.

The variety of regional free-trade agreements raised questions about the possibility of conflicting obligations should any of these nations join NAFTA. To simplify matters and strengthen their ability to compete, the leaders of Latin America's 19 largest nations reached an important agreement in June, 1994. They decided to combine the region's various free-trade pacts into one Latin American free-trade zone by 1999. The Latin American leaders stated their desire for freer trade with other nations, especially the United States. They also proposed the development of a common policy for the expansion of NAFTA.

1. *Explain how NAFTA has affected relations between the United States and Latin America.*
2. *State two examples of free-trade arrangements in Latin America.*

Section Review

Review NAFTA and Beyond, *and do the following:*

1. *Pretend you are the leader of a Latin American country that is deciding whether or not to apply for NAFTA membership. List advantages and disadvantages of NAFTA.*
2. *Develop a policy to help President Clinton. State your opinion about offering NAFTA membership to other countries.*
3. *Explain why you AGREE or DISAGREE with the claim that NAFTA is one of the great achievements of the Clinton Administration.*

America's War Against the Drug Lords

A major goal of U.S. foreign policy has been to stop the flow into North American cities of illegal drugs from Latin America. Colombia and Peru, especially, have been centers of "trafficante" activity. From drug production centers such as Medellín and Cali in Colombia, large criminal organizations, or *cartels,* control laboratories, ships, airplanes, and distribution networks. The drug lords who run these cartels are multimillionaires. Their private armies have waged war against local security forces as well as U.S. agents working with them.

In 1994, some observers charged the Clinton Administration with failing to properly direct its anti-narcotics strategy in Latin America. There appeared to be confusion over objectives and the means by which they should be pursued. Also, the intentions of some Latin American leaders engaged in the drug war have been open to question.

Between 1989 and 1994, the United States developed an extensive network to track drug-carrying airplanes. It includes ground-based radar installations in Peru, Colombia, and Ecuador, as well as American planes equipped with airborne warning and control systems (AWACS), based in Panama, that patrol the Andes region. This network made possible the identification of 600 suspected drug flights in Colombia in 1993. In the same year, information supplied by the Americans enabled Colombia to destroy 27 drug planes on the ground. In May, 1994, however, the Clinton Administration stopped flights of AWACS aircraft over Peru and Colombia and cut off the flow of information about possible drug-smuggling flights to those countries. The reason given for this decision was concern about the Peruvian and Colombian policy of shooting down drug-carrying aircraft. The Administration feared that American officials or military personnel might face criminal charges if people were hurt or killed when the Andean countries used American-supplied flight-tracking data to shoot down drug traffickers.

One result of this decision was an increase in drug flights in the Andes. Another was a storm of criticism from members of the U.S. Congress and from Latin American leaders. Fears arose that the decision would undermine anti-drug cooperation and create tension between the United States and the Andean nations.

Soon after the AWAC flights ended, Colombia said that it would expel ground-based American radar operations. Peru banned all American surveillance flights over its territory.

In June, 1994, the Clinton Administration reversed its stand and ordered a resumption of intelligence-gathering flights over the Andes. It prepared new legislation that would eliminate criminal liability for attacks on civilian aircraft by countries that face major threats from drug trafficking. Under interim agreements proposed to Colombia and Peru, American intelligence information could be used to identify illegal airstrips and to aid in the confiscation of drugs from aircraft once they have landed. However, no planes would actually be shot down.

1. *Define:*

   a. *drug wars*
   b. *drug lords*
   c. *trafficantes*
   d. *drug cartels*

2. *Explain why the United States assists Latin American governments against drug traffickers.*

3. *Describe the 1994 controversy between the United States, Colombia, and Peru.*

Questionable Policies

In 1994 and 1995, the Clinton Administration concluded that its anti-drug efforts in Latin America were having little impact on drug abuse in the United States. The attacks on drug cartels and their activities were not stopping the flow of drugs into the country or even increasing the street price of narcotics. However, Washington continued to finance the anti-drug war in

Latin America and to involve U.S. military and police agencies in the battle. Certain developments increased doubts about this policy.

The war against drugs in Colombia has been led by Prosecutor General Gustavo de Grieff, who is also his country's most prominent advocate of legalizing drugs. He has ridiculed the drug war; claimed that the huge profits made by the trafficantes has paid for the corruption of police, customs agents, and airport authorities; and declared that the jailing of drug lords and the efforts to stop their shipments have had no effect on the overseas prices of illegal drugs.

Although the Colombian government made clear its intention to replace the controversial Prosecutor General, who reached mandatory retirement age in 1994, the United States government accused him of frustrating efforts of the two countries to bring criminals to justice. De Grieff's arguments for legalization of drugs have received favorable responses from some U.S. mayors and police officials. However, the U.S. Justice Department stopped sharing criminal evidence with Colombia in March, 1994, claiming that de Grieff wanted to negotiate lenient prison sentences with major drug traffickers.

The Prosecutor General's warnings about the ability of the drug lords to corrupt government officials appeared to ring true in June, 1994. Ernesto Samper Pizano won Colombia's presidential election by a narrow margin of 2.2 percent. His opposing candidate played a tape recording at a news conference indicating that the campaign of the President-elect had been financed by a contribution of nearly $4 million from the leader of the Cali drug cartel. Samper denied the charge. Some journalists predicted that the scandal would fade away, as have other accusations of the drug lords' influence on Colombian politics. In 1991, for example, delegates to Colombia's Constitutional Assembly were videotaped accepting envelopes filled with cash from drug cartel messengers. The Assembly voted to bar the extradition of Colombian trafficking suspects to the United States for trial.

United States officials reacted angrily to the scandal. Assertions that the campaign was tainted by drug money worsened U.S.-Colombian relations, which had already been strained by tensions arising from the conflict between the Clinton Administration and Prosecutor General de Grieff.

These developments increased doubts about the wisdom of

continuing the policy of attempting to deal with drug abuse in the United States by fighting a war in Latin America. Events in Colombia were linked to problems elsewhere. In Peru, for example, funds provided by the United States to combat the trafficantes were reduced when it was found that the money was being used for other purposes. For the Clinton Administration, a careful consideration of future policy directions became necessary.

1. *Describe the conflict between the Clinton Administration and Colombian Prosecutor General Gustavo de Grieff.*
2. *Explain why the Colombian presidential election of 1994 raised doubts about U.S. policies in Latin America.*

Section Review

1. *Pretend you are a citizen of Colombia or Peru. Express your feelings about the presence in your country of U.S. police and military personnel engaged in anti-drug trafficking operations.*
2. *Explain why you AGREE or DISAGREE with the opinion of the Prosecutor General of Colombia that the best way to put the drug lords out of business is to legalize drugs.*

Democracy and Human Rights

While NAFTA was regarded as a U.S. foreign policy triumph, the crisis in Haiti was much publicized as being less than a victory.

The United States opposed the removal from office and exile of Haitian President Jean-Bertrand Aristide by the country's military in 1991. Aristide, a Roman Catholic priest, had been democratically elected, following a succession of dictators. Fearing a loss of their traditional power, Haiti's small class of wealthy landowners and military officers replaced Aristide with hand-picked civilian leaders. The real power, however, was exercised by a military "strongman," General Raoul Cedras, who used army and police forces to brutally crush support for Aristide among Haiti's small farmers and poverty-stricken city workers. Amid arrests, executions, and political murders, thousands of Haitians fled. Many lost their lives at sea, desperately attempting to reach the United States in small boats. The resulting human rights crisis provoked worldwide outrage.

CENTRAL AMERICA AND THE CARIBBEAN

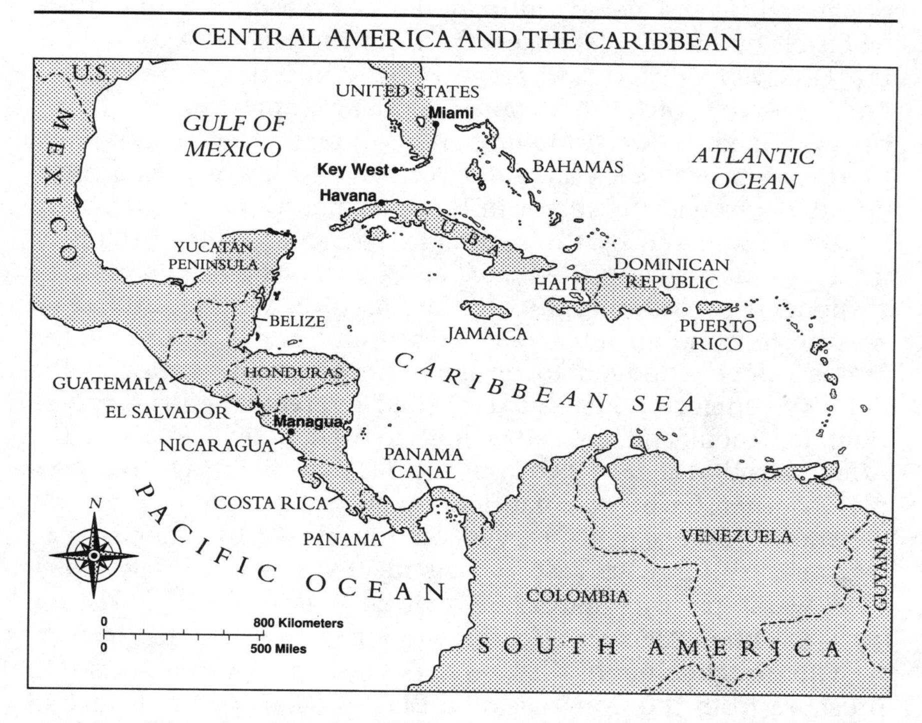

After his election in 1992, President-elect Clinton pledged intensified United States efforts, in cooperation with the United Nations and the Organization of American States (OAS), to restore President Aristide to office. This effort included a worldwide oil and weapons embargo. The trade sanctions were designed to put economic pressure on Haiti's ruling elite. In July, 1993, success appeared close when General Cedras and Aristide met on New York's Governors Island. They signed an agreement providing for the following: an interim civilian government headed by a prime minister appointed by Aristide; the resignation of Cedras and other top military and police officials; the stationing in Haiti of a foreign military force under U.N. supervision to reorganize and retrain the army and police; and Aristide's return to office by October 31, 1993.

Subsequently, the Haitian military rejected the Governors

Island agreement. Cedras did not resign and Aristide did not return to Haiti. Instead, repression intensified and a campaign of terror was aimed at Aristide's supporters. In the countryside, the military used "scorched earth" tactics, often destroying whole villages and the crops on which their occupants depended. The level of intimidation increased in July, 1994, when all human rights observers from the United Nations and the OAS were ordered to leave Haiti. While the United States and other nations broadened economic sanctions, the hardships caused by the trade embargo fell mostly on Haiti's poor.

President Clinton was widely criticized for not acting more decisively to end the terror in Haiti. Human rights groups were especially angered by the automatic return to Haiti of refugees intercepted at sea by the U.S. Coast Guard. The Administration responded by ordering the U.S. Immigration and Naturalization Service to conduct interviews at sea and admit to the United States refugees judged to be fleeing repression. However, the flood of refugees pouring out of Haiti overwhelmed the camps built for them and caused a halt to this policy. Instead, the Administration announced a new policy of diverting boat people to other Caribbean nations, such as Panama.

These developments moved Clinton closer to a decision to use military force to restore Aristide to power. In July, 1994, four warships carrying 2,000 marines were sent to Haitian waters. Other American forces practiced invasion tactics.

The toughening of Clinton's policy was partially due to pressure from the Congressional Black Caucus in the House of Representatives. In March, 1994, this group introduced a bill to tighten the economic embargo against Haiti, sever its commercial air links to the United States, halt the automatic repatriation of refugees picked up at sea, and block financial assets held in the United States by Haitian nationals. Almost all of these provisions were adopted as the President's policy toward Haiti.

The Caucus accused the Clinton Administration of racism in its treatment of Haitian refugees. Other groups advocating the rights of refugees also influenced the President to consider the use of military force as the only solution to a deepening crisis. By mid-1994, President Clinton was under extreme pressure to formulate some plan for decisive action.

In September, 1994, an American delegation sent by President Clinton negotiated an agreement with Haiti's military leaders. Cedras and his associates resigned, and thousands of U.S. troops took control of Haiti without opposition. President Aristide returned to Haiti and resumed office in October, 1994. In December, 1995, René Préval was elected President.

Haiti remained unstable. U.S. peacekeepers under U.N. command stayed until late 1996. They had been scheduled to leave in June, but several apparently political kidnappings and murders made the Security Council vote for an extension.

1. *Explain how a crisis developed in Haiti in the 1990's.*
2. *List steps by the Clinton Administration to deal with the crisis.*
3. *State reasons for the widespread criticism of President Clinton's Haitian policy.*

Other Human Rights Problems

Some efforts to protect democracy in the Western Hemisphere have succeeded. In 1990, U.S. forces invaded Panama and arrested its dictator, General Manuel Noriega, who had been aiding the transport of drugs from South America to the United States. The Americans helped install a more democratic government.

The United States also reacted when President Alberto Fujimori of Peru dissolved its Congress and courts in April, 1992. Claiming that they were obstructing his fight against terrorism, Fujimori assumed dictatorial powers. The United States then reduced its economic aid to Peru until a newly elected Congress took office in January, 1993.

In addition, the United States stopped most of its aid to Guatemala in May, 1993, after President Jorge Serrano Elias dissolved that nation's Congress and Supreme Court and suspended constitutional rights. Serrano wanted to repress labor unions and student groups that had protested his economic austerity measures. The United States joined the OAS and nearly every other nation in the Western Hemisphere to oppose Serrano's assumption of dictatorial powers. This international response, combined with the opposition of many Guatemalans, forced Serrano to resign. Ramiro de Leon Carpio, a civil rights prosecutor, became president, thus allowing constitutional democracy in Guatemala another chance to develop. In 1994, however, attacks on Americans in Guatemala were viewed by human rights advocates as part of an effort by antidemocratic forces to weaken U.S. influence in that country.

El Salvador has not been an American foreign policy success. During the 1980's, the United States aided the government of El Salvador in its struggle against local Communist guerrillas. The long civil war ended in 1991 with a cease-fire agreement between the government and the guerrillas. In 1993, El Salvador again became a focus of attention when it was revealed that human rights abuses committed during the civil war against American civilians, and those of other nationalities, were done with the knowledge of the U.S.-supported government. In June, 1994, Armando Calderon Sol, leader of the right-wing National Republican Alliance (ARENA), was elected President. Calderon's election was an indication that ARENA, which had been the ruling party during the civil war, had not lost its ability to control the country's political processes. Despite the desire of many Salvadorans for change, the lack of a strong, unified opposition to the government made the development of real democracy unlikely.

Although the poverty and discrimination suffered by Mexico's Indians are often ignored by Americans, as they have been by the Mexican government, an armed uprising by Maya Indians in the state of Chiapas in early 1994 captured media attention in both countries. The Indians demanded that President Carlos Salinas de Gortari meet with them. After listening to their complaints about poverty, discrimination, and injustice, Salinas promised paved roads, new schools, health clinics, and economic development plans.

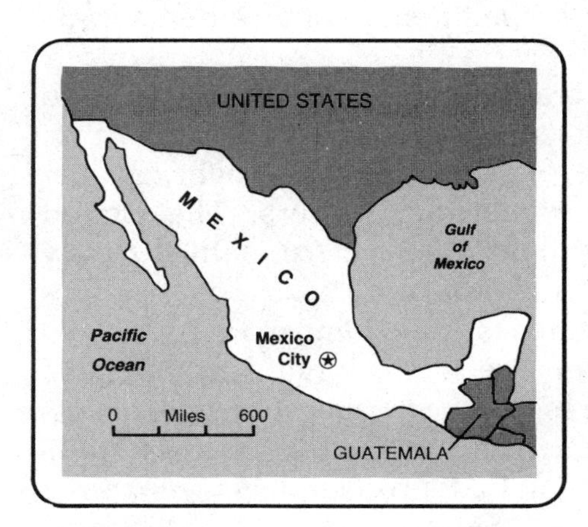

The rebel Zapatista Liberation Army rejected the proposals, demanding more democracy on a national level and a voice in decision and policy making. In early 1995, negotiations broke down. The new President, Ernesto Zedillo, ordered government troops into Zapatista territory.

In February, 1996, the Zapatistas, the Mexican government, and the state government of Chiapas signed the first of six peace agreements. It gave Mexico's Indians more political power within Mexico and the right to adopt traditional forms of local government.

President Zedillo also inherited an economic crisis. Although 1995 economic reports suggested an improving economy, the average Mexican still faced many hardships. In September, 1996, a disaffected guerrilla group, the Popular Revolutionary Army, attacked police and military posts in southern Mexico. The attacks were a major threat to the government. Leaders feared that the violence would discourage foreign investment and slow down economic recovery.

Significant human rights abuses have been common throughout Latin America. Argentina, Brazil, Colombia, and Venezuela have been high on the list of problem areas. Despite its emphasis on human rights as a foreign policy goal, the ability of the Clinton Administration to effect improvement has been limited by other policy concerns. Chief among these has been the anti-drug war.

1. *Describe the action taken by the United States to deal with human rights problems in Panama, Peru, Guatemala, and Mexico.*
2. *Identify:*
   a. *Manuel Noriega*
   b. *Alberto Fujimori*
   c. *Ramiro de Leon Carpio*
   d. *Armando Calderon Sol*
   e. *Carlos Salinas de Gortari*
3. *Explain why El Salvador has been unable to achieve real democracy.*

Section Review

1. *In a 1994 public opinion poll, 53 percent interviewed stated that President Clinton was effectively managing the problems in Haiti and the Caribbean. Why do you AGREE or DISAGREE?*
2. *American public opinion was divided, in mid-1994, on the question of an invasion of Haiti by U.S. military forces. Develop and list your own arguments for and against this action.*
3. *PROVE or DISPROVE: The United States has been effective in protecting democracy and human rights in the Western Hemisphere.*

The United States and Cuba: Background

During the first half of the 20th century, Americans owned many businesses in Cuba. They also controlled the sugar industry, which produced Cuba's main export crop. In 1959, Fidel Castro and his followers overthrew the Cuban government and came to power. Castro, a Marxist, took control of U.S.-owned businesses, and sought economic help from the Soviet Union. In time, Soviet aid was extensive enough to enable the Soviet Union to dominate Cuba.

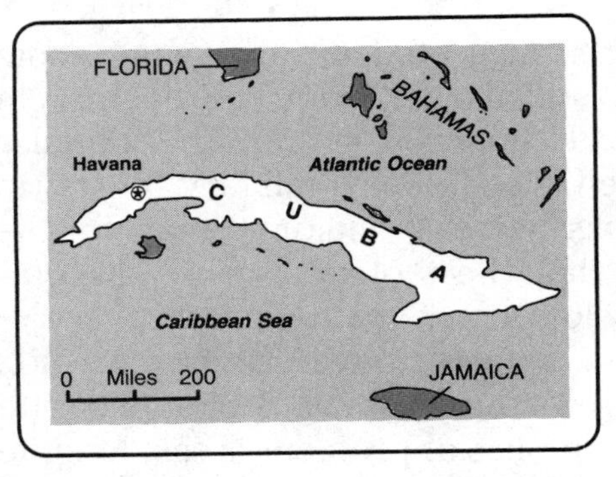

In 1961, the United States supported the effort of anti-Communist Cubans to invade the island and overthrow the Castro dictatorship. The "Bay of Pigs" invasion failed because the Cuban people did not support the American-trained force.

The following year, the United States and the Soviet Union nearly went to war over Cuba. The Soviets had placed in Cuba nuclear missiles capable of reaching the United States. President John F. Kennedy demanded that Premier Nikita Khrushchev remove the missiles. After the United States ordered a naval blockade of Cuba, the Soviets agreed to Kennedy's demand. Soviet aid to Cuba continued until the dissolution of the Soviet Union in 1991. Since then, the Cuban economy has suffered a severe decline.

During the cold war, 72 percent of Cuba's foreign trade was with the Soviet Union and the Communist nations of eastern Europe. In the 1990's, diminished trade and foreign investment further damaged the Cuban economy. Fuel shortages have limited both industrial and agricultural production. Also, the Cuban economy continues to suffer from the trade embargo maintained by the United States since 1962.

1. *Describe the development of hostility between the United States and Cuba.*
2. *Explain why Cuba's economic situation became desperate in the 1990's.*

The Cuban Policy Debate

In 1993, President Fidel Castro and the Communist Party leadership attempted limited free-market reforms. Citizens were allowed to form small private businesses, legally possess foreign currency, and establish their own agricultural cooperatives. However, as many Cubans turned eagerly to capitalism, Castro ended the experiment. The businesses which had sprung up were closed down by mid-1994. In addition, Castro rejected all efforts to improve production by providing incentives for the self-employed or opening free markets for farmers.

Nor has political freedom been permitted. Human rights abuses continued in 1995, including the arrest and harassment of dissidents. There was even a crackdown on "parabolicas," the antennas with which Cubans pick up foreign television.

Nevertheless, foreign investors were welcomed. WilTel, an American telecommunications firm, negotiated an agreement with the Cubans to build the first fiber optic link between Cuba and Florida. In June, 1994, Mexico became Cuba's most important foreign investor. During a visit by Mexico's President Carlos Salinas de Gortari, Castro agreed to sell 49 percent of Cuba's antiquated telephone system to a Mexican conglomerate. This $1.4 billion deal placed the island's future telecommunications development in the hands of the Mexican firm. Businesses from Canada, Spain, and other nations have also arranged to invest in Cuba.

Such investment activity, especially by the Latin American nations, represented a rejection of American policy toward Cuba. Latin America has called upon the United States to end its diplomatic and economic boycott of Cuba. Spain and Portugal have supported this demand. At a June, 1994, meeting of the OAS, a Panamanian delegate referred to the 1962 suspension of Cuba from that organization as "a relic of the cold war." This opinion was echoed by some of the most powerful OAS members—Brazil, Canada, Mexico, and Venezuela—and by most of the Central American republics. The OAS Secretary-General received a standing ovation when he called for the readmission of Cuba to the Latin American family.

Opinion in the United States has been divided. The State Department was angered by Mexico's telephone deal with Cuba. Congress demanded that pressure be exerted to dissuade the Mexicans from doing business with Castro. While

Mexican investors made it clear that they regard the Communist-ruled island as a wide-open field for expanding their business operations, the ban on trade with Cuba has cost U.S. companies an estimated $6 billion a year in lost opportunities. In response, Representative Charles Rangel, Democrat of Manhattan, sponsored a bill to lift the trade embargo. In mid-1994, however, the Clinton Administration showed no sign of changing its policy on this issue.

Starting in 1993, Clinton took some steps to end the hostility between the United States and Cuba. The belligerent tone and aggressive rhetoric common to official statements about Cuba have been calmed. This change has been publicly recognized by the Cuban government. Also, the way was opened for improved telephone and mail links, increased flows of humanitarian aid, and limited cooperation on drug trafficking and immigration.

Opposition to the resumption of trade and diplomatic relations with Cuba has been especially strong among Cuban Americans, most of whom entered the United States as refugees from the Castro dictatorship. This conflict between the desires of a politically powerful voting bloc in the United States, the need of American businesses for increased investment opportunities, and the demands of Latin American nations for a change in U.S. policy has become one more foreign policy dilemma for President Clinton.

The dilemma worsened in 1994 when more than 30,000 refugees left Cuba by boat in search of a better life in the United States. The Clinton Administration decided to detain the refugees in camps rather than grant them free entry to the United States. The tide of refugees ended after a new U.S.–Cuba emigration agreement was reached in September, 1994.

In March, 1996, Clinton responded to Cuba's downing of two U.S. civilian planes over international waters by signing a law that tightened the embargo on Cuba and penalized foreign investors in Cuba. European nations, as well as Mexico and Canada, protested this extension of "United States law into other jurisdictions."

1. *Explain how disagreement among the United States and other nations arose over Cuba.*
2. *Describe the Cuban policy of the Clinton Administration.*

Section Review

1. *Study the map of Cuba on page 196 and answer the following questions:*
   a. *Why was President Kennedy so concerned about Soviet missiles in Cuba in 1962? Was he right or wrong to risk war to force their removal? Explain the reasons for your answer.*
   b. *Why do you think Florida became the center of the Cuban-American community?*
   c. *What position do you think should be taken by Florida's representatives in Congress on the question of lifting the diplomatic and trade embargo on Cuba?*
   d. *Should U.S. policy change, why might Cuba be attractive to American tourists?*
   e. *Should the President of the United States visit Cuba, in what city would he be received? Why?*
2. *For decades, the United States has maintained a large naval base at Guantanamo Bay, in Cuba. Do some research to find out why this has been done and how the Cubans have reacted.*
3. *Develop arguments for or against the resumption of trade and diplomatic relations with Cuba by the United States. Present your arguments from the viewpoint of each of the following:*
   a. *the Cuban-American community*
   b. *the Organization of American States*
   c. *the American business community*
   d. *the Cuban government*

Plebiscite in Puerto Rico

On November 14, 1993, Puerto Rican voters went to the polls to express their preference for the political future of their island. At stake was their status as citizens of a self-governing commonwealth. As such, Puerto Ricans have American citizenship, but not all the rights and responsibilities that go with it. Nearly two million eligible voters, a record 80 percent of the electorate, chose from among the traditional three options for Puerto Rico—independence, statehood, or commonwealth. The decision was for maintenance of the commonwealth. However, this was not a victory for the status quo. All those who participated in the plebiscite agreed that change in the relationship between Puerto Rico and the government of the

United States is necessary. Some regarded the historic vote as a possible first step toward decolonization.

Puerto Rico was ceded to the United States by Spain after the Spanish-American War (1898). In 1952, the people voted in favor of commonwealth status. As such, Puerto Rico is a self-governing part of the United States. The island's citizens have the same control over their internal affairs as do the citizens of the 50 U.S. states. Although they can vote in primary elections to help select national candidates, they cannot vote in national elections. No federal income tax is collected from residents on income earned from local sources in Puerto Rico. As part of the U.S. legal system, Puerto Rico is subject to the provisions of the U.S. Constitution. Most federal laws apply here as they do elsewhere in the United States. The commonwealth is represented in the U.S. Congress by a resident commissioner. This official can participate in debates and discussions, but can vote only in committees, not in floor votes.

Puerto Rico's language and culture are primarily Hispanic. Traditionally, the islanders refer to their relationship with the rest of the United States as "estado libre associado" (free associated state). But their island is subject to the absolute power of Congress. Some Puerto Ricans regard this as colonialism. They would like a new relationship, based upon a negotiated agreement between a sovereign Puerto Rico and the United States.

1. *Define Puerto Rico's commonwealth status.*
2. *State the purpose of the plebiscite vote of November 14, 1993.*

Issues and Options

In his first State of the Union address, in January, 1989, President George Bush asked Congress to consider granting statehood to Puerto Rico. In elections for the governorship of the island, pro-statehood candidates had been winning ever-larger percentages of the vote for 37 years. Bush called for a referendum on this issue, but Congress did not approve it. Under the First Amendment of the Constitution, Puerto Rico now had the right to petition Congress for a redress of grievances. This meant a vote by the islanders. In 1992, Puerto Rican Governor Pedro Rossello, of the pro-statehood New Progressive Party, placed a bill before the island's Legislative Assembly that called for a plebiscite on November 14, 1993. The bill was approved and all three local political parties—the New Progressive Party, the pro-commonwealth Popular Democratic Party, and the Puerto Rican Independence Party—agreed to participate.

President Clinton supported the plebiscite and promised to accept any decision made by the Puerto Ricans. From Congress, however, came warnings that the Senate would not vote for statehood. Increased federal aid for poverty programs, beyond the $8.5 billion a year currently received by the commonwealth, was a consequence the budget-wary senators were not prepared to accept.

In Puerto Rico, the pro-statehood party claimed that it wished to preserve Puerto Rican culture, while gaining the rights of a state. The pro-commonwealth party emphasized the benefits of maintaining "the union that works" with the United States and preserving "the best of two worlds." The Independence Party called for a ten-year transition period of United States friendship and aid as a prelude to complete independence.

A number of issues determined the outcome of the plebiscite. Many Puerto Ricans became concerned about the financial consequences of statehood. As a territorial possession of the United States, the island is a tax haven for multinational corporations. This benefit, along with jobs and income, would be lost if it became a state. So would the benefits of other tax breaks.

Fears surfaced that statehood would require that English become the first and the only official language of the island. Fiercely proud of their 500-year history as a Caribbean culture, Puerto Ricans worried that statehood might cause assimilation and a loss of cultural identity.

The November, 1993, plebiscite resulted in 48.4 percent of the votes being cast for continuation of the commonwealth.

Statehood was chosen by 46.2 percent of those participating, while only 4.4 percent voted for independence. For the pro-statehood movement, the loss of 60,000 voters who had indicated their support in polls in 1992 was a painful reverse. The move toward independence was soundly rejected.

Despite the plebiscite, the question of Puerto Rico's relationship with the rest of the United States remains open. Although the islanders have stated that they wish to remain a commonwealth, they have also petitioned Congress for legislation to end their territorial status and enable them to negotiate new agreements as a sovereign equal. How Congress will respond remains to be seen.

◆ *State the results of the plebiscite vote in Puerto Rico on November 14, 1993, and review the reasons for them.*

Section Review

1. *Indicate what choice you would have made if you were a Puerto Rican voter in November, 1993, and give the reasons for your choice.*
2. *Why do you think the 2.6 million members of the Puerto Rican community on the United States mainland demanded that they be allowed to participate in the plebiscite? Why do you think the Puerto Rican government refused?*
3. *Evaluate the roles played by President George Bush and President Bill Clinton in the events leading to the plebiscite. Did they provide effective leadership? Why or why not?*

Chapter 9 Review

A. *For each question, indicate the correct response.*

1. *A major reason for the concern of the United States with Latin American development is (a) fear of the spread of communism (b) the benefits of trade with expanding economies (c) Latin American aggression toward the United States.*
2. *A country that might be considered for admission to an expanded NAFTA is (a) Haiti (b) Chile (c) El Salvador.*

3. *The Southern Cone Common Market is a (a) military defense arrangement (b) law enforcement agency (c) regional free-trade agreement.*

4. *The Clinton Administration has been criticized for its (a) conduct of anti-drug operations in Latin America (b) response to demands for a hemispheric free-trade arrangement (c) proposals for hemispheric defense.*

5. *The United States has disagreed with Colombia about (a) the shooting down of aircraft suspected of carrying drugs (b) charges of collaboration between Colombian officials and drug cartels (c) both of these.*

6. *The goal of the Clinton Administration's Haitian policy in the 1990's has been (a) the election of Raoul Cedras as President of Haiti (b) the return to power of Jean-Bertrand Aristide (c) the annexation of Haiti by the United States.*

7. *Successful attempts of the United States to protect democracy and human rights in the Western Hemisphere included actions in (a) Panama and Guatemala (b) El Salvador (c) Colombia.*

8. *U.S.–Mexico trade relations were strained when President Salinas (a) negotiated a telecommunications deal with Cuba (b) withdrew from the OAS (c) arranged a cease-fire with the Zapatista Liberation Army.*

9. *In 1994, most Latin American nations demanded (a) an end to the American diplomatic and trade embargo of Cuba (b) a halt to U.S. Air Force flights over the Andean countries (c) cancellation of a U.S. invasion of Haiti.*

10. *The relationship between Puerto Rico and the rest of the United States can best be described as (a) domination of a conquered Latin American nation by a colonial power (b) an agreement negotiated by sovereign and equal powers (c) a special arrangement between a federal government and a territory with special privileges.*

B. *Write an essay on ONE of the problems of the Clinton Administration in Latin America by answering one of the question groups:*

1. *Why has the war against drug trafficking stalled? What are the alternatives open to the United States? Which alternative do you favor? Why?*

2. *Why did the Congressional Black Caucus and human rights groups criticize President Clinton's Haitian policy? Do you agree with them? Why or why not?*

3. *Should the Clinton Administration continue the diplomatic and economic isolation of Cuba? Why or why not? What has been the reaction of the other nations of the Western Hemisphere? What are the President's alternatives?*

C. *Organize a debate in your class to argue the pros and cons of ONE of the following propositions:*

1. *NAFTA should be expanded to include all nations in the Western Hemisphere.*
2. *The use of narcotics should never be legalized in the United States or Latin America.*
3. *No Haitian or Cuban refugees should be admitted to the United States.*
4. *Puerto Rico should be offered statehood and be allowed to retain its territorial tax benefits.*

Unit II Review

A. *After the cold war, the United States and other nations created a new world order. While doing so, American leaders have attempted to promote democratic governments, free-market economies, and human rights. Use information from Unit II to evaluate America's global role by doing the following:*

1. *Identify and describe ONE major foreign policy problem faced by the United States in the 1990's in each region: Europe, Asia, the Middle East, Africa, and Latin America.*
2. *Develop answers to the following questions:*
   a. *Has the United States been successful in achieving its goals? State the reasons for your opinion.*
   b. *What have been America's successes and failures in promoting democratic government, free-market economies, and human rights?*

B. *Review* Chapter 5, The United States and Europe. *Then explain why you AGREE or DISAGREE with each of these statements:*

1. *President Boris Yeltsin of Russia has proven himself to be worthy of continuing American political and economic support.*

2. *American military forces should be sent to Bosnia-Herzegovina as peacekeepers.*
3. *The United States should commit itself to the defense of the eastern European nations and the former Soviet republics against Russian aggression.*
4. *It is the responsibility of the United States to find a solution to the strife in Northern Ireland.*
5. *American foreign policy should be more concerned with Asia and Latin America than with Europe.*

C. *Use information found in Unit II to write an article to accompany ONE of the following newspaper headlines:*

CLINTON FORMS PARTNERSHIP FOR PEACE

U.S. OFFERS JAPAN MISSILES FOR TECHNOLOGY

AMERICAN SECRETARY OF STATE VISITS MIDDLE EAST

THE NEW SOUTH AFRICA GETS AMERICAN SUPPORT

CONGRESSIONAL BLACK CAUCUS CONDEMNS CLINTON'S HAITIAN POLICY

D. *By mid-1994, President Clinton's foreign policy was under heavy criticism. Use information from Unit II to form your own opinion. Make sure you do each of the following:*

1. *Explain why the President drew criticism from so many sources; e.g., Republicans, the Congressional Black Caucus, the business community, human rights groups, and foreign governments.*
2. *Evaluate the performance of the President and his Administration in TWO crises or problem situations described in Unit II.*
3. *Offer an alternative to the course of action taken by the Clinton Administration in ONE crisis or problem situation described in Unit II.*
4. *Write a letter to the President to propose changes or improvements in his foreign policy.*

UNIT III

AMERICA'S ROLE IN BUILDING GLOBAL SECURITY AND PROSPERITY

The end of the cold war did not bring an era of peace and security. Although Americans were no longer concerned about the twin threats of Communism and nuclear war, other problems developed. In Rwanda, Somalia, Bosnia, Cambodia, Haiti, and elsewhere, oppression and civil wars caused suffering and death for thousands. And dictators, such as Saddam Hussein of Iraq, repressed their own people and threatened their neighbors.

Other nations expected the United States to take the lead in finding solutions to these problems. Yet many Americans questioned the extent to which they should take responsibility for problems beyond their borders.

The growth of a new global economy also involved the United States. Beyond the establishment of NAFTA, America played a leading role in the Group of Seven (G-7), the General Agreement on Tariffs and Trade (GATT), the International Monetary Fund (IMF), and the World Bank.

Chapter 10

The Peacemakers

When Bill Clinton took office in 1993, Americans and their allies understood that his Administration's chief concern would be finding solutions to the troubling domestic problems that had made George Bush a one-term president. Nevertheless, America remained the world's sole military superpower. A U.S. leadership role was expected in both the United Nations and the North Atlantic Treaty Organization (NATO), the two major organizations responsible for maintaining international security. Regional organizations, such as the Association of Southeast Asian Nations (ASEAN), also looked expectantly to America.

For President Clinton, the problem was complex—how to

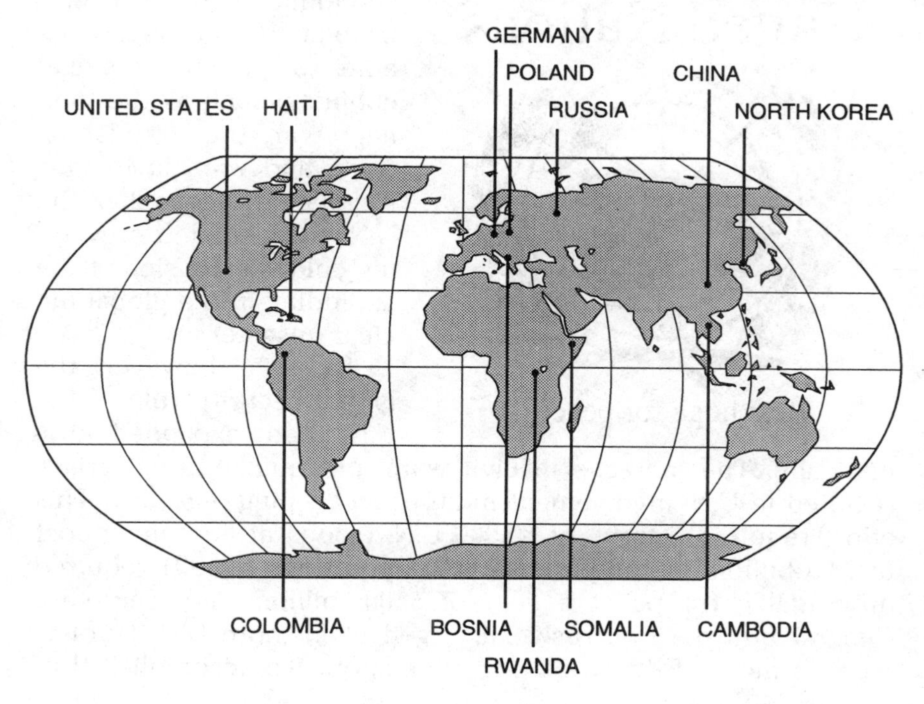

avoid surrendering global leadership without involving American troops in a series of dangerous crises. A related security issue was the need to reduce the size and cost of U.S. military forces in order to fund health care and other domestic programs. All of these were thorny issues, involving potential combat risks for American forces and political headaches for the President.

1. *Explain why the end of the cold war did not bring global peace and security.*
2. *Describe the problem facing President Clinton.*

The United States and the U.N.

The United Nations was created by the victorious Allies at the end of World War II. Its purpose was to prevent another world war by providing member nations with a forum for the settlement of potential conflicts. To preserve the peace by attacking the root causes of war, the U.N. was organized to deal with global social, economic, and health problems. Although unable to prevent regional conflicts, such as the Vietnam War, the Arab-Israeli wars, and wars in Bosnia, Angola, and Somalia, the U.N. succeeded in preventing cold war tensions from exploding into a global nuclear disaster.

Best hope for peace?

By 1994, however, the global security role of the U.N. had expanded dramatically. The increase in civil wars and humanitarian crises resulted in U.N. involvement in 20 peacekeeping missions. This effort required a force of 80,000 U.N. troops at an annual cost of $3.5 billion. In comparison, U.N. operations in 1991 required only 12,000 troops at a cost of $400 million. And Secretary General Boutros Boutros-Ghali urged even more U.N. involvement in more of the world's trouble spots. To accomplish this, the U.N. leader called upon member nations to contribute additional troops, money, and resources to peacekeeping operations. For the United States and the Clinton Administration, the time had come to question whether the role of international policeman was in America's best interests.

1. *Compare the original purpose of the U.N. with its global security role in the 1990's.*
2. *Explain why the term "international policeman" has been applied to the U.N.*

Originally a strong supporter of U.N. intervention in crises, President Clinton adopted a new policy after American soldiers were killed in Somalia. Presidential Decision Directive 25, issued in May, 1994, set cautious guidelines for American involvement in peacekeeping missions. The directive made clear the requirement that the trouble spot be one in which the United States has national interests. Other requirements included evidence of a real threat to international peace, clear objectives for the mission, and identification of an end point to U.N. participation. The new policy was applied to the crisis in Rwanda in mid-1994.

When U.N. Secretary General Boutros-Ghali proposed the immediate movement of 5,500 U.N. troops to Rwanda (see map, p. 172) in May, 1994, the United States refused to authorize it. As a permanent member of the Security Council, the U.S. must approve all peacekeeping missions. Despite the rising number of deaths in Rwanda, as the Rwandan Patriotic Front (RPF) battled government forces for control of this African nation, the U.S. demanded a modest first-wave U.N. force and careful planning before a full-scale mission. This insistence reflected the intention of the Clinton Administration to apply its strict new guidelines on peacekeeping to all U.N. operations, not just the ones in which the United States might play a central role. Despite the criticism of other nations and human rights organizations, the Administration refused to reverse its position.

The new policy placed the Clinton Administration in direct conflict with the U.N. Secretary General Boutros-Ghali had attempted to obtain from member nations enough troops to form a U.N. standing army. When that effort failed, Boutros-

Ghali attempted to persuade the United States and other nations to commit large numbers of specialized forces and equipment to the U.N. on a standby basis. Desperately short of funds for peacekeeping operations, he has also sought larger contributions from U.N. members.

The United States responded to these demands with little enthusiasm. Taking a dim view of Boutros-Ghali's desire for involvement in an increasing number of global crises, the Clinton Administration refused to pay more than one-third of the peacekeeping costs demanded of it. The Administration also refused to place U.S. troops under non-American command.

These decisions led to accusations that the United States was failing to exercise its leadership role as the world's sole military superpower. The Clinton Administration, however, had learned an important lesson from its experience in the failed peacekeeping mission in Somalia. It would not again commit troops to operations which lacked the approval of the Congress and the public.

Following the deaths of American soldiers in Somalia, the President was under intense pressure to withdraw our troops. This was an important reason for rejecting the plan for immediate dispatch of U.N. forces to Rwanda. In addition, there was a lack of enthusiasm for American military action on the part of either Congress or the public. By July, 1994, however, the rising number of sick and dying refugees pouring across the Rwandan borders into neighboring countries alarmed Americans. The Administration responded by sending specialized forces to Rwanda, Zaire, and Uganda to participate in U.N. efforts to provide food, water, and medical services to the refugees.

Despite the caution exercised by the Administration, it also recognized the need to assist the United Nations to become more effective at dealing with crises. (In July, 1994, for example, President Clinton sought U.N. approval for a possible invasion of Haiti to restore President Jean-Bertrand Aristide to power.) How to accomplish this without giving the U.N. a blank check in the form of troop availability has been the question debated in Washington. Among the issues under consideration in 1995 were whether the United States should designate standby forces for service with the U.N. and whether a separate national chain of command should be established if and when U.S. troops are made part of a multinational force.

The Secretary General's personality was a factor in the ongoing U.S.–U.N. relationship. Boutros-Ghali, described as an "imperious" administrator, operated with a small, loyal team of Third World advisers and often clashed with U.S. officials. In 1994, he dismissed U.S. representative Melissa Wells as Under-Secretary for Management because they disagreed over basic organizational matters.

In 1996, when Boutros-Ghali's first term ended, the Clinton Administration opposed his reelection. Most members of the Security Council, however, were at first supportive of Boutros-Ghali, even though U.S. cooperation is vital to U.N. leadership. The United States then used its veto to defeat Boutros-Ghali. The Security Council shortly nominated, and the General Assembly confirmed, Kofi Annan of Ghana to be the new U.N. Secretary General.

1. *Identify Presidential Decision Directive 25.*
2. *Explain how this document was applied to the Rwandan crisis.*
3. *Describe the disagreement between the Clinton Administration and the U.N. Secretary General.*
4. *List the global security issues under consideration by the United States in the 1990's.*

Section Review

1. *Develop arguments for and against the Clinton Administration's refusal in May, 1994, to approve the sending of 5,500 U.N. peacekeepers to Rwanda.*
2. *In July, 1994, President Clinton ordered a small number of American soldiers to fly to Rwanda with food, fuel, medicine, and other supplies. Explain why you AGREE or DISAGREE with the claims of some critics that his actions were "too little, too late."*
3. *Contrast the positions on peacekeeping operations of the Clinton Administration and the U.N. Secretary General. With which position do you agree? Why?*

4. *PROVE or DISPROVE: By 1994, the United States had abandoned its leadership role in the United Nations.*

The United States and NATO

In June, 1994, officials of Russia, the United States, and the North Atlantic Treaty Organization (NATO) signed an agreement to forge closer military ties. Regarded as an historic event, the agreement was intended by the Clinton Administration to bind the Russians closer to the West.

Russia (see map, p. 100) became the 21st country to join President Clinton's Partnership for Peace. This program permits the non-NATO countries of Eastern Europe to hold joint military exercises with NATO nations, cooperate in peacekeeping matters, and exchange information on military tactics and weapons. The former Communist nations did not become NATO members and thus were not guaranteed the alliance's protection from attack. The Russian government opposed full NATO membership for the East Europeans, regarding such a step as a threat to Russia's security.

The signing of the agreement followed several months of difficult negotiations. Russia had originally rejected the Partnership for Peace, demanding a broader military relationship with the United States. Russian officials had insisted on special treatment in recognition of their country's status as a nuclear power.

The new agreement was regarded by some as a triumph for the Clinton Administration. However, the United States and Russia remained at odds over such key issues as peacekeeping and military exercises. In May, 1994, for example, the Russians canceled a joint military exercise. And they have been slow to fulfill a treaty requiring them to dismantle nuclear weapons and disclose the extent of their chemical-weapons program.

The new security agreement, therefore, was largely symbolic. However, it calmed Russian fears that the East European nations would be admitted to NATO and become part of a military alliance that excluded Moscow. The Clinton Administration developed the plan for this loose alliance as a compromise between two conflicting goals. The Administration wanted to move the former Communist nations closer to NATO. And it also wanted to meet Russia's objection to the addition of new members to NATO. In Russia's view, such an expansion would simply move the former cold war frontier closer to Russia's western border.

The East Europeans hope the Partnership for Peace will lead eventually to full NATO membership and the protection it would provide them. They want this because of their distrust of Russia, the nation which dominated them for so long. Under the Partnership for Peace, the United States and NATO have promised to consult with the East Europeans if they are attacked, but not to come to their defense.

These agreements were part of America's effort to respond to the security needs of post-cold war Europe without increasing U.S. military commitments. It included helping NATO develop a new mission, with changed security arrangements and more dependence on European forces. However, American leaders recognized that Russia's ambitions and policies might, at times, be troublesome for the United States and its NATO allies.

1. *Explain the importance of the security agreement signed by the United States, NATO, and Russia in June, 1994.*
2. *State the reasons for the desire of the Eastern European nations to join NATO and for Russia's objections.*

Section Review

1. *Explain why you AGREE or DISAGREE with the belief that Russia's agreement to join the Partnership for Peace in 1994 was a diplomatic triumph for the Clinton Administration.*
2. *Complete each sentence:*
   a. *The 1994 security agreement between the U.S., Russia, and NATO was a symbolic measure because _______.*
   b. *In the mid-1990's, the conflicting security goals of the United States in Europe have been _______.*
   c. *The United States wanted to help NATO _______.*

Other Security Concerns: Russia, Poland, and Germany

A post-cold war security risk to the United States has come from Russian-based organized crime. By 1994, some 160 Russian gangs with large sums of money and international connections were operating in more than thirty countries. They deal in drugs, prostitution, oil, minerals, and weapons. They are also involved in *money laundering* (investing money from criminal activities in legitimate businesses to disguise the origin). American law-enforcement officials have been especially concerned with narcotics trafficking, the illegal transfer of money, and the impact of Russian gangs on Russian immigrant communities in the United States. Also, the efforts of these gangs to acquire weapon-grade nuclear material is regarded as a significant long-term threat to the security of the United States.

The disorder in Russia following the fall of the Soviet Union and the movement from a Communist state-controlled economy to capitalism gave the gangs an opportunity to organize and expand their operations. By means of bribes and payoffs, they have gained the support of many underpaid policemen and officials.

In recognition of this problem, Federal Bureau of Investigation (FBI) Director Louis Freeh signed an agreement, in July, 1994, to cooperate with Russian authorities in the fight against organized crime. It provided for the exchange of information among police forces, cooperation in investigations, the detention of alleged criminals in each other's countries, and the training of Russian officers in the FBI's more modern techniques. It also called for the establishment of an FBI office in the American Embassy in Moscow.

A security matter on which the United States and Russia did not so readily agree, in mid-1994, was advanced chemical weapons. American intelligence gatherers have long believed that Russia has been developing binary chemical weapons. (Such a weapon consists of two different chemicals whose mixture produces a deadly type of poison gas.) However, when American and Russian officials met in May, 1994, to exchange information on their chemical-weapon programs, the data provided by the Russians made no mention of binary weapons. The conclusion reached by the Americans was that Russia was concealing this information. The exchange of data was part of a 1989 agreement between the two countries.

Russia's poison gas stock has been estimated at 40,000 tons, the largest arsenal in the world. Contrary to Russia's actions, the Clinton Administration supports a global treaty banning chemical weapons.

◆ *Identify a security area in which the United States and Russia cooperated in 1994, and one in which they did not.*

Hope and Demands from Poland

During the cold war, American leaders encouraged the Poles in their long opposition to Communism and Soviet domination. As the first nation to free itself from Communism and begin the development of democracy and a free-market economy, Poland has been held in special regard by the United States. When President Clinton visited Warsaw in mid-1994, he was met by Polish leaders who wanted his promise to work for Poland's admission to NATO. They feared that Russia might once again become an imperial power. While still the President of Poland, Lech Walesa warned that "the West doesn't understand the dangers of leaving the former Warsaw Pact countries alone." In 1993 and 1994, Walesa gave repeated lectures to American officials about Poland's need to join NATO. Referring to the Partnership for Peace, Walesa expressed the Poles' lack of faith in "paper guarantees."

Although Clinton praised Poland as having served as a model for its neighbors with its rapid adoption of political and economic reforms, he did not give Walesa the assurances he sought. Instead, he offered a $210 million aid package. Administration officials acknowledged that it represented only a token gift intended to encourage the Poles to move further toward a free-market economy. The largest part of the gift was allotted to a fund that would provide insurance to American companies investing in Poland. Poles worried about the United States' apparent favoritism toward Russia and lack of understanding of Poland's security problems.

In November, 1995, Aleksander Kwasniewski took Walesa's place as Poland's President. Although a former Communist, he worked hard to make Poland a member of NATO and to foster its free-market economy.

1. *State the reason for the special regard in which Poland is held by the United States.*
2. *Identify two of President Aleksander Kwasniewski's goals for Poland.*

Germany: America's Special Ally

In July, 1994, Germany's High Court ruled that the country's 1949 constitution did not prohibit German troops from joining United Nations peacekeeping or combat missions. This historic decision removed a longstanding obstacle to Germany's participation in global security projects. Since the reunification of East and West Germany in 1990, the agreement to remove Russian troops from German soil, and the collapse of the Soviet Union, German leaders have recognized the need for the country to participate fully as a U.N. member and engage in peacekeeping missions.

The memory of the Nazi era and the Holocaust had made Germany and its neighbors reject a German military role beyond the NATO area in Europe. This restriction had embarrassed Germany during the Persian Gulf War of 1991. As one of the economic superpowers of the world and a leader of the European Union, Germany felt obliged to contribute to the maintenance of international security.

A broader German role on the world stage had been sought by the United States and other allies within NATO. During a July, 1994, visit to Berlin, President Clinton declared himself fully comfortable with the High Court decision and urged a more assertive Germany. Using college-learned German, which drew roars of approval from the assembled crowds, Clinton promised the Germans that "America stands on your side now and forever."

Clinton also ordered the withdrawal of the Berlin Brigade from Germany. This U.S. Army unit had been sent to Berlin in 1961 at the height of the cold war. Its retirement was part of an American plan to withdraw all U.S. troops from Germany. Although thousands of American troops still remained in other sections of the country, U.S. policy for the 1990's was clear. A greater portion of Europe's security burden would be left to the Europeans, including the Germans.

1. *Explain why the 1994 decision of the German High Court was welcomed by President Clinton.*

2. *State the connection between the withdrawal of the U.S. Berlin Brigade from Germany and the policy of the United States on international security.*

Section Review

1. *Review the security arrangements made by the United States with Russia, Poland, and Germany. How do they differ?*

2. *Decide which of these statements is correct:*

   a. *In the 1990's, the United States and Russia were able to agree on some security issues, but disagreed on others.*
   b. *In 1994, the Clinton Administration committed the United States to the military defense of Poland.*
   c. *Fear of Germany's Nazi past caused the United States to oppose any expansion of Germany's global security role.*

3. *PROVE or DISPROVE: President Clinton's visits to European capitals in the summer of 1994 convinced most people that the United States would continue to provide strong leadership in the effort to maintain international security.*

America and the Security of Southeast Asia

The mid-1994 decision of the Clinton Administration to send equipment and military trainers to Cambodia represented a cautious U.S. reentry into the security problems of Southeast Asia. It was the first time since the 1970's that the United States provided direct assistance to the Cambodian army. However, the aid was nonlethal. It did not include weapons or ammunition, but consisted of equipment for road building and the clearing of millions of mines scattered over the Cambodian countryside during years of civil war. Cambodian military officials had requested American weapons and tactical advisers. These were under consideration by the Clinton Administration.

Cambodia's head of state, King Norodom Sihanouk, warned that American arms shipments are needed to prevent the brutal Khmer Rouge guerrillas from once again taking control of Cambodia. The Khmer Rouge is a radical Communist organization that overthrew an American-backed government in 1975. Under Khmer Rouge rule, hundreds of thousands of Cambodians were imprisoned, worked to death, or executed. The organization's control of Cambodia was ended by a Vietnamese invasion in 1979. Since then, the guerrillas have fought the Cambodian government forces. By 1994, the Khmer Rouge controlled large portions of western Cambodia.

Although the Khmer Rouge signed a United Nations-sponsored peace treaty in 1991, they later backed out of the agreement and refused to take part in national elections. Held in 1993, these elections produced the first freely-elected Cambodian government in more than twenty years. In 1994 and 1995, however, the future of this government was in doubt. Continuing warfare disrupted the harvest in the richest rice-growing areas. Banditry and extortion became common. The rural population, which comprised 80 percent of the population, received few benefits from the new government and became resentful.

Since 1973, the United States had been uninvolved in Indochinese affairs. However, the recent growth of American business interests in Vietnam and the ending of the trade ban with that country refocused U.S. concern there.

This concern grew in 1996. One of the Khmer Rouge, Ieng Sary, broke from that group, declared himself and his followers liberal democrats, and won political recognition from Cambodia's government. Western leaders feared that Sary's influence might destabilize Cambodia's fragile democracy.

1. *Explain why Cambodia needed U.S. aid in 1994.*
2. *Describe the U.S. aid given to Cambodia in 1994.*

The United States and ASEAN

An arms race began in the 1990's among the six nations of the Association of Southeast Asian Nations (ASEAN). The ASEAN nations are Malaysia, Thailand, Indonesia, Singapore, the Philippines, and Brunei.

In addition to the purchase of American, Russian, and British combat aircraft and a wide selection of cheaper weapons from China, the ASEAN members have also been building up their own domestic weapons industries. This military buildup reflected two things: unresolved tensions among the organization's members, and the growing uncertainty about security in Asia. The latter arose from doubts about American intentions.

America's rethinking of its Asian strategy after the end of the cold war resulted in a decline in U.S. troop strength in East Asia of approximately 24,000, or about 18 percent. This withdrawal has made the ASEAN members, who supported the United States during the cold war, nervous about the future. The growth of China's economic and military power and signs that Japan may become more assertive have increased their uncertainty.

Buying more weapons is only one part of ASEAN's response to these dangers. Its members have also decided to enlarge the organization by admitting four more countries: Vietnam, Laos, Cambodia, and Myanmar. In time, this might create a Southeast Asian bloc to balance the power of China and Japan, as well as India—Asia's other potential great power.

Out of these arrangements may emerge a Southeast Asia whose security depends less on American military strength and more on a new balance of power involving the United States, China, Japan, and the ASEAN members. As a first step in that direction, the ASEAN Regional Forum (ARF) was established in 1994. ARF's purpose is to bring together the ASEAN members, their traditional Western allies, and new powers previously excluded from ASEAN meetings, like China and Russia. ARF is regarded as a first step away from the old military arrangements between the United States and individual Asian countries, and the start of a broader international forum for resolving Asia's security problems.

The Clinton Administration hopes that ARF might eventually produce a regional peacekeeping force. This would contribute to the maintenance of security in Southeast Asia without requiring a stronger American commitment.

1. *Define* ASEAN *and* ARF *and explain the difference between the two organizations.*
2. *Identify one way in which recent developments in Southeast Asia are linked to American policies.*

Section Review

1. *Develop arguments for and against American aid to Cambodia.*
2. *PROVE or DISPROVE: The United States was responsible for the military buildup in Southeast Asia in the 1990's.*

America's Military Establishment: Leaner and Meaner

Faced with foreign policy crises in Haiti, Bosnia, Somalia, and Korea, the shrinking U.S. military has been stretched thin in the 1990's. To fund health care and other domestic programs, the Clinton Administration has battled Congress and others for reductions in the defense budget. This has meant a smaller military establishment, with periodic reductions in force and the offer of bonuses to career military personnel to retire early. However, military cutbacks began in the 1970's when the volunteer-army concept replaced the practice of filling the military ranks with *conscripts,* or draftees. As the Selective Service Act expired and the draft boards lost their authority to induct non-volunteers into the military, the armed forces increased pay and benefits to attract qualified recruits. To balance rising personnel costs, the size of the military establishment was reduced. From the more than two million in uniform during the 1970's, the active duty force was reduced to 1.6 million in 1994.

The rising costs of purchasing sophisticated military hardware and maintaining employment levels in defense industries also contributed to the reduction of personnel. In 1994, for example, the Senate voted to add $150 million to the 1995 defense authorization bill to fund the continued production of B-2 stealth bombers. The high-tech planes cost $2.2 billion each. The Clinton Administration's 1993 defense review concluded that 184 long-range bombers would be needed to meet its new policy of being able to fight two regional wars (e.g., Bosnia and North Korea) at the same time. Although the defense budgets projected for the remainder of the 1990's allow mostly for the older-model B-52s and B-1s, the U.S. Air Force has demanded more of the bat-wing stealth B-2 bombers. Two of these can do the work of 75 other bombers while risking the lives of only four aircrew members instead of 132. Should the generals get their way, higher military equipment costs may be offset by more personnel reductions.

It has become standard practice to respond to military crises with forces having special abilities. Among these are the 82nd and 101st Airborne Divisions, Marine amphibious units, airborne command and control squadrons, missile defense batteries, and special operations troops such as Army Rangers and Navy SEALS. These units have been constantly on call. For example, the 2,000 marines of the 24th Marine Expeditionary Unit returned to the United States in mid-1994 after six months at sea off Europe and Somalia. They were immediately ordered back to sea and sent to the Caribbean in anticipation of an invasion of Haiti.

This and similar situations have caused the Defense Department to worry that military morale and efficiency will suffer. The demands on the U.S. military have increased in the 1990's. Specialized units have been spending extended tours enforcing no-fly zones in Iraq and Bosnia, assisting the drug war in Colombia and Peru, and showing American strength in Korea and in Haiti.

For the Clinton Administration, the ability to make security commitments has diminished in the 1990's. A war in Korea, for example, could force the United States to withdraw its promise to send 25,000 troops to enforce a Bosnian peace settlement and to contribute some 10,000 more to maintain order and train police in Haiti. Despite the demands on America to play a leadership role in the maintenance of international security, military realities require cautious policies.

1. *State the size of the U.S. military establishment in 1994.*
2. *Indicate the reasons for the decline in uniformed personnel since the 1970's.*

Section Review

1. *List the military crises to which the United States has responded or promised to respond in the 1990's. Indicate the situations to which you would or would not commit U.S. forces if you were President.*
2. *Explain why you AGREE or DISAGREE with the policy of reducing the size of the military establishment to fund domestic programs.*

Chapter 10 Review

A. *For each question, indicate the correct response.*

1. *The purpose of the U.N. is to (a) preserve global peace (b) direct military operations around the world (c) overthrow dictators.*
2. *By 1994, the U.N. had experienced a dramatic increase in (a) cultural activities (b) industrial development (c) peacekeeping operations.*
3. *Following the loss of American soldiers in Somalia, President Clinton (a) withdrew America from the U.N. (b) set guidelines for U.S. participation in U.N. missions (c) committed more troops to foreign crises.*

4. *Specialized American troops were sent to support U.N. efforts in 1994 to help refugees in (a) Rwanda (b) Ghana (c) Kenya.*
5. *The Clinton Administration achieved a diplomatic triumph by persuading Russia to join (a) NATO (b) the Partnership for Peace (c) the European Union.*
6. *A nation disappointed by U.S. security arrangements in Europe in 1994 was (a) Germany (b) Poland (c) Britain.*
7. *Russia and the United States failed to agree on (a) chemical-weapons production (b) anti-crime measures (c) immigration.*
8. *The American assistance given to Cambodia in the 1990's did not include (a) road-building equipment (b) technical advisers (c) weapons.*
9. *The arms buildup in Southeast Asia in the 1990's resulted from concern about (a) the reduction of U.S. military forces in Asia (b) American aid to Cambodia (c) increased U.S. trade with Vietnam.*
10. *A factor that limited U.S. security commitments in the 1990's was (a) the decline in the combat readiness of specialized units (b) insufficient numbers of B-2 bombers (c) the reduction in military personnel since the 1970's.*

B. *Write a brief essay on America's commitment to international security by answering these questions:*

1. *Is it in the best interests of the United States to assume the role of international policeman?*
2. *How has the United States supported the peacekeeping efforts of the United Nations in the 1990's?*
3. *To what extent have American interactions with NATO and ASEAN helped to preserve global peace?*
4. *How have crises in global trouble spots involved the United States?*
5. *What recommendations would you make to the President of the United States about the ways America can help to maintain international security?*

C. *Select ONE of the leaders below and explain how he has supported or obstructed American policies on international security:*

1. *Boutros Boutros-Ghali*
2. *Boris Yeltsin*
3. *Lech Walesa*

Chapter 11

The United States and the Global Economy

As one of the seven most industrialized nations, the United States has aided the formulation of policies which emphasized free trade and the development of market economies. In pursuit of these goals, the Clinton Administration brought to a successful conclusion negotiations for a new General Agreement on Tariffs and Trade (GATT). This feat required skillful bargaining with the economic representatives of many nations, especially those of the European Union.

America has played a leading role in building the new world economic order of the 1990's.

America also reviewed its economic policies toward Europe and Asia and assisted the expansion of its businesses into foreign markets. These steps were taken to promote the development of more cooperation among nations and more economic opportunities for Americans and the citizens of other nations.

America and the Group of Seven (G-7)

At the 19th annual conference of the world's leading industrial powers—Britain, France, Germany, Italy, Japan, Canada, and the United States—in Tokyo, in 1993, the key global concerns of the 1990's were addressed. These included stimulating world trade by lowering tariffs; ending global recession; reducing chronic unemployment; promoting human rights; limiting nuclear proliferation; and finding a solution to the crisis in Bosnia-Herzegovina.

Also considered was Boris Yeltsin's demand that Russia be

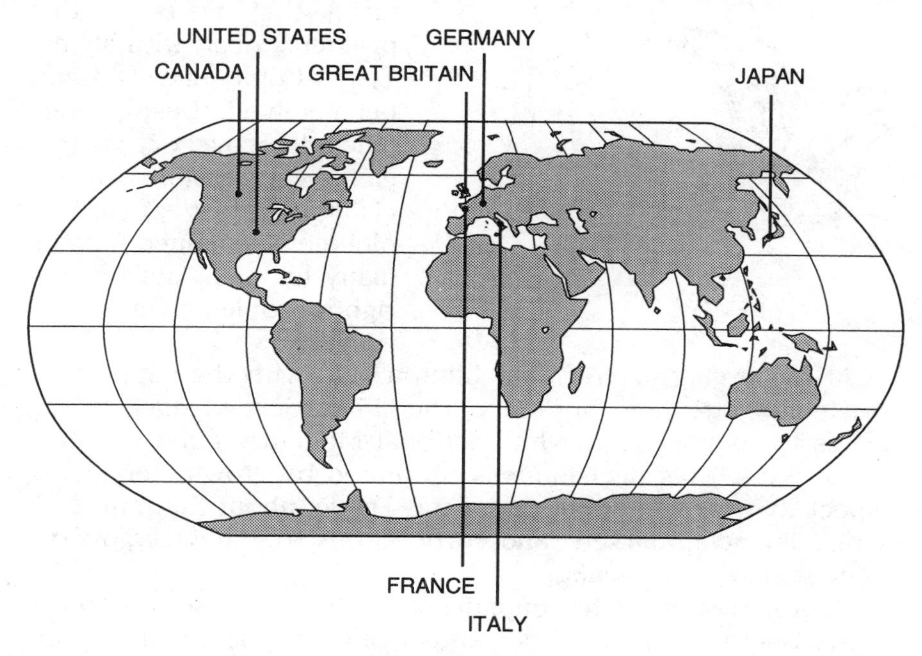

admitted to the Group of Seven. Although Russia's request was denied in 1993, it was granted the following year at the G-7's 20th annual meeting in Naples. As a first step toward strengthening the post-cold war economic and political order, Russia was added to the political decision-making council of the Group of Seven. However, Russia was considered too weak to be included in the economic half of the world summit conference.

Yeltsin was delighted at the outcome of his long diplomatic battle for acceptance by the world's economic leaders. It was a victory made possible by the support of President Clinton. The American and Russian presidents agreed to meet in September, 1994, to speed up the participation of the East European nations in the West's trading and financial systems. Support for the demands of the former Communist countries for equal economic rights and an end to cold-war trade barriers has been the policy of the Clinton Administration.

The effort to find financial, diplomatic, and humanitarian solutions to the growing number of trouble spots, including Bosnia, Haiti, and Rwanda, followed an attempt to find a way of

building a better global economic and financial organization. It was recognized that many of the problems dealt with at the Tokyo Conference had not been solved. Despite significant recovery from the global recession, especially in the West, unemployment remained high in many nations. And human rights problems were multiplying.

At the urging of President Clinton, and with the support of President Mitterrand of France, the G-7 leaders pledged themselves to reorganize the International Monetary Fund and the World Bank. This decision was prompted by growing concern, especially in Washington, Paris, and Tokyo, about the power of banks, financial markets, and corporations to influence government policies and goals.

Clinton demonstrated impatience at the risk posed to American economic growth by demands from the global markets for actions to limit inflation, such as raising interest rates. At his insistence, the final economic statement of the Naples Conference stressed jobs and economic growth as the top priorities of the G-7. As part of the effort to aid economic growth, the G-7 committed itself to debt relief for the poorest Third World nations.

1. *List the members of the Group of Seven.*
2. *Indicate how American policies influenced the Naples Conference.*

Section Review

1. *Write a brief speech for President Clinton in which he urges the G-7 leaders to admit Boris Yeltsin to their group.*

2. *Explain why the United States should or should not support each of the following decisions of the Naples Conference:*
   a. *The IMF and the World Bank must be reorganized.*
   b. *The poorest Third World nations must be assisted to reduce their debts.*
   c. *A new global economic and financial framework must be developed.*
   d. *Economic growth and jobs must remain top G-7 priorities.*

GATT: America's Long Diplomatic Struggle

In December, 1993, Mickey Kantor, Trade Representative of the United States, and Sir Leon Brittan, who held the same position for the European Union, came to agreements about global trade. As a result, the organization known as GATT (General Agreement on Tariffs and Trade) successfully concluded negotiations which had begun in Uruguay in 1986. These negotiations were known as the *Uruguay Round.* The task of those representing the 111 GATT member nations at these discussions was to stimulate world trade by limiting government protection of certain industries and products, and by reducing tariffs. The most important issue included in the Uruguay Round discussions was services. This included banking, insurance, telecommunications, construction, aviation, shipping, tourism, advertising, and broadcasting. Services represent the fastest growing area of world trade.

Created by treaty in 1947, GATT is an international organization that creates rules governing global trade. It also provides its members with opportunities to make deals and settle trade disputes. The primary purpose of GATT is to expand world trade by reducing commercial barriers. All members of GATT must benefit from "Most Favored Nation" (MFN) treatment. This means that a country's products can enter foreign markets under terms no less favorable than those enjoyed by any other country. The MFN provision is designed to make global trade freer and fairer for all 111 treaty members.

During the 1970's and 1980's, GATT was weakened by the desire of the industrialized nations to be more competitive and less cooperative. The United States, Japan, and other nations responded to global recession by practicing protectionism.

They used tariffs and other means to protect endangered industries and products. As MFN requirements were evaded, GATT became unable to prevent disputes such as the trade war between the United States and Japan.

The collapse of GATT would have dealt a severe blow to international cooperation on trade. To prevent this from happening, the Clinton Administration had to ensure a successful conclusion to the Uruguay Round of talks, which had been dragging on for seven years. Failure to reach agreement on the most vital issues by the end of 1993 (the deadline set by GATT's Director-General Peter Sutherland) was a distinct possibility.

U.S. Trade Representative Kantor and EU Commissioner Brittan worked hard to end the Uruguay Round in December, 1993. The United States and the European Union agreed to reduce tariffs on each other's goods by 50 percent on average. Tariffs on goods from the rest of the world would be cut less. It was also decided that industrial nations should lower agricultural tariffs by 36 percent and developing nations by 24 percent. However, negotiators could not reach agreement on free-trade rules involving films, television programs, and music; civil aircraft; shipping; and financial services like stock brokerage and banking. These unresolved issues may cause future disagreements.

The 1993 GATT agreements are expected to stimulate business and investment activity. U.S. exporters, for example, will encounter lower tariffs in major foreign markets on a wide variety of goods. The agreements will also result in the establishment of a World Trade Organization to further expand global trade and settle trade disputes. Supporters of President Clinton regarded the outcome of the Uruguay Round as a major foreign policy victory for his Administration.

1. *Define or identify: GATT, Mickey Kantor, Leon Brittan, MFN, Uruguay Round.*

2. *State some of the agreements reached in December, 1993.*
3. *List those areas in which GATT negotiators could not agree.*

Section Review

- *Explain why you AGREE or DISAGREE with each statement:*
  a. *The collapse of GATT would be a global disaster.*
  b. *The Uruguay Round was a diplomatic triumph for the Clinton Administration.*

America's Trade Partners: Direction Changes in the 1990's

In mid-1994, a report, entitled "Shrinking the Atlantic: Europe and the American Economy," was published. It reflected the conclusions of a series of working groups in Washington. Organized by the European Institute, the purpose of the project was to consider future U.S.-EU cooperation after the completion of the GATT trade talks.

During its first year in office, the Clinton Administration indicated its belief that Europe should no longer be the main focus of American foreign and economic policy. According to Secretary of State Warren Christopher, the United States had been "too Eurocentric for too long." Seeing that U.S.-Asian trade in 1993 reached a record $350 billion, the Administration's trade-oriented policy makers declared that much of America's economic future lay across the Pacific. At this time, too, Europe's trade was experiencing a slowdown because of a recession.

By 1994, however, the tilt toward Asia seemed to be over. Despite the possibility of future trade profits, a number of problems developed. The nuclear crisis with North Korea, the MFN argument with China, and trade disputes with Japan made the Pacific Rim seem more of a headache to the Administration rather than a source of financial opportunities.

In contrast to the Clinton Administration policy, a new report by the Economic Strategy Institute focused on trade patterns in terms of quality rather than quantity. It cited data showed the United States exporting $130 billion worth of goods and services to Asia in 1993, compared to $110 billion to Europe. And it showed the U.S. importing $241 billion from Asia, and only $114 billion from Europe. While U.S.-European trade was in approximate balance, America's 1993 trade with Asia had resulted in a deficit for the U.S. of about $100 billion.

Not only was the transatlantic flow of trade more balanced, it was also healthier and more productive for both partners. In 1993, Europe had $250 billion invested in the United States, in companies which employed 3 million Americans and paid $20 million in American taxes. In contrast, Asia's 1993 investment of $107 billion in the U.S. produced fewer than one million American jobs and paid only $7 million in taxes.

European companies have spent over three cents on research and development in the United States for every dollar invested. Asian companies spent 1.4 cents per investment dollar. A 1991 comparison of European and Japanese businesses in the United States showed that while they exported about the same amount of goods, the Japanese imported many more products from their parent companies in Japan.

Since 1980, the United States has often had a trade surplus with Europe, exporting to that region more than it imported. The Economic Strategy Institute report also referred to the broad agreement between the Atlantic countries and the United States on most of the major issues shaping the global economy. These included labor rights, investment issues, competition policy, and many other matters.

Lane Kirkland, former head of the AFL-CIO, called for "a real NAFTA." Instead of the North American Free Trade Agreement signed in 1993, he proposed a new North Atlantic Free Trade Association that would bring together the United States and the European Union in a free-trade area that would account for more than half the world's economic output.

At the United States–European Union summit in Madrid, Spain, in December, 1995, world leaders discussed a number of proposals for furthering U.S.–European cooperation. This so-called New Transatlantic Agenda included plans to build a New Transatlantic Marketplace by reducing or eliminating tariffs and other barriers to the flow of free trade.

Unfortunately, in 1996, the United States experienced a rising trade deficit with Western Europe. It grew from $800 million in June of that year to $4.2 billion in July.

1. *Describe the changing focus of the Clinton Administration's economic policy.*
2. *Explain why this has happened.*

Formulation of a policy on trade with Japan remained a problem for the Clinton Administration throughout 1994. Central to the problem was the disparity between the continuing flow of Japanese products into the United States and the limits imposed by Japan on American exports to that country. In March, the rising deficit prompted Mickey Kantor, the nation's top trade official, to dismiss Japan's latest proposals for reducing the imbalance as inadequate. Kantor stated the refusal of the United States to reopen trade talks until the Japanese offered stronger measures for opening their markets to American goods.

In May, 1994, the Clinton Administration signaled a new tactic in its trade policy. The Justice Department reached a settlement in a lawsuit against a British glass company whose patents and licenses had prevented American glass companies from operating overseas. The case had little to do with the glass market in the United States. Instead, it sought to make sure that American companies could freely operate in other countries. The action against Pilkington PLC, the world's largest manufacturer of flat glass, was the first such legal case in many years. The Justice Department refused to say whether similar actions were planned against Japanese companies in connection with the Clinton Administration's effort to open Japan's markets to American businesses. It was stated, however, that investigations of other foreign companies were under way.

The case against Pilkington PLC asserted the right of the Justice Department to have jurisdiction over foreign companies operating in the United States. It was recognized that this could be a powerful trade weapon in the future. The Japanese denounced the tactic as a violation of international law.

The United States took an even tougher position in July, 1994, after another collapse in trade talks. The Clinton Administration formally accused Japan of discriminating against American companies when it came to awarding government contracts there for medical equipment and telecommunications gear. To support the claim of discrimination, the office of U.S. Trade Representative Mickey Kantor published figures on Japanese imports of the disputed products. They showed that imports, mostly from the United States, occupy only 5 percent of the market in Japan for telecommunications equipment, compared with 25 percent of the market in other industrialized countries. Also, American companies supply less than 20 percent of the Japanese medical equipment market, compared to nearly 40 percent of the European Union market. In short, a lot more American medical and telecommunications equipment is sold in Europe than is permitted into Japan. Kantor blamed this on discrimination by the Japanese government.

In early 1995, however, it appeared that U.S. goals for the sale of auto parts to Japanese companies would be reached. Hopes declined for a similar increase in the sales to Japan of American cars and other goods. In response, the Clinton Administration threatened a 100 percent increase of tariffs on Japanese cars imported to the United States.

1. *State the objective of the Clinton Administration in its business relations with Japan.*
2. *Describe the tactics used in 1994 and 1995 to achieve this objective.*

Section Review

1. *Explain why you AGREE or DISAGREE with each statement:*
    a. *The focus of American economic policy must remain on Europe.*
    b. *The expanding economies of Asia in the 1990's make trade with that region more important than trade with any other region.*
2. *State your reaction to the desire of AFL-CIO leader Lane Kirkland for a North Atlantic Free Trade Association.*
3. *Develop arguments for and against restrictions on Japanese imports to the United States.*

U.S. Corporations: Overseas Investments and Expansion

By 1994, American businesses were rapidly expanding their operations in other countries. For many, the urge to spread factories, offices, stores, and jobs overseas became irresistible. Lower labor and production costs made overseas operations attractive. While a weak dollar and declining labor costs made it easier to sell American products abroad, overseas investment rose at twice the rate of exports. And the sale of American goods manufactured and distributed abroad earned for U.S. companies twice what was earned from goods made in America and exported. Experts urged American firms to grow by producing in many countries.

This trend troubles American workers and labor unions. Fearing the loss of jobs to Europeans, Asians, and Latin Americans, they would prefer to see American businesses expand at home. In 1994, American companies employed 5.4 million people overseas, 80 percent of them in manufacturing. From the ranks of labor have come appeals for the production of those goods and services by Americans.

Expansion abroad, however, contributes to the growth of the global economy and the influence of U.S. firms in world markets. Also, American investment overseas has been largely concentrated in manufacturing, which was more of a growth area in the 1980's than it is in the 1990's. Today, service industries provide more jobs to Americans seeking to enter the labor market than does manufacturing.

It should be noted that the opening of American-owned enterprises abroad does not necessarily result in the closing of plants or the reduction of operations in the United States. For instance, Wal-Mart's retail investments in Canada, Brazil, and Mexico have not led to job reductions at home. The same has been true of Morgan Stanley, an investment banking firm, which has eight offices in East Asia.

Expanding economies in such East Asian countries as China,

Singapore, and Hong Kong have drawn American investment. So has nearly every Western Hemisphere country, especially Canada, Mexico, Argentina, and Bermuda. Bermuda has been an offshore haven for American banking and insurance companies. Canada, Mexico, and Argentina have attracted mainly investment in manufacturing.

1. *Describe the movement abroad of American businesses in the 1990's.*
2. *Explain why this trend has worried labor unions.*

Many prominent American businesses have moved their manufacturing operations abroad. They develop a market for their products in the same area where they manufacture. For example, the Gillette Company, which makes razors and razor blades, prefers to manufacture and sell abroad rather than export its products. One reason is that sales have been greater elsewhere than in America. Over the years, Gillette has put 62 factories into 28 countries. The company has found that being close to local markets in foreign countries brought better profits than did shipping their products from the United States. In 1994, Gillette employed 7,700 people overseas.

In April, 1994, the Ford Motor Company announced its most sweeping reorganization in 25 years. It took steps to improve its competitive position in the coming decades in its established North American and European markets and in the potentially huge car and truck markets developing in Asia. The plan called for the consolidation of its North American and European operations into a single unit, Ford Automotive Operations, which would do business globally. Ford's Asian-Pacific and Latin American operations would remain separate for the time being.

Ford has factories in 30 countries and more than 322,000 employees worldwide. The reorganization will enable America's second-largest automaker to reduce the costs of materials and other development expenses. A wider variety of cars and trucks will be produced more cheaply for diverse markets around the world.

Another American giant also expanded its global operations. The Sprint Corporation announced in June, 1994, that it would form a global alliance with the state-owned telephone

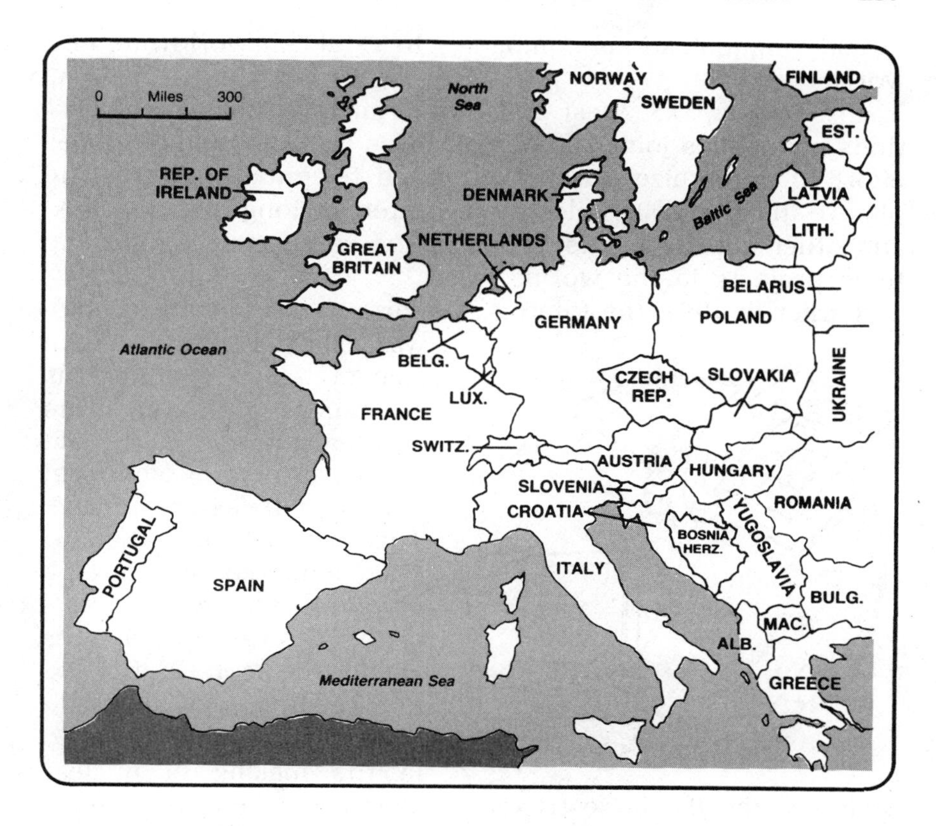

companies of France and Germany to compete in the fast-growing international communications business. The deal would make Sprint the technical pacesetter in a partnership with Europe's two largest telecommunications companies, Deutsche Telekom and France Telecom. While each company would control its operations within its own country, the three would combine forces for a global network and an international operating company. If approved by the U.S., French, and German governments, the arrangement would enable Sprint, the third-largest American long distance carrier, to better compete with its bigger rivals, AT&T and MCI Communications.

A week after the announcement by Sprint, AT&T formed an alliance with the telephone companies of Sweden, Switzerland, and the Netherlands to provide advanced communication services to multinational companies. Also at this time, MCI Communications obtained approval from the Justice Department to form an alliance with British Telecommunications. These events reflected a major development of the 1990's: the race by all communications companies to establish worldwide networks.

In addition, U.S. West and other American telecommunications companies joined European firms in a multibillion dollar effort to modernize Russia's outdated telephone system. The plan to install 31,000 miles of new intercity long distance lines and other improvements is one of the largest telecommunications projects in the world.

Earlier in 1994, the Clinton Administration abandoned cold-war export controls on the sale of telecommunications equipment and computers to China, Russia, and most other former Communist countries in Eastern Europe. This move is expected to open a market worth $150 billion over the next decade. Although restrictions would be kept on the export of supercomputers and material that could be used in the making of nuclear weapons, the list of restricted products was being shortened so that American companies could take better advantage of growing markets in China and the former Soviet bloc. U.S. manufacturers welcomed the news.

American firms expanded their operations into the former Communist countries with a variety of projects in 1994 and 1995. Rockwell International Corporation embarked on a space-age modernization of Russia's air traffic control system. Chevron, the U.S. oil giant, formed a joint venture with the former Soviet republic of Kazakhstan to invest $20 billion to develop the vast Tengiz oil field near the Caspian Sea. This area contains some of the richest sources of oil and gas on earth. The Kellogg Company moved into Latvia to sell corn flakes and other breakfast cereals, opening a new factory on the outskirts of Riga, the capital.

In Eastern Europe, negotiations began between McDonald's and the Polish city of Cracow. The government of this historic medieval city was not enthusiastic about the presence of the fast-food vendor in its main square, although McDonald's has thirteen restaurants in other cities of Poland. In impoverished Albania, Coca-Cola opened a $10 million bottling plant.

1. *Give examples of American business expansion abroad in:*
   a. *telecommunications*
   b. *automobiles*
   c. *food services and products*
2. *State the motivation for the desire of U.S. companies to build factories and invest in foreign countries.*

Section Review

1. *PROVE or DISPROVE: The movement of American business operations to foreign countries is good for the global economy, but bad for the United States.*
2. *Complete the following sentences:*
   a. *By opening factories and offices in foreign countries, American businesses can increase profits by ______.*
   b. *American telecommunications firms have taken steps to ______.*
   c. *The Clinton Administration removed export limitations on ______.*

The Fall and Rise of the Dollar

In the early years of the 20th century, the United States practiced *Dollar Diplomacy.* This involved the use of American military power to protect U.S. business interests wherever threatened. Throughout Latin America, political turmoil and disruption resulted in the invasion of countries by U.S. forces to restore order and prevent damage to American-owned businesses and property. This policy, widely regarded as a form of imperialism, earned America considerable hatred. Dollar Diplomacy ended with the presidency of Franklin D. Roosevelt (1933–45), who replaced it with the *Good Neighbor Policy.*

In the view of some economists, President Clinton practiced a new form of Dollar Diplomacy in the 1990's. It involved using the value of the dollar to achieve economic goals and protect

American economic interests. In mid-1994, the value of the dollar abroad fell to its lowest level since World War II. Measured against the Japanese yen and the German mark, which are the strongest currencies in world financial markets, the dollar moved from approximately 110 yen (in January) to an unprecedented 100 yen (in June) and from 1.6 marks to 1.5 marks (in July). It also fell against the Canadian, British, and some other European currencies. The dollar declined even further in early 1995.

A decline in the value of the dollar increases the cost of living for all Americans, whether traveling abroad or remaining at home. The dollar fell in the summer of 1994 for a variety of reasons. The most important was the continuing weakness of the American economy. For a long time, America has spent too much and saved too little. The result has been both a federal deficit and a trade deficit. America has purchased more than it can afford from many countries, especially Japan. The flow of imports has been paid for in dollars. By 1994, our trading partners had an oversupply of American currency, thus driving down the price of the dollar.

The Clinton Administration was expected to take action to reverse the fall of the dollar. By persuading the Federal Reserve Board to raise interest rates, Americans would be encouraged to save more and spend less. Secretary of the Treasury Lloyd Bentsen stated, in July, 1994, that a stronger dollar was in everyone's interest. Administration officials, however, noted that the value of the Japanese yen was rising as the dollar was falling. Washington began to hope that this would make American products cheaper for the Japanese to buy, thus reducing our trade deficit with Japan. While creating problems for American consumers, such a strategy might benefit U.S. industries. As the dollar continued its fall, Clinton was accused of "dollar bashing" and of practicing a new form of Dollar Diplomacy.

◆ *Describe the fall of the dollar in mid-1994 and explain why this was bad for consumers.*

In late July, 1994, however, the Administration denied that it wanted to use a weakened dollar as a weapon against Japan. Concern that the decline of the dollar would lead to price inflation led to efforts to "talk the dollar up" in world financial markets. Administration officials made statements about the possibility of a rise in interest rates to stabilize the dollar. Eventually, the Federal Reserve Board did raise interest rates. This increased confidence and the dollar began to slowly rise against the yen, the mark, and other currencies. It was recognized, however, that the underlying problems which had caused the decline of the dollar remained. This was demonstrated when the dollar fell again in early 1995. A major reason for its decline was an economic crisis in Mexico which drove down the value of the peso. Fears arose that the Clinton Administration would give large amounts of aid money to Mexico. This would further increase the federal deficit. Demands were made for another increase in interest rates.

The events of mid-1994 brought a reexamination of the policy of increasing the cost of Japanese products by driving up the value of the yen. Economists pointed out that although the dollar had been declining against the yen for years, the only result was a yearly deficit with Japan of $60 billion.

In October of 1996, the dollar, though still weak, reached a new 33-month high against the yen. This rise was caused by the slow-paced recovery of Japan's economy and the election victory of its Liberal Democrat party. Both developments were considered signs that Japanese interest rates would remain low.

The dollar, however, fell against other currencies. Historically, countries with large deficits and weak currencies have declined in prosperity. The Clinton Administration has been urged to study the example of countries like Chile and Argentina. Their efforts to reduce government spending and balance their budgets have begun to improve living standards.

◆ *Explain why President Clinton was accused of "dollar bashing" in mid-1994.*

Section Review

1. *PROVE or DISPROVE: The U.S. continues to spend too much and save too little. The falling dollar is the world's way of canceling America's credit card.*

2. *Develop arguments for and against using the decline in the value of the dollar to solve the trade problems of the United States.*
3. *List some ideas for improving the value of the dollar.*

Chapter 11 Review

A. *For each question, indicate the correct response.*

1. *At the 1994 conference of the Group of Seven, the United States supported (a) the building of NATO bases in Eastern Europe (b) admission of Russia to the G-7 (c) abolition of GATT.*
2. *The final economic statement of the Naples Conference reflected President Clinton's policies by stressing (a) jobs and economic growth (b) increased interest rates (c) devaluation of currencies.*
3. *The Clinton Administration succeeded in bringing to a conclusion in 1993 the trade negotiations known as the (a) Tokyo Conference (b) Moscow Summit (c) Uruguay Round.*
4. *Among the agreements reached by GATT members in 1993 was (a) elimination of all tariffs (b) creation of a World Trade Organization (c) regulation of films and television programs.*
5. *Upon taking office, the Clinton Administration focused economic policies on trade with (a) Asia (b) Europe (c) Africa.*
6. *In 1994, the Clinton Administration's concern with balanced trade and investment in the United States resulted in renewed focus on trade with (a) Asia (b) Europe (c) Africa.*
7. *A trend of American business activities in the 1990's has been (a) reduction of foreign operations and investments (b) opening factories and offices abroad (c) withdrawal of American employees from foreign countries.*
8. *American companies have been active in finding foreign partners in the field of (a) telecommunications (b) computer technology (c) weapons and military equipment.*
9. *In 1994, the dollar dropped severely in value against the (a) pound (b) lira (c) yen.*
10. *President Clinton was accused of attempting to use the decline of the dollar to (a) reduce inflation (b) increase savings (c) decrease trade deficits.*

B. *Write an essay about the role of the United States in shaping the global economy by answering each of the following questions:*

1. *How successful has American leadership been in the Group of Seven and GATT?*
2. *How does America gain both benefits and problems from its trading partners?*
3. *How have steps taken by U.S. corporations in the 1990's strengthened the global economy?*
4. *How can America be hurt by a falling dollar?*

C. *Identify these officials and explain how each has contributed to the development of U.S. economic policy:*

1. *Mickey Kantor*
2. *Lloyd Bentsen*

Unit III Review

A. *As the world's sole military superpower, the United States has been expected to play a major role in creating a safer and more prosperous world. This has raised a number of problems for American policy makers.*

Use information from Unit III to describe the ways in which the United States has responded to each of the following:

1. *By 1994, the global security role of the United Nations had expanded dramatically. More troops and funding were demanded of the United States.*
2. *Russia has opposed full NATO membership for Eastern European nations.*
3. *Germany's leaders wish their country to play a full role in NATO and U.N. peacekeeping.*
4. *Cambodia is in danger of another Khmer Rouge takeover.*
5. *The ASEAN nations have had doubts about America's commitment to their security.*
6. *Problems discussed at the Tokyo Conference of 1993 were not resolved by the G-7.*

7. *The collapse of GATT in 1993 would have dealt a severe blow to international cooperation on trade.*

B. *Use information from Unit III to write a speech for President Clinton to be given to the students of your school. Help the President to do the following:*

1. *Describe the security problems which America must face in the 1990's.*
2. *Explain the global economic goals of the United States and how they might be accomplished.*

C. *Use information found in Unit III to write an article to accompany ONE of the following newspaper headlines:*

U.S. SECURITY COMMITMENTS INCREASING

CLINTON ADMINISTRATION DEVELOPS NEW TRADE TACTICS

AMERICAN BUSINESSES EXPANDING OVERSEAS

PRESIDENT ACCUSED OF DOLLAR BASHING

D. *Provide arguments FOR or AGAINST each of the following opinions:*

1. *The U.S. should play a stronger role in maintaining international security.*
2. *American trade policies strengthen the global economy.*
3. *The decline of the dollar is bad for American consumers, but good for American industries.*

UNIT IV

THE AMERICAN AGENDA FOR THE 1990'S: ISSUES AND PROBLEMS

In every age, Americans have struggled to overcome problems threatening the quality of their lives. The 1990's have been no exception. At home and abroad, great issues have demanded attention, including environmental destruction, the global drug trade, and international terrorism. These strike at the heart of American life and raise doubts about the nation's future.

Another problem requiring a response from the government has been nuclear proliferation. As the last of the superpowers, America has led the effort to limit the number of members of the world's "nuclear club."

Finally, the 1990's has been the decade when Americans seek to set their goals for the upcoming 21st century.

Chapter 12

The Battle for the Environment

During the 1990's, Americans became increasingly determined to save the planet Earth from environmental destruction. The efforts of concerned individuals and organizations such as the Sierra Club, Earthwatch, Greenpeace, and the Audubon Society have sharpened awareness of the dangers to air, water, soil, forests, and wildlife.

To guard the environment from its enemies, several efforts have begun. Some involve community programs such as recycling of garbage and other waste materials. Educational institutions have introduced courses of study in environmental science. New laws have restricted the production of chemicals which pollute the atmosphere and limited the disposal of toxic wastes. Greater stress has been placed on non-polluting forms of energy such as solar power, nuclear power, windmill power, natural gas, and fuels which do not burn carbon. Pressure has been exerted on the automobile industry to reduce emissions and to develop an electric car.

America alone cannot save the environment. The battle must be global and involve many other countries and the United Nations. The United States has entered into many international treaties to limit the manufacture and use of pollutants, and also to protect endangered wildlife.

At home, environmentalists and concerned citizens have strongly pressured political leaders to secure the environment for future generations. Public opinion, however, has not been unanimous. Some Americans have resisted the impact of environmental measures on their lives, resorting to legal action to protect property rights and other interests.

Political change has also affected the environmental struggle. In early 1995, the Republican-dominated House of Representatives approved sweeping changes in the enforcement of environmental regulations. Their new bill emphasized economic concerns. Environmentalists opposed the antiregulatory position taken by the House. The environmental battle of the 1990's has included the search for a balance between environmental protection and individual rights.

1. *List the things that environmentalists wish to protect.*
2. *Describe some of the actions taken by Americans to protect the environment.*

Environmental Politics

Although the main issue in the 1992 and 1996 U.S. Presidential election campaigns was the economy, the environment also played an important role. In 1992, the Clinton campaign benefited from the charges of groups working for the environment that previous Republican Administrations had neglected environmental concerns. Many voters favored environmental preservation in 1992, but they were more worried at that time about job opportunities and income. Long before the elections, however, experts had already debated whether the environment or economic recovery should receive the most funding.

The argument extended into a number of areas. One of the most important was the survival of endangered wildlife species. In the 1990's, for example, the duck population had its steepest decline since the 1930's. To protect this population, environmentalists demanded that limits be set on the economic development of wetlands, the habitat of ducks and other threatened species. Such groups as construction companies and real estate developers resisted this proposal.

On the other side of the issue, environmentalists protested over a reduction in regulations limiting the amount of pollutants that businesses can emit into the air.

Efforts to clean up water and air pollution by energy sources included a 1992 federal energy law that set new standards for lighting and electric motors. It imposed safeguards at hydroelectric plants to protect fish and other wildlife. The law also held out incentives for developing sources of clean energy, such as solar and wind power. Public utility companies joined the effort to reduce the demand for electricity by promoting the use of high-efficiency appliances and better methods of home insulation.

Attempts were also made to preserve the nation's older forests. The courts have periodically halted the logging of the forests of the Pacific Northwest because this area is the habitat of the endangered northern spotted owl. Environmentalists have been encouraged by the movement of some of the logging industry from the Northwest to the South, where fewer endangered species exist.

To prevent soil erosion, an increasing number of farmers began to use conservation tillage methods. This involves leaving a third of each field unplanted. Besides preventing erosion, conservation tillage lowers the cost of some crop yields and reduces the need for pesticides and fertilizers.

Overgrazing by livestock also causes soil erosion. Environmentalists and ranchers have argued bitterly about the grazing of cattle on public rangelands. In early 1995, the Interior Department made changes in grazing policy designed to better protect millions of acres of federal land used by livestock. It did not, however, raise grazing fees for ranchers.

1. *Why did a debate over national priorities begin in the 1990's?*
2. *State two examples of the environmental controversy.*

The Environment in the 1996 Campaign

In 1996, the economy had improved enough for voters to focus more on environmental problems. During the last year of his first term, Clinton signed several environmentally friendly measures. Among these were the Safe Drinking Water Act, signed on August 6, 1996, and an order, signed on September 18, to create the Utah Land Monument. The first act tightened the standards set in the Safe Drinking Water Act of 1974. This bill easily passed the House and Senate to become law. Clinton's order to create the Utah Land Monument was more controversial, however. Since the order forbade development and mining in this coal-rich area, the Utah legislature and the state's mining companies threatened to challenge in the courts Clinton designation of the land as a monument.

Clinton's campaign platform included a promise to invest $2 billion for expediting projects to reduce pollution. The plan's main feature was an allocation of about $1.3 billion to clean up toxic waste sites. The President also planned to use large amounts of the funding to reduce industrial pollution.

Clinton also endorsed a new plan to prevent destruction of the Florida Everglades by fertilizers in the run-off water from sugar plantations. The proposal was contested by sugar growers, who mainly objected to a tax that the plan imposed. Other Floridians, however, seemed to welcome this effort to restore the Everglades, which are important to Florida's tourist industry. Clinton made much of this idea in his Florida campaign, which cheered environmentalists. Florida voters, however, indicated that they wanted no new tax on sugar growers.

Section Review

1. *List an environmental development in each area:*

   a. wildlife *c. water* *e. forests*
   b. air *d. energy* *f. soil*

2. *State an example of conflict between environmental and economic concerns.*

Environmentalists vs. Property Owners

The Clinton Administration has taken a strong pro-environment position. Leaders in the environmental movement have been given top government jobs, and Vice President Gore is the author of a best-selling book on the subject. In 1994, however, the movement faltered. Environmentalists ("greens") came under media attack as dreamers who did not care about the problems of ordinary working people. Moreover, the movement suffered political setbacks. A green Bureau of Land Management chief left office, and a bill that would have made the Environmental Protection Agency (EPA) an executive department with cabinet rank was killed in Congress.

Some regarded these events as the opening shots of a war between environmentalists and a growing political force known as the *property-rights* movement. Its advocates have challenged the Clean Water Act, the Endangered Species Act, and other environmental laws. The property-rights people maintain that the government should compensate landowners whenever green regulations lower the value of property. Claiming that government regulation of privately owned land is a form of theft, they seek to restrict the use of laws and rules designed to protect the environment.

The property-rights movement developed in the 1980's. By 1994, it had become a powerful force composed of hundreds of organizations backed by conservative and special-interest groups. Among their supporters are loggers, farmers, land developers, miners, and oil and gas producers. To support their claim that government regulation of private property without compensation is a denial to property owners of due process of law and other Constitutional protections, they cite the Fifth Amendment. This portion of the Bill of Rights contains a clause which says ". . . nor shall private property be taken for public use, without just compensation."

1. *Identify the issue which has divided environmentalists and property-rights activists.*

2. *List some of the groups which have supported the property-rights movement.*

The Legal Struggle

Property-rights activists have fought their anti-environmentalist campaign in the courts. Despite winning several legal victories in the 1990's, they have not been permitted to bypass all government regulation. In a number of landmark cases, the Supreme Court has stated that reasonable regulation of land use is constitutional, and that the government need not pay complainants every time regulations lower property values. However, the Supreme Court did rule that compensation must be given for two reasons: if a property owner suffers a permanent "physical occupation," such as government mandated cable television lines; or if environmental regulation causes the property to lose all economic value.

Unable to win a total victory in the Supreme Court, the property-rights movement carried its campaign to Congress. There they have attempted to attach property-rights amendments to every important piece of environmental legislation. In so doing, they placed obstacles in the path of the Clinton Administration's environmental efforts. In October, 1993, for example, a proposed property-rights amendment to legislation authorizing a government survey of plant and animal species was so heavily debated that the renewal of the Endangered Species Act was delayed for a year. Property-rights advocates won a victory in March, 1995. The House of Representatives passed a bill that would prohibit federal agencies from protecting wetlands or endangered species unless landowners are compensated for any resulting decline in their property's value. The bill, however, was defeated in the Senate.

Property-rights activists have also taken their fight to the state legislatures. Between 1992–94, they persuaded 39 states to consider property-rights legislation. Most of these measures would require states to consider the potential cost of compensating property owners before writing any new environmental regulations. By 1994, only four states—Delaware, Utah, Indiana, and Washington—had passed such laws. The other 35 states defeated the bills, fearing that basic health and environmental protections would be undermined.

The controversy between the environmentalists and the property-rights movement has become a question of how to balance private rights with the public good. It also involves the need to ensure that corporations and businesses can use the land they own to expand economic operations without jeopardizing land, water, air, and wildlife.

Section Review

1. *PROVE or DISPROVE: Environmental laws and regulations prevent farmers, loggers, oil producers, and others from earning a living. These laws are, therefore, a denial of the rights of private property owners to use their land as they see fit.*
2. *Explain why you AGREE or DISAGREE with the argument of environmentalists that profits and economic growth are less important than the survival of the land.*

Protecting Wildlife at Home and Abroad

In April, 1994, the Clinton Administration took two important steps to change government management of logging operations in the nation's remaining ancient forests. They first directed the U.S. Forest Service to cancel a 50-year contract with the Alaska Pulp Corporation. Environmentalists had attacked the corporation because it permitted the cutting of timber in the Tongass National Forest in southeastern Alaska. The second requested Judge William Dwyer of the U.S. District Court in Seattle, Washington, to allow some logging in the old forests of the Pacific Northwest.

In 1989, Judge Dwyer issued the nation's most comprehensive order against logging in old forests. The court orders resulted in the closing of lumber mills in the Northwest and the unemployment of thousands of workers. The Clinton Administration was concerned about both the environment and the economy. To put some of the people back to work, a partial resumption of logging operations was needed. But the Northern forests are the home of the spotted owl and other endangered species the Administration had to protect.

To satisfy Judge Dwyer's strict standards for environmental protection, the Clinton Administration presented a panoramic plan for environmental management across a landscape of millions of acres and hundreds of species. It was the most ambitious example to date of the new science of ecosystem management. (An *ecosystem* is the interaction of living organisms with their environment.) The Clinton Administration has identified itself with this new science.

The Administration plan requires careful analysis of the impact of logging on rivers, streams, and wildlife while providing economic stimulation to the Northwest. It has been attacked by the environmentalists, who argue that it does not provide sufficient protection to endangered wildlife, and is intended to appease the logging industry. The timber interests have also rejected the plan because it does not increase the logging operations.

Legal challenges in federal courts are expected to prevent the Clinton environmental management plan from going into effect for a long while. The strategy of the logging industry has been to create conflicting court decisions. This might encourage Congress to write a law allowing a greater amount of timber to be cut.

1. *Identify the environmental actions taken by the Clinton Administration in 1994.*
2. *Describe the conflicting reactions to these measures.*

Poachers: The Wildlife Killers

According to the U.S. Fish and Wildlife Service, there are few species that enterprising Americans have been unwilling to kill or kidnap in the country's national parks. *Poaching* (illegal hunting) has been a problem since the parks were founded in the 19th century. In the 1990's, however, the illegal hunting of protected wildlife has soared. Wildlife enforcement officials, for example, estimated in 1994 that 3,000 American black bears are taken illegally every year.

Poachers operate in nearly half of America's 366 park areas, the very places designated for the preservation of wildlife. Poachers supply animal parts to illegal traffickers who do business in at least 17 states. They sell bear paws as food delicacies and bear gallbladders for medicinal ingredients. Rare butterflies are netted for collectors around the world. Deer, elk, and moose are beheaded for decorations. The illegal killing of animals is a $200 million a year business. The victims include large animals and more than 100 other species. The Park Service has warned that at least 20 of these wildlife species could become extinct in the 21st century if the killing continues at the current rate.

Snake poaching is a multimillion-dollar industry. Poachers sell skins and live specimens to pet shops and private collectors through mail-order houses. In 1994, scientists studying a plague of rats in communities surrounding Big Bend National Park in Texas concluded that the problem resulted from the absence of snakes. The natural predators of rats had been nearly poached out. As part of the effort to prevent this ecosystem destruction, an anti-poaching unit of the U.S. Park Service arrested 27 people in July, 1994. All were part of a crime ring, extending from Texas to Florida, engaged in snake poaching.

There are an estimated 7,200 state and federal wildlife agents, 200 of whom are special agents of the U.S. Fish and Wildlife Service. Their assignment is to protect 750,000 square miles of national parks across the United States. This is a very small force struggling to control a big problem. For example, at Yellowstone National Park, 60 full-time rangers patrol an area larger than Delaware and Rhode Island combined.

Environmentalists have urged the hiring of more rangers and passage of tougher federal laws, already quite rigorous. Under existing law, poaching penalties can go as high as $250,000 and up to five years imprisonment. Law enforcers also try to use state laws to prosecute poachers caught in national parks. In August, 1994, the Center for Wildlife Law, in Albuquerque, New Mexico, reported an ongoing effort to strengthen federal laws and coordinate them with state laws.

1. *Describe the poaching problem in our national parks.*
2. *State the danger arising from this problem.*

Wildlife Diplomacy

The United States is also engaged in efforts to protect endangered wildlife in other countries. In April, 1994, the

Clinton Administration announced that it was imposing trade sanctions on Taiwan for refusing to halt the sale of tiger bones and rhinoceros horns. This was the first time that the American government employed economic weapons to protect the environment. While trade sanctions have often been used by the United States as a lever to promote human rights or to lower trade barriers imposed by other countries, they had never been used to protect endangered wildlife.

Tiger and rhinoceros parts are used by people in Taiwan and many other Asian nations as medicines. Demand has become so widespread that an underground trade has developed. The number of these animals still alive has been in steep decline. President Clinton warned that the species could be extinct in five years if the illegal trade in rhinos and tigers is not stopped.

The American environmental actions drew attention to the fact that as trade becomes more global and as barriers between countries come down, the environmental consequences can be enormous. When advances in hunting techniques are combined with lower trade barriers and rapidly growing populations that demand medicines derived from wildlife, a species can be quickly wiped out. The tiger is especially in danger. In 1900, the world's tiger population was estimated at about 100,000. In 1994, fewer than 6,000 remained. The same has happened to the rhinoceros. Its numbers declined from more than 65,000 African black rhinos in 1970 to fewer than 1,800 of that species in 1994.

Wildlife diplomacy has also brought the United States into conflict with Norway and Japan. Despite a worldwide ban on commercial whaling, both nations revived their whaling industries in the 1990's. In 1993, Japan killed more than 300 minke whales in Antarctica. An exemption to the international ban allows whale hunting for scientific study. Japan has satisfied its consumers' demand for whale meat by selling the meat from their scientific hunts.

Antarctic waters are the largest feeding ground for whales. It is one of the last areas of the world in which the minke whale is still plentiful. All other types of whales that have been hunted in the past have been reduced to a fraction of their original numbers.

In May, 1994, the United States voted with a majority of member nations of the International Whaling Commission to create a vast sanctuary for whales in Antarctica. The measure put nearly a quarter of the world's oceans, including all waters south of Australia, Africa, and South America, permanently off-limits to commercial whaling. Only Japan voted against the measure. Norway abstained.

1. *Describe the Clinton Administration's 1994 efforts to protect wildlife abroad.*
2. *Explain why the increase in global trade has made "wildlife diplomacy" necessary.*

The California Desert Protection Act of 1994

The largest land and wildlife conservation measure since the 1980 Alaska Lands Act was approved by Congress in mid-1994, when it designated 9.4 million acres of California desert as a national park. The area includes 90 mountain ranges, sand dunes as high as 700 feet, Indian rock paintings, the world's largest forest of cactus-like Joshua trees, the only known dinosaur tracks in California, and more than 2,000 species of plant and wildlife, including the endangered desert tortoise.

The creation of this park was a major victory for environmentalists. They had made protection of the desert area a prime goal. However, the bill also created a new Mojave National Preserve, a lesser designation that allows hunting, trapping, and fishing. The Sierra Club called the Desert Protection Act "the most significant land protection measure ever considered for the lower 48 states." In addition to the desert tortoise, the area is home to deer, bighorn sheep, rabbits, and quail.

- *Explain the importance to environmentalists of the California Desert Protection Act.*

Section Review

1. *Evaluate the efforts of the Clinton Administration to protect wildlife at home and abroad. Identify measures never before taken by the United States government. Express your opinion of these measures.*

2. *Develop arguments for and against harsh penalties for those caught poaching in national parks.*
3. *Explain why you AGREE or DISAGREE with those who argue that economic activities, such as logging, are more important than wildlife protection.*

Technology and the Environment

In May, 1994, the Clinton Administration announced its intention to give the agricultural biotechnology industry broad authority to market genetically engineered crops without intensive government review. This allowed farm products that have been genetically altered to grow bigger and better to be sold to consumers without interference from government regulators.

President Clinton and Vice President Gore strongly supported the new technology, which they considered largely harmless and favorable for economic growth. Under current regulations, the Department of Agriculture requires biotechnology companies to advise the government of field tests of genetically engineered crops. Since 1987, approximately 2,000 field trials have been conducted without problems in 42 states and Puerto Rico. Vegetables, fruits, and grains containing genes from a variety of sources have been tested.

Under the Clinton plan, most of the new crops will be exempt, after field testing, from further federal monitoring when they are sold to the public. The only altered crops the Administration wants to observe more closely are those containing bacterial genes that produce a natural defense against insects. The marketing of these plants will be monitored by the Environmental Protection Agency (EPA).

However, while biotechnology executives shared the enthusiasm of the President and the Vice President, some Americans have been skeptical about genetically altered crops. Scientists from Michigan State University, for example, have questioned the adequacy of the government's regulation of the new crops. They raised the possibility that plants engineered to be resistant to viruses might lead to new types of viruses that could cause widespread damage to American crops. A debate began within the scientific community. Some supported the caution of the Michigan State University researchers. Others accused them of overestimating the risks. The Department of Agriculture gave assurances that the government was doing all that was necessary to ensure public safety.

Among the new farm products approved for marketing in 1994 were a tomato engineered to stay on the vine longer, to improve taste, and a genetically altered cow hormone. The cow hormone, sold to farmers to increase milk production, alarmed some consumers. In New York, Seattle, Atlanta, and other cities, protests arose about the safety of milk.

1. *Explain the Clinton Administration plan to stimulate economic growth in the farm industry.*
2. *State the concerns of some scientists and consumers.*

American Efforts to Prevent Global Warming

Environmentalists anxious about possible changes in the world's climate were heartened by President Clinton's pronouncements in August, 1994. He decided that the 1992 international treaty, the Earth Summit, to reduce the threat of global warming, required energetic support.

Signed during the Bush Administration, the treaty calls for a reduction in the amount of certain "greenhouse gases" from the atmosphere, the air that we live in. Greenhouse gases, mainly carbon dioxide, result from the burning of fuels that are used principally in automobiles.

When the amount of carbon in the atmosphere increases dramatically, the carbon-rich air surrounding the globe prevents the heat, generated on Earth, from escaping to the upper atmosphere. This condition, by which the temperature of Earth's atmosphere is raised, is called the *greenhouse effect.*

In October, 1993, the Administration adopted a short-term plan to control carbon dioxide and other greenhouse gases. By mid-1994, however, it was acknowledged that the plan would not meet the emissions targets set for the year 2000. Lower than expected oil prices encouraged higher gasoline consumption. Also, some power plants increased their use of coal, rather than natural gas. And stronger economic growth increased industry's use of carbon-burning energy.

In response, federal agencies were ordered to develop new methods for reducing emissions of greenhouse gases from automobiles. Energy Secretary Hazel O'Leary stated her desire to put more emphasis on alternative-fuel vehicles (those which do not burn gasoline), especially the electric car.

While encouraged by the government's favorable reaction to the problem, environmentalists were less satisfied with the reluctance of the Administration to raise federal standards for fuel efficiency in automobiles. They sought to require automakers to build cars which could run farther on less gasoline. Instead, the government indicated its preference for reducing automobile emissions by steps that would cut gasoline consumption.

During his campaign for the Presidency, Clinton promised to set higher standards for automobile fuel efficiency. His Administration, however, preferred to rely upon voluntary measures by industry to reduce the use of carbon-burning fuels. Environmentalists claimed that the voluntary approach did little to reduce automobile pollution. By mid-1994, the Administration was convinced of the need for tough measures. However, it became difficult to sell this idea to the Republican-dominated Congress in 1995. The Contract With America called for less government regulation.

1. *Explain why environmentalists were pleased by some, but not all, of the conclusions reached by the Clinton Administration in mid-1994.*
2. *State the approach of the Clinton Administration to the task of reducing air pollution.*

The Race to Build Electric Vehicles (EV)

By 1994, more than half of California's 30 million residents lived in areas in which air pollution regularly reached unhealthful levels. Since half of the pollution had been caused by automobile emissions, state laws were passed to reduce the amount of poisonous gases emitted by cars into the air. Now, new cars emit 97 percent fewer pollutants than old ones. Nevertheless, California has not enjoyed a cleaner atmosphere, because residents drove 260 billion miles in 1993, nearly triple the number driven in 1973.

California was determined to solve the pollution problem and gradually achieve zero automobile emissions. In May, 1994, California regulators reaffirmed that by 1998, some 2 percent of the vehicles sold in the state by major automakers must be electrics. This number will increase to 5 percent by 2001 and 10 percent by 2003. New York and Massachusetts will require EV's by 1999. Similar measures are being considered by 10 other Eastern states and the District of Columbia.

To meet the new demand, the Big Three—Ford, General Motors, and Chrysler—and the rest of the automobile industry throughout the world have moved fast to develop EV's.

In the 1980's, General Motors built a solar-powered vehicle called Sunraycer. It crossed the Australian Outback desert region in record time. This encouraged GM to design the Impact, a battery-powered two-seater for sale in the 1990's. GM also has under consideration an electrified Geo Prizm compact.

Ford developed the Ecostar, a battery-powered minivan. However, this prototype was abandoned. Instead, Ford may develop an electric version of the Taurus or some other popular model.

In 1994, Chrysler developed plans to build gasoline, electric, and natural gas versions of its next minivan.

For all automobile manufacturers, key questions must be answered. The most important one is, who will buy the EV's? By California's 1998 deadline, EV's will not match gasoline vehicles in performance or price. Their 80- to 100-mile range per 8-hour charge may not appeal to consumers accustomed to driving up to 400 miles per tank and refueling in five minutes. Expensive EV battery packs can burn out in two years and cost thousands to replace. Many potential customers lack proper outlets for recharging.

In their search for answers to these problems, the automobile industry is enlisting the aid of utility companies. Utilities may, for example, install quick-charge stations that recharge batteries in 15 minutes. They may also lease batteries to consumers to lower the cost of early failure. Some utility companies have already begun to seek temporary rate increases to subsidize the installation of recharging stations.

No matter how these problems are solved, and whatever the environmental benefits, the successful development and sale to consumers of EV's will cause the most dramatic change in the automobile industry since 1902. In that year, a gasoline-powered vehicle captured the land-speed title from an electric car.

1. *Describe the role of California in EV development.*
2. *Discuss the EV development problems faced by the automobile industry.*

Section Review

1. *Complete each sentence:*
   a. *When considering genetically altered farm products, President Clinton pleased businesses, but alarmed some environmentalists and scientists by ______.*
   b. *To strengthen efforts to prevent global warming, the Clinton Administration ______.*
   c. *Environmentalists favor the development of EV's because ______.*
2. *PROVE or DISPROVE: The technology of the 1990's has provided answers to a wide range of environmental problems.*

Chapter 12 Review

A. *For each question, indicate the correct response.*

1. *In the 1990's, Americans have debated the allocation of funding to environmental protection instead of (a) foreign aid (b) economic growth (c) defense.*
2. *Environmentalists are concerned with the preservation of the quality of air, water, soil, and (a) roads and highways (b) national monuments (c) wildlife.*
3. *The environmental policies of the Clinton Administration have been opposed by the (a) property-rights movement (b) Sierra Club (c) EPA.*
4. *The 1994 forest management plan of the Clinton Administration was designed to protect the environment and (a) assist farmers (b) increase hydroelectric development (c) stimulate the economy of the Pacific Northwest.*
5. *The federal agency most concerned with the effects of poaching is the (a) U.S. Park Service (b) EPA (c) Department of Agriculture.*
6. *Among the endangered species the United States has attempted to preserve are (a) raccoons and beavers (b) hawks and sparrows (c) tigers, rhinoceroses, and whales.*
7. *A major land and conservation measure was approved by Congress in 1994. It affected the (a) Rocky Mountain states (b) California desert (c) Great Plains.*
8. *A technological development approved by the Clinton Administration is (a) genetic engineering of farm products (b) selective killing of the genetically weaker wildlife species (c) EPA testing of toxins on surplus farm animals.*
9. *To limit global warming, the United States supported the 1994 demands of European nations for steps to (a) increase the use of carbon-burning fuels (b) reduce emissions of greenhouse gases (c) make automobiles more fuel-efficient.*
10. *In 1994, California announced new laws which will force the automobile industry to (a) design smaller cars which consume less gasoline (b) eliminate cars with fuel injection (c) manufacture and sell electric vehicles.*

B. *Explain why you APPROVE or DISAPPROVE of the actions taken by the Clinton Administration to protect the environment.*

C. *Environmental issues have involved controversy and debate. Among those argued in the 1990's have been*

Property rights
Commercial use of forests
Hunting in national parks
Genetic engineering of farm products
Reduction of greenhouse gases

Select TWO of these issues. For each, explain the opposing views, and state your own opinion.

Chapter 13

Survival in a Dangerous World

During the cold war, the threats to American security came from the Soviet Union and its Communist allies. In the new world order of the 1990's, the United States has directed its military and intelligence operations against other organized global enemies. Terrorists and narcotics traffickers have headed the list. The American struggle against these destructive forces is expected to continue into the 21st century.

A less violent, but equally determined effort has been maintained to prevent the spread of nuclear weapons. This struggle has involved efforts to curb the illegal use of technology and fissionable materials.

America's Fight Against Global Terrorism

The capture by French security forces of Ilich Ramirez Sanchez in August, 1994, was a turning point in the war against terrorism. Better known as "Carlos the Jackal," the 44-year-old Venezuelan was one of the most infamous of political murderers. Among the crimes for which Carlos has been blamed was a 1975 raid on a meeting of the Organization of Petroleum Exporting Countries (OPEC) in Vienna. Carlos and five followers kidnapped and then killed three oil ministers. Their announced purpose was to seize oil wealth for the benefit of the Arab people and other inhabitants of the Third World.

Carlos recognized no moral limits. His killings were indiscriminate and included innocent bystanders. His terrorist activities were made possible by the support of several governments, a practice that the United States called "state-supported terrorism." By the 1990's, however, this kind of

support for the Jackal and his friends began to diminish. After years of hiding in Syria, Carlos was told by the authorities in that country to leave in 1991. Refused entry by Yemen and Libya, he found temporary refuge in Jordan. In late 1993, Carlos slipped into Sudan with a false Yemeni passport. The intelligence services of several countries cooperated in tracking him down. The Sudanese government was persuaded to arrest the Jackal and hand him over to French security agents. (It was rumored that, in exchange, France had given Sudan's military government satellite pictures to aid its fight against rebels.)

For the United States government, the arrest of Carlos was highly significant. The kind of terrorism he and others practiced in the 1970's and 1980's had helped to shape the political and religious violence of the 1990's. As the number of governments willing to engage in state-sponsored terrorism decreased, it became possible to focus more sharply on those regimes that still supported terrorism. Carlos's arrest also indicated that the nature of terrorism was changing.

- *Identify "the Jackal," and explain why his arrest was so important to the United States and other nations.*

America's Experiences with Terrorism

During the period of U.S. involvement in the Vietnam War (1965–73), an organization called the Weathermen engaged in acts of violence to force a withdrawal of American forces from Southeast Asia. Government offices, military installations, and industrial firms with defense contracts were their targets. The Weathermen, and other groups which used violence to effect changes in foreign or domestic policies, attracted the young and disaffected. They were not, however, supported by foreign governments. Although they represented America's first experience with terrorism, most of these groups faded away after the Vietnam War ended and the *draft* (the conscription of non-volunteers into the armed forces) was discontinued.

In the late 1970's, the U.S. government made the issue of terrorism a major part of its foreign policy. A list was compiled of countries believed to be supporting such activities. Special military units were set up to prevent terrorism and to retaliate against terrorist acts, when appropriate.

In 1979, an Islamic Revolution in Iran brought to power the fundamentalist government of the Ayatollah Khomeini, a Muslim religious leader of great influence. This was followed by an increase in international terrorism. Iranian militants held 52 American hostages in Iran for 444 days, until early 1981. A terrorist on a suicide mission blew up the U.S. Marine headquarters in Lebanon, in 1984, causing the death of 241 Americans. A passenger ship, the *Achille Lauro,* was hijacked in 1985, and an American was killed. Several Americans and Europeans were kidnapped and held prisoner for years by terrorists based in Lebanon. In 1986, the U.S. Air Force bombed two Libyan cities in response to a terrorist attack on American military personnel in Europe. A terrorist bomb aboard Pan Am Flight 103 exploded over Lockerbie, Scotland, in 1988, killing 270 passengers. In 1989, Lebanese terrorists kidnapped and executed a U.S. Marine officer. In that year, the Pentagon reported the existence of 52 terrorist groups in various parts of the world. Many targeted Americans because of their resentment of U.S. policies, especially the support given to Israel.

During the 1970's and 80's, the United States followed an official policy of refusing to deal with terrorists. However, an exception was made in 1986, when the Reagan Administration secretly sold weapons to Iran in exchange for the release of American hostages in Lebanon. The profits from the sales of the weapons were used to support the Contras, a rebel organization fighting the Communist government of Nicaragua. This violated an act of Congress that forbade aid to the Contras. During the scandal and investigation that followed, President Ronald Reagan was cleared of lawbreaking, but some officials of his Administration were convicted of lying to Congress.

1. *Describe the impact of terrorism on Americans during the 1970's and 1980's.*
2. *Explain how the Iran-Contra affair of 1986 violated official U.S. policy.*

Terrorism's New Face

Terrorism took on new forms in the 1990's. Often it arose from the efforts of Muslim fundamentalists to replace secular governments with Islamic rule. In several countries, shadowy, unstructured groups formed around mosques with radical sheiks. Many of the modern Islamic terrorists are veterans of the Afghan War (1979–92) against the Soviet occupation of that country. During the war, some of these ex-soldiers received training and support from the Central Intelligence Agency (CIA). Although state-sponsored terrorism appears to be declining, a few countries continue to practice this policy.

In 1993, the U.S. State Department branded Iran the world's most dangerous state sponsor of terrorism. It called the Iranian-supported, Lebanon-based Hezbollah organization the most aggressive and lethal terrorist group in the world. Other radical organizations that have spearheaded global terrorism in the 1990's include Islamic Jihad, Hamas, the Muslim Brotherhood, and the Islamic Salvation Front.

The terrorists' war was transported to the United States in early 1993. In January, an immigrant from a region of Pakistan that borders Afghanistan, stood outside the headquarters of the CIA in Langley, Virginia. He shot and killed two CIA employees, wounded three others, and then fled the country.

The bombing of New York City's World Trade Center in February, 1993, was the second most destructive terrorist act ever committed on American soil. Plans for attacks on U.N. headquarters and the Lincoln Tunnel were prevented. The mastermind of the conspiracy was alleged to be Sheik Omar Abdel Rahman, the spiritual leader of fundamentalists in Egypt and elsewhere in the world. Four of his followers were convicted of conspiracy, assault, and other charges in connection with the bombing deaths of six people. In September, 1996, Ramzi Ahmed Yousef (see page 155), the suspected organizer of the World Trade Center bombing, was tried and convicted of plotting to blow up 12 U.S. airliners.

The World Trade Center tragedy raised American fears of a large-scale terrorist conspiracy aimed against the United States. This concern was renewed in March, 1994, when a Lebanese cabdriver in New York City shot up a van in which Hasidic Jewish students were riding, killing one boy. Reports that the gunman and two accomplices were part of a terrorist ring under surveillance by the FBI proved to be false. However, the fear of terrorism had become a part of American life.

A wave of bombings in July, 1994, struck at a Jewish community center in Buenos Aires and the Israeli Embassy in London. Approximately 100 people were killed. American and Israeli diplomats and intelligence officials blamed the attack on Hezbollah and Hamas, as well as on the government of Iran, which supports these terrorist groups. Secretary of State Warren Christopher told a House of Representatives committee that the United States must not let those responsible for the bombings succeed, and called for the defeat of Hezbollah and the containment of Iran. He also pledged American leadership of a concerted international response to the bombings. Full cooperation among the intelligence services of several nations to track down those responsible was promised.

The Secretary of State also criticized some of the allies of the United States for trading with Iran, saying that they were indirectly supporting state-sponsored terrorism.

In April, 1995, terrorists bombed a federal office building in Oklahoma City. The blast left 167 dead. The suspected bombers, Timothy McVeigh and Terry Nichols, were caught and scheduled for trial in early 1997.

Such acts of domestic terrorism are committed by Americans—members of right-wing militias opposed to having their activities, however extreme, subject to government regulation. Found throughout the United States and known variously as "freemen" or white separatists, they promote racism and terrorism. To prevent such tragedies as the Oklahoma City bombing, President Clinton demanded that Congress approve wide-ranging new FBI powers to infiltrate terrorist networks, tap their telephones, and check the credit and travel records of activists suspected of engaging in treasonable acts.

1. *Describe the arrival of terrorism in the United States in the 1990's.*
2. *Explain why the Clinton Administration branded Iran an "outlaw nation" in 1994.*

Section Review

1. *Review the American experience with terrorism from the 1960's to the 1990's. How do you think the United States should respond to the kind of terrorism practiced in recent years?*
2. *Explain why you AGREE or DISAGREE with the belief that terrorism is more of a problem for other nations than it is for the United States.*
3. *Write a brief analysis of the terrorist mentality. Why do you think terrorists operate the way they do?*

The American Drug Scene

In mid-1994, new, powerful blends of heroin began appearing on the streets of American cities. Deaths from overdoses and other drug-related causes increased. To law enforcement agencies, it was an indication that a change in the drug scene had come. For years, cocaine had been the substance most favored by drug users. Now, heroin appeared to be making a comeback. And, as several deaths illustrated, heroin abuse is no longer mainly a practice of the poor and the unemployed. Addiction has been increasing among the working and middle classes as well. White-collar professionals have become frequent customers of drug pushers, who offer their wares in the financial districts of major cities. In Washington, D.C., drug deals have been made even in the park across the street from the White House.

Drug abuse has long been regarded as the root cause of a number of American social problems, especially violent crime. The rising demand for drugs by affluent people has raised the street price and made the habit more expensive to support. Addicts need money any way they can get it.

◆ *Explain why drug abuse is a danger to the addict and to the community in which he or she lives.*

America has responded to the drug threat in a number of ways. New laws have mandated stiffer prison sentences for dealers. Educational programs and public-service media warnings have pointed out the harmful effects of drugs and other forms of substance abuse. Neighborhood community centers and schools have been made drug-free zones. During the 1980's, First Lady Nancy Reagan introduced the phrase "Just say no!" And in 1994, President Bill Clinton responded to the suggestion of the U.S. Surgeon General that drug use be legalized and placed under government control by saying "It's not going to happen!"

These strategies had little effect. A long-term decline in drug abuse by high school and college students continued into 1992. Surveys made in 1993, however, showed an increase in drug abuse by students in both groups, beginning with grade eight. The use of marijuana, cocaine, crack (cocaine mixed with baking soda and water), LSD, other hallucinogens, stimulants, and inhalants was on the rise again. Although crack use in the 1990's appeared to be more common among adults than among teens, older users often depend upon younger suppliers. Much of the violence of the inner cities arose from teenage dealers and neighborhood gangs competing for sales territories.

1. *Explain why drug-related deaths increased in 1994.*
2. *Describe the changing patterns of drug abuse in American cities.*

Drug Abuse Through the Decades

Data collected by the National Institute on Drug Abuse (NIDA) in 1991 indicated that 75.4 million Americans age 12 and older reported some use of an illegal drug at least once during their lives. According to NIDA, drug abuse resulted in

400,000 admissions to hospital emergency rooms in 1991. There were 6,601 deaths due to drug abuse in the same year.

Addiction, however, became part of the American scene long before the 1990's. Opium dens became known during the 19th and early 20th centuries. For those who did not care to smoke themselves into oblivion in the company of others, it was possible to buy the drug in pharmacies. Nevertheless, drug abuse was not regarded as a major social problem until after World War II. Depressed economies and general disorder abroad after the war made it easy for organized crime to import large quantities of narcotics into the United States. Markets were quickly developed in the poverty-stricken inner cities and elsewhere. By the 1950's, police forces around the country were sending undercover officers into schools to track the sources of marijuana and heroin. In a famous motion picture of the era, *The Man With the Golden Arm,* Frank Sinatra gave a riveting performance as a tormented addict fighting to free himself from the destructive effects of his habit.

During the 1960's and 70's, the era of the Vietnam War and the civil rights struggle, American society was in turmoil. As part of their rebellion against authority, young people turned to "doing drugs" to demonstrate their independence. Some combined drug abuse with mysticism to "liberate" their minds. LSD and other hallucinogens became popular on college campuses. In the inner cities, a "drug culture" developed. People whose lives were based on the acquisition and use of drugs came together to pursue their self-destructive lifestyle.

Military operations in Southeast Asia brought Americans into contact with the Golden Triangle, an area in which the borders of China, Burma, and Thailand come together. The altitude, weather, and soil of the Shan Plateau is ideal for the growing of poppies and the production of opium. In the Golden Triangle, fortunes were made from deals with warlords who imported drugs to Vietnam for sale to American troops. Large-scale addiction resulted. A growing market was created in the United States as addicted veterans returned home with their habits intact.

◆ *State reasons for the expansion of drug addiction during the 1960's and 70's.*

As the American market grew, narcotics found their way into the United States from a variety of sources. The international drug trade developed routes through Turkey and the Middle East; China, Hong Kong, Taiwan, and a variety of other Asian nations; and from major production centers in Latin America, especially Colombia, Peru, and Bolivia. By the 1980's, the American Mafia was fighting Colombian and Vietnamese gangs for control of drug territories in the United States. And in the 1990's, organized Russian gangs from the former Soviet Union muscled their way into the drug trade in American cities.

America's Losing Battle

Between 1982 and 1992, the federal government increased spending on drug control programs from $1.7 billion to $12 billion. Much of this funding has gone to the Drug Enforcement Agency. DEA agents have been the frontline soldiers in the war to stop the flow of illegal narcotics into the United States. Some of these agents have come to believe that this war cannot be won.

DEA teams have been stationed in a variety of countries and in American cities. In the course of highly dangerous operations, some have lost their lives. In August, 1994, five DEA agents were killed in a plane crash in Peru. The agents involved in this worst incident in DEA history were on a surveillance mission in the Huallaga Valley, an area of heavy jungle and mountains. They were searching for drug-carrying airplanes, secret airstrips, and drug laboratories. Their flight was part of Operation Snowcap, a cocaine-fighting program in Peru and Bolivia. Peru is the source of 60 percent of the world's coca, from which cocaine is manufactured. The intelligence gained from such DEA missions is given to national police agencies. They conduct raids in which DEA agents participate. The agency also uses observation planes, along with satellite images, to monitor growth patterns of coca throughout South America.

◆ *Describe the work of the DEA.*

It was not the first time Americans had lost their lives in this dangerous area. In 1989, two DEA agents were killed in a similar plane crash. However, most narcotics agents who are killed are shot on American streets fighting drug dealers.

Despite DEA heroism and the efforts of the U.S. Coast Guard ships and other military units assigned to anti-drug operations, an estimated 80 percent of the illegal narcotics directed to the United States arrives there. Peruvian coca accounts for approximately 65 percent of the cocaine entering the United States. Regardless of the number of raids made on drug labs and other narcotics production centers in that country, coca remains Peru's largest export. Its sale earns more than $1 billion a year. As many as one million of the country's 21 million people are believed to be involved in the drug trade.

Nor have American efforts been successful in preventing foreign drug dealers from operating in the United States. In 1994, the DEA expressed concern about the takeover of a large part of the California drug market by Mexican nationals. Once under the unchallenged control of motorcycle gangs like the Hell's Angels, the illegal production of methamphetamine (speed) has been taken over by well-organized Mexican syndicates. These traffickers have established networks involving heroin, marijuana, and cocaine. In the 1990's, they have used their organization, labor force, and access to large supplies of chemicals to take control of the production of methamphetamine in the deserts of southern California.

◆ *State the evidence that DEA efforts have not been completely successful.*

President Clinton rejected the suggestion of Surgeon General Joycelyn Elders to put the drug dealers out of business by legalizing drug use. On moral and political grounds, his decision was supported by many. For his Administration, however, the problem and the question remain. If America's long war against the drug dealers and traffickers cannot be won, what is the answer?

Section Review

1. *Explain why you AGREE or DISAGREE with President Clinton's decision not to legalize drug use.*
2. *Briefly describe the history of illegal narcotics in the United States.*
3. *Develop arguments FOR and AGAINST the suggestion that the war against the traffickers be halted and federal funding be used to stop drug abuse and narcotics dealing in other ways.*

Nuclear Smuggling and Other Proliferation Problems

To keep both America and the world secure, the United States has stood strongly against nuclear proliferation. Efforts to prevent nations without nuclear weapons from developing or buying them have been an important part of American foreign policy. To this end, the United States has supported the work of the International Atomic Energy Agency (IAEA) and the Nuclear Nonproliferation Treaty of 1968 (NPT). Founded in 1957, the IAEA is an independent United Nations agency. Its task is to encourage peaceful uses of atomic energy while discouraging the building of nuclear weapons. The NPT is an agreement among 135 nations to halt the spread of nuclear weapons and to allow IAEA inspections of nuclear facilities.

In 1995, the Clinton Administration began an effort to make the NPT a global agreement; all nations would sign the treaty. The Administration also pushed for an indefinite extension of the treaty.

For the Clinton Administration, the task of keeping the "nuclear club" (the United States, Russia, China, France, and Britain) limited has been complex. Starting in 1993, the United States has struggled to keep North Korea from developing nuclear weapons. (See Chapter 6.) Intense negotiations resulted in a suspension of that Communist nation's decision to withdraw from the NPT. Suspicions grew, however, that the North Koreans had already built at least one nuclear bomb. This possibility worried South Korea and Japan, both in range of the Communists' Redong missiles. Confirmation was prevented by the North Koreans' refusal to allow complete IAEA inspections of their nuclear facilities. Attention focused on North Korea's supply of plutonium. Had they extracted from their nuclear reactor enough weapons-grade plutonium to build a nuclear arsenal?

1. *Define:*

   a. nuclear proliferation
   b. IAEA
   c. NPT

2. *Explain why North Korean actions became a problem for the Clinton Administration in the 1990's.*

The Geneva Talks

In July, 1994, the death of President Kim Il Sung of North Korea brought to power his son, Kim Jong Il. While his ability to retain control seemed uncertain, the younger Kim showed signs of being more willing to negotiate with the United States. Three days of discussions between the two nations were held in Geneva in August, 1994. The result was a joint statement which lessened the threat of confrontation by promising cooperation on several nuclear issues:

1. North Korea stated its willingness to conform to the NPT and to denuclearize the Korean peninsula.

2. The United States agreed to an exchange of diplomatic liaison offices and eventual full normalization of relations. Assurances against the threat or use of nuclear weapons against North Korea were also offered.

In addition, the North Korean negotiators offered to shut down their nuclear reactor if the United States would replace it with more modern light-water reactors. Extraction of plutonium from such a reactor would be difficult. North Korea also offered to freeze the construction of two larger reactors.

The American negotiators agreed to provide the new reactor, which would cost $1 billion, only as part of an overall settlement. Included must be regular, full inspection of all North Korean nuclear areas. The Communists were also required to reveal the amount of plutonium they had stockpiled. If the North Koreans met these conditions, the United States would gather international financial support for the ten-year project. South Korea stated its willingness to help fund the project.

The Geneva negotiations resumed in September, 1994, and led to an agreement that confirmed the joint statement of August. Implementation halted, however, when North Korea objected to South Korea as the supplier of the reactors. In December, 1995, North Korea dropped this objection. U.S. leaders were not entirely reassured by these agreements. No IAEA inspections would take place until the light-water reactors were installed. During the five years that installation would require, it was feared that, as in the past (see page 136), North Korea might engage in secret nuclear activity.

1. *State the solution to the North Korean crisis reached in Geneva in December, 1995.*
2. *Explain why the future of North Korea's nuclear program remained uncertain.*

The United States vs. Russia

Surplus plutonium became the focus of nuclear proliferation fears in the summer of 1994. Between May and August, German authorities conducted raids on smugglers believed to be obtaining weapons-grade plutonium from Russia. Some 300 grams of contraband plutonium and uranium were seized. It is highly radioactive material; even in small quantities it is capable of causing mass destruction.

The incidents caused an upheaval in government and security circles. Both Germany and the United States called the illegal trade in nuclear materials a major threat to their security. President Clinton scheduled talks with Boris Yeltsin.

Although it was not proven that the nuclear materials smuggled into Germany originated in Russia, attention was drawn to the poor security at the latter country's nuclear sites. Early in 1994, Russian safety officials complained about the lack of any law regulating the use of nuclear materials. After a check was made of 5,500 of the 14,500 organizations and individuals licensed to work with radioactive materials, some 20,000 safety violations were found.

1. *Describe the 1994 incidents which alarmed the United States and Germany.*
2. *Explain why Russia's nuclear program has worried the West.*

While in the employ of the Soviet Union, nuclear officials controlled ten secret cities with a total population of 700,000 people. Located there were the top scientists who designed Soviet nuclear weapons and the technicians and workers who built them. They were the best-paid, most privileged citizens of the Soviet Union. In the 1990's, budget cuts and reductions in the manufacture of weapons have impoverished the nuclear cities. However, their reactors are still producing weapons-grade plutonium.

As the plutonium has piled up and its producers have gotten poorer, the temptation to engage in smuggling has grown. Security controls are inadequate, and the Russian Mafia is ready to buy nuclear materials. International terrorists and outlaw governments provide the Russian gangsters with customers.

Surplus plutonium became the cause of a growing disagreement between the United States and Russia. To the Americans, the nuclear material is a threat to global security and should be destroyed. The Russians regard it as a "national treasure,"

WHICH SIDE, PLUTONIUM?

to be saved for future energy production. While the United States has searched for a safe way to get rid of plutonium no longer needed for weapons production, the Russians are planning increased plutonium output. A new generation of nuclear power plants called breeders will be built in Russia. They will create more plutonium than the nuclear fuel they consume. This material will be usable by bomb makers.

Americans fear that Russian plans will heighten long-term security risks. Since Russia will keep its surplus plutonium in a pure form (the form used in weapons), it will be quite attractive to terrorists or nations that want a nuclear bomb. Less than ten pounds of plutonium, a chunk smaller than a fist, would be sufficient to make such a weapon.

Even without thefts, large stores of surplus plutonium in either the United States or Russia are dangerous. Giant nuclear arsenals could be rebuilt in a short time, thus expediting a return to the cold war. The United States has argued that disposal of plutonium now could help protect future generations. The Russians do not agree. They regard plutonium production as the best way to provide fuel for future generations.

1. *State the opposing positions of the United States and Russia on plutonium production.*
2. *Explain why Russia's plans to build breeders worry the United States.*

Additional Nuclear Headaches

Despite the efforts of the Clinton Administration, the nuclear club appears to be growing. India is suspected of having a small nuclear arsenal for possible use against Pakistan. (These two countries are divided by long-standing quarrels over religion and territory.) Pakistan has pursued the development of its own nuclear weapons.

In 1994, the Clinton Administration took a hard look at Pakistan's atomic weapons program. There was no doubt that Pakistan, like other nations, had forced its way into the nuclear club. The United States recognized that there was little it could do to reverse this. However, an effort was made to impose limitations. Pakistan was asked to limit its arsenal to 10–15 bombs and to prove that it has no plans to build additional nuclear weapons. In exchange, the United States offered to deliver 38 American-made F-16 jet aircraft that Pakistan had paid for but had not received. This strategy drew criticism. The CIA warned that if war flared up again between Pakistan and India, the Pakistani air force might use its F-16s to drop nuclear bombs on India.

In 1989, it was known that Israel had built several hundred nuclear weapons for use as a last resort against its Arab neighbors. In early 1995, Israel refused to sign the NPT. This strained relations with Egypt, a signer of the NPT. Secretary of State Christopher returned to the Mideast to negotiate a resolution.

Libya is suspected of developing nuclear weapons. After the Persian Gulf War, strong efforts were necessary to prevent Iraq's development of nuclear weapons. In 1995, the United States attempted to persuade China to stop helping Iran develop nuclear weapons.

As the nuclear club expands, the danger grows of an outlaw regime passing nuclear weapons to terrorist organizations. It has been pointed out that even one bomb could produce great damage in critical situations. Washington has also been warned of the possibility of more nuclear proliferation. North Korea's nuclear program, for example, could pose a threat to neighboring South Korea, Japan, and Taiwan, and cause them to conclude that they too must have nuclear weapons.

Preventing nuclear proliferation has been the clear policy of the Clinton Administration. However, the desire of several nations to develop nuclear arsenals to increase their security and prestige has challenged this policy.

- *State examples of the growth of the nuclear club.*

Section Review

1. *Evaluate the efforts of the United States to prevent nuclear proliferation. How successful has this effort been? What problems have developed in the 1990's? Why is prevention of nuclear proliferation a policy of the Clinton Administration?*
2. *Analyze the statements below by answering the following questions:*
   - a. *How do these statements reflect an argument between the United States and Russia?*
   - b. *Which policy do you think is correct? Give reasons for your opinion.*

STATEMENTS

> The plutonium we no longer need for weapons is a global security risk.
>
> —*Hazel O'Leary, U.S. Secretary of Energy*

> We have spent too much money making this material [plutonium] to just mix it with radioactive wastes and bury it.
>
> —*Viktor N. Mikhailov, Russia's Minister of Atomic Energy*

3. *President Clinton was urged to go to war, if necessary, to prevent North Korea from building nuclear weapons. What do you think?*

Chapter 13 Review

A. *For each question, indicate the correct response.*

1. *In the 1990's, there has been a decline in (a) all forms of terrorism (b) state-supported terrorism (c) religiously motivated terrorism.*
2. *Since the 1970's, the official policy of the United States towards terrorists has been (a) no dealings (b) limited dealings (c) frequent dealings.*
3. *Many Islamic terrorists are veterans of the (a) Vietnam War (b) Persian Gulf War (c) Afghan War.*

4. *The most destructive terrorist act ever committed on U.S. soil was the 1995 bombing of the (a) World Trade Center (b) United Nations (c) Oklahoma City federal building.*
5. *Among the social problems most strongly rooted in drug abuse is (a) poverty (b) illiteracy (c) violent crime.*
6. *In 1993, drug abuse among high school and college students (a) increased (b) decreased (c) remained at 1992 levels.*
7. *Drug abuse in the United States was increased by the (a) Afghan War (b) Vietnam War (c) Persian Gulf War.*
8. *Support of the IAEA and the NPT is part of America's policy of opposing (a) nuclear testing (b) nuclear proliferation (c) nuclear power.*
9. *The 1994 Geneva Talks resulted in agreements for cooperation on nuclear issues between the United States and (a) Japan (b) Russia (c) North Korea.*
10. *Disagreement between the United States and Russia in 1994 concerned the manufacture of (a) surplus plutonium (b) long-range missiles (c) nuclear submarines.*

B. *Write articles to accompany TWO of the following newspaper headlines:*

THE JACKAL IS CAPTURED AT LAST

AMERICANS FEAR TERRORISM AS NEVER BEFORE

HEROIN MAKES A COMEBACK

DEA FIGHTS GLOBAL WAR

NUCLEAR SMUGGLING THREATENS U.S. SECURITY

C. *In the 1990's, the United States has used negotiation, as well as military and intelligence operations, in efforts to solve critical problems. Write one or two paragraphs about America's approach to ONE of the following:*

Global terrorism
Drug abuse
Nuclear proliferation

Chapter 14

Preparing for the 21st Century

In the last decades of the 20th century, Americans wondered, hopefully, about the 21st century. What changes would it bring? What new problems would present themselves?

Most feel sure that the United States will remain the world's sole military superpower. It is also expected that America's continued global leadership will depend upon its ability to find answers to nonmilitary problems. Experts have predicted that economic competition will shape the 21st century. To compete successfully in the new global marketplace, America must deal with the changes brought by continuing technological advances. Solutions must also be found to ongoing environmental and social problems.

The cold war has been won. It remains for Americans to create a new and better future.

The Population Crisis: Controversy and Decision

In September, 1994, the International Conference on Population and Development met in Cairo. The delegates came together to discuss methods of dealing with the crisis of overpopulation on Earth. The world's 5.7 billion people are headed toward a possibly disastrous 10 billion by the year 2050. By that time, food, water, and other resources may be insufficient to support so many people.

The United Nations, which sponsored the conference, intended it to be a harmonious gathering of nations. However, the United States delegation, led by Vice President Al Gore, soon found itself under attack and embroiled in controversy. The Americans and other delegations agreed that the key to curbing population growth lies in giving women more control over their own health and reproductive ability. In a final "plan of action," adopted by more than 150 nations, the focus was upon women's rights. It was recognized that of the 960 million illiterate people in the world, two-thirds are women. It was also noted that 90 million girls around the world are denied primary education. The conference conceded that many men and women would choose to have fewer children if they were given adequate information, health care, and access to a wide choice of contraceptive methods. The emphasis on female education and employment represented support for a new empowerment for women.

1. *State the purpose of the Cairo Conference of 1994.*
2. *List the principles supported by the United States delegation.*

America Under Attack

The conference was in danger of falling apart before it even got started. Proposals for extending contraceptive services directly to adolescents and protecting women from unsafe abortions drew fire from Roman Catholic and Muslim leaders. The Vatican strongly denounced Vice President Gore for the U.S. role in setting the agenda of the conference. The Vatican has had a long-standing opposition to birth control and abortion. In the Islamic world, abortion is generally forbidden.

Gore vainly attempted to calm the controversy by stating that the United States did not seek to establish any international right to abortion. In response, a Vatican spokesman accused the Vice President of misrepresenting the American position on abortion.

While the Vatican chose to be strongly represented at the Cairo Conference, some Muslim nations boycotted it. Saudi Arabia, Sudan, Lebanon, and Iraq refused to send delegates. Also, two prominent women, Prime Ministers Tansu Ciller of Turkey and Begum Khaleda Zia of Bangladesh, did not attend. Neither did President Suharto of Indonesia, the most populous Muslim nation. Saudi Arabian religious leaders condemned the Cairo Conference as "a ferocious assault on Islamic society."

♦ *Explain how the Cairo Conference embroiled the United States in an international controversy.*

America, Women's Rights, and the Future

Preparation for the 21st century requires the United States to be concerned about population control. A 1994 total of 261 million Americans is expected to expand to more than 325 million by the year 2050. To meet this challenge, the United States will have to develop more efficient ways of providing education and economic opportunity to increasing numbers of people. A key part of this task will be the steps taken to advance the empowerment of women.

The U.N.-sponsored conference in Cairo was about more than population. Its real topic was women's rights, now and in the future. By its leadership in the preparation of the final action plan, the United States committed itself to a policy designed to move the world more strongly toward gender equality. For America and the 150 nations which signed the plan, the empowerment of women will be the cornerstone of future population programs. Such a policy is bound to cause friction between the societies of the U.S. and others.

In terms of birth control, the notion that what happens to a woman should be her decision and entirely within her control has long been the rallying cry of American feminists. In recent years, this idea has been expressed as "the right to choose." For many Americans, the principle that all individuals have rights is easy to accept. Other cultures, however, do not find such views acceptable. Some Muslim religious leaders have accused the United States of "cultural imperialism." As America presses for more empowerment for women—meaning more education, employment opportunities, and decision-making power—it can be expected that the kind of "culture clash" that occurred at the Cairo Conference will continue into the 21st century. Nevertheless, women are entering the global work force in ever-increasing numbers, taking jobs ranging from prime minister to factory worker. American support for women's rights will help shape the future.

1. *Define:*
   - *a.* gender equality
   - *b.* the right to choose
   - *c.* empowerment of women
2. *Explain why American population-control policies may cause "culture clash" to continue into the 21st century.*

Section Review

1. *Biologists predict that population growth will increase competition for food and other resources and lead to starvation and global misery. Economists claim that the growth of free markets and technology will enable supply to keep pace with demand.*
   - *a. With which position do you agree? Give reasons for your answer.*
   - *b. How might each position affect the development of U.S. policies on population control?*
2. *Examine the statements that follow, and explain how the views expressed reflected developments at the 1994 International Conference on Population and Development.*

> The United States does not seek to establish any international right to abortion.
>
> —*Vice President Al Gore*

> The draft document contradicts, in reality, Mr. Gore's statement.
>
> —*A Vatican spokesman*

> We all live in one boat. No country can withdraw, set itself aside, and those who do this are defeatists.
>
> —*Dr. Maher Mahran, Egyptian Population Minister*

Global Economics: How Competitive Will America Be in the 21st Century?

In the late summer of 1994, the Allies formally ended their 49-year occupation of the city of Berlin. The victors of World War II withdrew the last of their troops from the German capital. As ordinary Berliners were toasting the departing American soldiers, Germany's business leaders were greeting a delegation of top U.S. corporate executives. Among the American businesspeople were the leaders of General Motors, IBM, Goldman Sachs, Motorola, and Morgan Stanley. Their meeting with the German executives was for the purpose of ensuring that the post-cold war era would be profitable for the United States. For nearly 50 years, the relationship between Europe and America had been basically military. Now, a new emphasis on trade and economics was beginning.

Whether or not America can compete successfully in the 21st century will depend upon its ability to increase its exports. The world must be persuaded to buy American products. Recognition of this economic necessity has shaped the policies of the Clinton Administration. The President has devoted much effort to international business deal-making in pursuit of a national export policy.

In the summer of 1993, Clinton persuaded King Fahd of Saudi Arabia to buy $6 billion worth of Boeing and McDonnell Douglas civilian aircraft. In May, 1994, the President helped AT&T close a $4 billion deal to modernize Saudi telecommunications. He came through again for U.S. industry in June, 1994, when he persuaded Brazil's government to award a $1.4 billion radar project to Raytheon, Inc.

These deals boosted the sale abroad of American goods and services and increased the profits of U.S. corporations. America's national export policy is also expected to create 13 million new jobs at home by the year 2000.

Before his death in an April, 1996, plane crash while on a mission to Bosnia, Secretary of Commerce Ron Brown was a key figure in implementing this policy. Corporate executives vied for seats on his plane when he traveled in search of new business opportunities. He concentrated on emerging Asian and Latin American markets. China also holds great promise for U.S. exports. As it rapidly industrializes during the next five years, it is expected to buy $1 trillion in foreign technology. In September, 1994, Brown led 24 U.S. executives to the Asian giant. They negotiated deals worth $6 billion, including the sale of 11 Boeing 757 passenger jets, a telecommunications contract for AT&T, and construction of an electric power plant by Entergy Corporation.

1. *Define the term* national export policy *and describe the efforts of the Clinton Administration to implement this policy.*
2. *Explain how the national export policy is part of the preparation of the United States for the 21st century.*

The Stubborn Trade Gap

In June, 1994, the export of goods and services by the United States hit an all-time monthly high of $58.2 billion. Among the reasons for this economic strength were the policies of the Clinton Administration, economic expansion in all major industrial countries, a weak U.S. dollar, and the North American Free Trade Agreement. U.S. exports increased by 7.5 percent in 1995, reaching $685 billion.

A wide variety of American industries participated in this

export boom. Among the Big Three automakers, for example, Ford Motor Company's exports increased by 90 percent over 1993 levels. Mexico and Japan were the countries to which Ford sold the most additional cars. Chrysler Corporation's overseas car sales increased by 34 percent in the first half of 1994. Many cars were sold in South America, which has proved to be one of the fastest growing automobile markets in the world.

With American goods and services in so much demand overseas, expectations arose that the trade deficit might be reduced. Instead, the trade imbalance grew because Americans continued to import more than they exported.

Americans have not been willing to give up foreign products such as luxury cars from Germany and Japan or consumer electronics from Singapore and other Asian producers. Other factors also contribute to the growing trade gap. One is the increasing number of foreign-owned factories in the United States that merely assemble parts imported from abroad. Once assembled, these products may be shipped overseas. However, the profit from their sales does not benefit American manufacturers. More significant is the American preference for buying, rather than saving. As a result, U.S. imports keep climbing. For the month of June, 1994, imports to the United States exceeded $65 billion.

As America approaches the 21st century, its need to compete successfully in the global marketplace requires a reduction of the trade gap. In order to accomplish this, the U.S. savings rate must be doubled. Also, consumers must be encouraged to "buy American." Attaining these objectives poses a serious challenge for the Clinton Administration.

1. *Describe the 1994 U.S. export boom.*
2. *Explain why the trade deficit continues to grow and why this is significant as America approaches the 21st century.*

Section Review

1. *Draw up a list of popular foreign products. Which of these products have American-made counterparts? How would you organize a*

campaign to persuade people you know to "buy American"? Why is "buying American" more important in the 1990's than it might have been in previous decades?

2. *Evaluate the national export policy of the Clinton Administration. Should it be continued into the 21st century? Why or why not?*
3. *Explain why you AGREE or DISAGREE with those who believe that the President of the United States should not be assisting U.S. corporations to make international business deals.*

America the Violent

In September, 1994, Walter Mondale, U.S. Ambassador to Japan, spoke to the National Press Club in Washington, D.C. The Ambassador described the efforts being made by representatives of both nations to resolve differences over trade. He discussed the need for Americans and Japanese to recognize and respect their cultural differences as they developed ways to cooperate and resolve problems. Mondale was clearly optimistic about the future of Japanese-American relations.

There was one matter, however, that worried the Ambassador. He spoke of the Japanese perception of the United States as an extremely dangerous place, in which Americans were obsessed with guns and violence. Mondale warned his audience about the dangers of this kind of global image. He urged Americans to take steps to control the acts of violence which were gaining so much attention throughout the world.

In a 1994 civil case in Louisiana, a judge awarded damages and funeral costs to the parents of a Japanese exchange student who was shot and killed two years before. The 16-year-old boy had been shot by a homeowner who felt threatened when the boy approached the house while wearing a Halloween costume. The shooting provoked outrage in Japan, where gun ownership is rare. The civil court judgment was reported by the Japanese media in terms of America's need to come to terms with gun violence. After the shooting, the parents of the slain boy campaigned in the United States for gun control.

Always a part of the American scene, crime and violence captured world attention in the 1990's. The Japanese are not alone in considering the United States to be a place in which acts of brutality occur more frequently than in other countries.

Many Americans agree, fearing for the future of the nation and its quality of life. Preparing for the 21st century has included a national struggle to bring violence under control.

◆ *Explain how violence damages both the quality of American life and the international reputation of the United States.*

The Violent Crime Control and Law Enforcement Act of 1994

In September, 1994, after months of political struggle, Congress finally passed President Clinton's crime bill. The legislation was the first major crime bill enacted in six years. It allocated $30 billion over six years to hire 100,000 local police officers, build state prisons, and launch crime-prevention efforts. The new law also bans 19 assault weapons and large gun clips. It expands the use of the federal death penalty and imposes life imprisonment on repeat violent offenders.

Strong opposition from President Clinton's political opponents and the National Rifle Association made this a bitter struggle. The NRA, long an opponent of gun control legislation, objected to the weapons ban and attempted to have the bill killed. However, the randomness and viciousness of sensational crimes had raised public anxieties about violence. By 1994, it had become the nation's top concern.

The crime bill was a response to the country's rising fear of crime. However, law-enforcement experts doubted that it would be effective in stopping the ever-increasing street violence. The law will spread the 100,000 new police officers to be hired by cities and towns so thin that critics doubt they will make a difference. It bans the manufacture, sale, and possession of 19 military-assault weapons, but leaves in circulation many thousands of the same firearms. It imposes the death penalty for about 60 offenses. Some of these rarely occur. It provides cash grants to cities for social programs. Many of these have been ineffective in reducing crime in the past. The building of more prisons will take many criminals off the streets. However, the prison construction boom of the 1980's has not reduced the crime rate.

Nevertheless, supporters of the crime bill regarded it as a good beginning. It indicated a stronger role for the federal government in fighting crime. It was hoped that the new law would begin to restore public confidence in the ability of the federal government to take the offensive against crime.

The National Rifle Association has long proposed an alternative solution. NRA supporters demand an end to all gun control laws and weapons bans. This would enable all Americans to have free access to weapons. Armed citizens, the NRA claims, would then be able to exercise their right to defend themselves against violent criminals. For some, this solution represented the path to the abandonment of law and order and the eventual breakdown of civilization in the United States.

Americans have agreed, in the 1990's, that the means of bringing violent crime under control must be found, hopefully before the 21st century.

1. *List the main provision of the Violent Crime Control & Law Enforcement Act of 1994.*
2. *State the criticisms of this law by law-enforcement experts.*

Section Review

1. *Visitors to the United States often express fears for their personal safety. How would you respond to such people? What advice would you give them? How do you feel about your own safety? How does the violent crime issue reflect upon your pride in your country?*
2. *Give your opinion about the following anti-crime measures by explaining why you APPROVE or DISAPPROVE of each:*

    a. *gun control and weapons bans*
    b. *increased funding for expanded police forces*

c. construction of more prisons
d. greater use of the death penalty
e. more job-development and other social programs

Technology: Where Is It Taking Us?

Among the forces reshaping the way Americans live and work, technology is predominant. Industrial historians forecast that the 1990's will be a period of dramatic change for the nation's businesses. The adoption of information technologies is a major reason.

Whether competing at home or abroad, American businesses require information. Success or failure is determined largely by the amount and quality of the information they receive and the speed with which they get it. This realization has spurred the United States to develop the technology necessary to obtain and process information. Vice President Al Gore has devoted himself to the building of an "information superhighway" on which computers and telecommunication facilities would give the U.S. superior competitive capabilities in the global marketplace.

♦ *Explain the connection between information and global competition.*

The Cutting Edge

Americans have embraced the latest technology to be on the cutting edge of global competition. Businesses have spent billions of dollars on computers, networks, and related information technologies. This huge investment has increased the productivity of manufacturing, retailing, and services. It has also changed the way in which companies operate. America is far ahead of other nations in the development and use of technology. In the United States, for example, there is roughly one computer for every four Americans compared with one for every 10 Germans, one for every 12 Japanese, and one for every 1,500 Chinese.

The new hardware and software have had a powerful influence on the organization of businesses. The restructuring of U.S. corporations in the 1990's has been made possible by information technologies. They extend a supervisor's range of control and make team efforts easier to run. As a result, fewer managers and fewer layers of organization are required. And improvements in telecommunications (see Chapter 4) have given businesses much more freedom to choose where they will locate. Information technology has become a strategic weapon. Used properly, it can support American efforts to win the economic battles of the 21st century.

1. *Compare American use of information technology with that of other nations.*
2. *Describe the impact of information technology on U.S. businesses.*

The Job Scene: How Is It Changing?

Many predictions have been made about the nature of work in the 21st century. One such forecast is that by the year 2000 technology will have so changed the workplace that jobs, as we know them, may not exist.

For example, technology has made it possible to automate the production of goods and the provision of services. Production has become customized. Big firms, where most of the good jobs used to be, are farming out production processes to smaller companies.

In many states and cities, public services are being privatized. Government bureaucracy, a source of so many lifetime jobs, is being reduced in size. In both the public and private sectors of the American economy, *downsizing* (reduction of personnel) has become common. Technology has made it possible to do more with fewer workers.

In response to the need for greater flexibility, some businesses have been replacing full-time jobs with temporary workers (*temps*) to accomplish short-range tasks and projects. The business organizations of the 21st century are expected to allocate much of their work to changing labor forces which can grow and shrink and reshape to meet the requirements of each new project.

As improvements in technology make production faster and more efficient, the management of workforces composed of temps, part-time workers, consultants, and contract workers will require different skills and techniques. Traditional business firms may find themselves in difficulty after the year 2000 if they are unable to change.

Some firms have already introduced the practice of assigning a newly hired person to a project. As it changes over time, the person's responsibilities change with it. Then the person is assigned to other projects, which also change. This requires working under several team leaders, keeping different schedules, being in various locations, and performing a number of different tasks. Technology is required to make such business operations succeed. Databases and networking are among the most important. Such technology is transforming the American workplace.

1. *Explain how employment in the 21st century may differ from what has been traditional.*
2. *Describe the impact of technology on the labor force.*

Section Review

1. *Below are examples of 1990's technology. Select ONE and explain how it will help Americans in the 21st century.*

   Computer databases and networks
   Telecommunications
   Information superhighway

2. *Explain why you AGREE or DISAGREE with each of the following statements:*

   a. *To be competitive in the 21st century, American businesses will have to change the way they employ and manage people.*

b. By the 1990's, technology had become a disadvantage to American workers.

Chapter 14 Review

A. *For each question, indicate the correct response.*

1. *The purpose of the Cairo Conference of 1994 was to discuss the crisis caused by (a) global recession (b) international terrorism (c) population growth.*
2. *At the Cairo Conference, the United States came under attack for its position on (a) birth control and women's rights (b) economic development (c) agricultural technology.*
3. *To compete economically in the 21st century, America must increase its (a) imports (b) exports (c) foreign loans.*
4. *President Clinton has assisted U.S. corporations by (a) lowering business taxes (b) reducing tariffs (c) negotiating international business deals.*
5. *American businesspeople have prepared for the 21st century by increased use of (a) information technology (b) foreign labor (c) large, complex management.*
6. *Among the economic changes expected in the 21st century is a reduction in the number of traditional (a) service industries (b) jobs (c) stock exchanges.*
7. *By the 1990's, many American businesses had begun to change the way in which they (a) employ and manage people (b) finance projects (c) market products.*
8. *Among the provisions of the 1994 federal crime law was funding for (a) community hiring of more police (b) distribution of weapons to qualified citizens (c) deportation of convicted criminals.*
9. *The National Rifle Association has opposed anti-crime measures which include (a) mandatory sentencing (b) increased prison construction (c) gun control and weapons bans.*
10. *Critics of the 1994 federal crime law claim that its provisions (a) are too expensive to implement (b) will not stop the rise in street violence (c) have no public support.*

B. *In order to prepare for the 21st century, Americans have addressed the problems of population control, economic competitiveness,* *technological change, and violent crime. Select the ONE problem that you think will most affect the United States after the year 2000, and do the following:*

1. *Explain why you think this issue is so critical.*
2. *Describe the ways in which it has been approached in the 1990's.*
3. *State your ideas for dealing with this problem.*

C. *Consider the United States as it moves through the 1990's into the 21st century. What will improve and benefit Americans? What will not improve or change, but will threaten the quality of American life?*

Write a speech for delivery on national television by the President of the United States. His theme will be ''America in the Next Century.'' Help the President to give Americans a glimpse into their future.

Unit IV Review

A. *Many issues in the 1990's have been the subjects of intense national debate. Develop arguments FOR and AGAINST each of the following opinions:*

1. *Protection of the environment is more important than economic growth.*
2. *Global terrorism threatens the security of the United States more than do the international drug trade and nuclear proliferation.*
3. *In response to the population crisis, the United States must lead the fight for women's rights.*
4. *American success in the global marketplace depends on closing the trade gap and using information technology.*
5. *More police and stricter gun control are the only answers to America's rising level of violent crime.*

B. *Use information found in Unit IV to write an article to accompany ONE of the following newspaper headlines:*

CLINTON ADMINISTRATION TAKES ACTION AGAINST GLOBAL WARMING

DEA BATTLES DRUG TRAFFICKERS

U.S. TRIES TO LIMIT MEMBERSHIP OF NUCLEAR CLUB

V.P. GORE UNDER ATTACK AT CAIRO CONFERENCE

TRADE GAP CONTINUES TO GROW

CLINTON GETS CRIME BILL

C. *Two officials of the Clinton Administration—Ronald Brown and Al Gore—have played key roles in dealing with the American issues of the 1990's. Use information found in Unit IV to do the following:*

1. *Identify each of these officials by job or title.*
2. *State the issue or problem addressed by each.*
3. *Describe the role or actions taken by each.*

Index